MW00999549

"This is a well-designed, thoughtful, penetrating and ⟨...⟩ ⟨...⟩
and role of European security. The exercise is timely, given the unfolding of important
changes in regional and global security. It will be an invaluable guide to students, teachers
and researchers interested in the topic."

Emil J Kirchner, Emeritus Professor, University of Essex, UK

"European security has been on an incredible journey over the past 30 years. Precisely
because of the fluidity and complexity, *Contemporary European Security* is a topic that is difficult for students to grasp and that seems impossible to squeeze into a textbook. Nevertheless,
Galbreath, Mawdsley, and Chappell have done just that in an excellent way. Students and
teachers of European Security stand to benefit enormously."

Trine Flockhart, Professor, University of Southern Denmark

"*Contemporary European Security* is a comprehensive and timely volume that addresses the
major issues confronting Europe and its strategic partners in the twenty-first century. It ties
the discussion of a wide range of security challenges to the theoretical debates in a manner
that gives students of International Relations an accessible look at the state of the discipline
as it relates to European security."

Zachary Selden, Associate Professor, University of Florida, USA

Contemporary European Security

Contemporary European Security explores the complex European security architecture and introduces students to the empirical, theoretical and conceptual approaches to studying the subject. Written by experts in each subfield, it addresses key topics within the wider strategic context of international security.

Presenting traditional and critical debates to illuminate this ever-changing field, it addresses specifically:

- European security since 2000 and the end of the Cold War.
- The evolution of International Relations theories in understanding security in Europe.
- The role of NATO in the post-war period and its strategy, impact and enlargement.
- The institutionalisation of the CSCE and the political tensions within the OSCE.
- The EU's Common Security and Defence Policy and recent policy initiatives in defence.
- Feminist conceptions of European security.
- European military innovation.
- Security challenges in the post-Soviet space and the growing instability in the Middle East and North Africa.
- The emergence of human security.
- Internal and societal security.

This essential textbook will be of key interest to students and scholars of European Security, Security and Military studies, Strategic Studies, European Politics and International Relations.

David J. Galbreath is Professor of International Security and Dean of the Faculty of Humanities & Social Sciences at the University of Bath, UK.

Jocelyn Mawdsley is Senior Lecturer in European Politics at Newcastle University, UK.

Laura Chappell is Senior Lecturer in European Politics at the University of Surrey, UK.

Contemporary European Security

EDITED BY DAVID J. GALBREATH, JOCELYN MAWDSLEY, AND LAURA CHAPPELL

LONDON AND NEW YORK

First published 2019
by Routledge
2 Park Square, Milton Park, Abingdon, Oxon OX14 4RN

and by Routledge
52 Vanderbilt Avenue, New York, NY 10017

Routledge is an imprint of the Taylor & Francis Group, an informa business

© 2019 selection and editorial matter, David J. Galbreath, Jocelyn
Mawdsley, and Laura Chappell; individual chapters, the contributors

The right of David J. Galbreath, Jocelyn Mawdsley, and Laura
Chappell to be identified as the authors of the editorial material,
and of the authors for their individual chapters, has been asserted in
accordance with sections 77 and 78 of the Copyright, Designs and
Patents Act 1988.

All rights reserved. No part of this book may be reprinted or
reproduced or utilised in any form or by any electronic, mechanical,
or other means, now known or hereafter invented, including
photocopying and recording, or in any information storage or
retrieval system, without permission in writing from the publishers.

Trademark notice: Product or corporate names may be trademarks
or registered trademarks, and are used only for identification and
explanation without intent to infringe.

British Library Cataloguing in Publication Data
A catalogue record for this book is available from the British Library

Library of Congress Cataloging in Publication Data
Names: Galbreath, David J., editor. | Mawdsley, Jocelyn, editor. |
    Chappell, Laura, 1980- editor.
Title: Contemporary European security / edited by David Galbreath,
    Jocelyn Mawdsley and Laura Chappell.
Description: Abingdon, Oxon ; New York, NY : Routledge, 2019. |
    Includes bibliographical references and index.
Identifiers: LCCN 2018055404| ISBN 9780415473569 (hardback) |
    ISBN 9780415473576 (pbk.) | ISBN 9781351235600 (epub) | ISBN
    9781351235594 (mobipocket/kindle)
Subjects: LCSH: National security—Europe—Textbooks. | Europe—
    Military policy—Textbooks. | Security, International—Textbooks. |
    Europe—Politics and government—1989—Textbooks. | Europe—
    Foreign relations—1989—Textbooks. | Europe—Strategic
    aspects—Textbooks.
Classification: LCC UA646 .C674 2019 | DDC 355/.03304—dc23
LC record available at https://lccn.loc.gov/2018055404

ISBN: 978-0-415-47356-9 (hbk)
ISBN: 978-0-415-47357-6 (pbk)
ISBN: 978-1-351-23562-4 (ebk)

Typeset in Dante
by Swales & Willis Ltd, Exeter, Devon, UK

To the University Association for Contemporary European Studies (UACES)
and to its late Executive Director, Luke Foster (d. 2015)

Contents

Figures

Tables

Boxes

Contributors

André Barrinha is Lecturer in International Security at the University of Bath and a researcher at the Centre for Social Studies, University of Coimbra.

Raphael Bossong is a researcher at Stiftung Wissenschaft und Politik in Berlin.

Laura Chappell is Senior Lecturer in European Politics at the University of Surrey.

David J. Galbreath is Professor of International Security and Dean of the Faculty of Humanities & Social Sciences at the University of Bath.

Hendrik Hegemann is a Lecturer in International Relations and Peace and Conflict Research at the University of Osnabrück.

Peter Viggo Jakobsen is Associate Professor in the Department of Strategy at the Royal Danish Defence College and Professor (part-time) at the Center for War Studies, University of Southern Denmark.

Jocelyn Mawdsley is Senior Lecturer in European Politics at Newcastle University.

Sarah da Mota is an independent researcher based in Switzerland.

Simon J. Smith is Associate Professor of Security and International Relations at Staffordshire University.

James Sperling is Professor of Political Science at the University of Akron.

Katharine A. M. Wright is Lecturer in International Politics at Newcastle University.

Acknowledgements

From the original inception of this book to its eventual publication, 'contemporary' European security has been in flux. Originally signed in 2008, the goal was to capture European security in what it had become: increasingly European and stable. Reflecting over ten years later, Europe seems to be creaking at the seams, with the UK headed, at the time of writing, towards Brexit, an increasingly uninterested and sometimes hostile US Administration under Donald Trump, a Russian supplied secessionist war in Ukraine plus the occupation and incorporation of Crimea into the Russian Federation, the population flows from the wars and instability in Syria, Egypt, Tunisia, Democratic Republic of Congo and beyond, to the perpetuation of radical religious violence and the resurgence of ultra-nationalist violence in Europe, to the increasingly nationalists governments in Turkey, Hungary and Poland. While the institutions of European security such as NATO, the EU and OSCE continue to play an important role, they are not able to address many of issues that face contemporary European security. Rather, from climate change to a resurgent Russia, there is a distinct lack of a European response to these destabilising circumstances. In other words, had this book been published in 2010 when it was originally scheduled, it would have looked a lot different.

Originally planned as a single authored text, then multi-authored and then multi-edited (by the past and contemporary editors of *European Security*), the book had to change with the changing character of European security. The editors bring together a variety of contributors who work in and around European security, though from a variety of different perspectives. As editors and contributors, we recognise that textbooks are increasingly unrewarding as everything from the Research Excellence Framework (REF) in the UK to the drive to 'publish or perish' puts increasing pressure on how scholars use their time. Nevertheless, we have overcome these changes in European security and pressures on the contemporary scholar to deliver what we believe is a textbook that can inform students of European and international politics about the core themes and key changes in European security. We do take a commitment to our students as the foundation for this book.

Together, we would like to thank the contributors who were able to make this textbook a more representative and informed collection and Alex Neads for his help with the final editing of the manuscript. We would also like to thank at Routledge, publishing editor Andrew Taylor for his patience and support, and editorial assistant Sophie Iddamalgoda, as well as Craig Fowlie, who started all this, Nicola Parkin, Peter Harris, and Charlotte Endersby.

David J. Galbreath would like to thank in the first instance Jocelyn Mawdsley and Laura Chappell. Without their role in this project since they joined me as authors and editors, I would not have been able to deliver. Second, I would like to personally thank Craig Fowlie, who pressured me over an espresso in Turin, Italy at an ECPR SGIR conference to take on the book in the first place. Third, I would like to thank my European security students at the University of Aberdeen from 2004 and 2010 and the University of Bath from 2010 to 2013. Finally, I would like to thank my wife, who has to suffer my often over-commitment in an otherwise time poor position as Dean of Faculty.

Jocelyn Mawdsley would like to thank her family and friends who have heard far too much about this book, as well as the Newcastle University Politics students, who have helped her to think through the challenges of teaching contemporary European security.

Laura Chappell would like to thank her colleagues in the Department of Politics, as well as her students, both past and present, at the University of Surrey. Our discussions on European security have helped to shape some of the content in this textbook. Finally, she would like to thank her friends and family, and particularly Darren, for their support.

A changing security architecture

1

*Laura Chappell, David J. Galbreath
and Jocelyn Mawdsley*

Introduction

Contemporary European security is as complex and complicated as it has always been. One only needs to pick up a paper or go online to see high-profile issues such as Britain's nuclear deterrent, terrorist attacks in European cities, crises in Europe's periphery from the invasion of Ukraine by a resurgent Russia to the ongoing civil war in Syria and the resulting refugee crisis. Gone are the days when the main threat to Europe was a nuclear war between the two superpowers. At the same time, while Europe seems to be no longer the staging ground for a nuclear holocaust, the insecurity that states and their people experience continues to dominate global, regional and local communities. *Contemporary European Security* analyses the changing nature of European security since the end of the Cold War and represents an insightful study into the importance of how regional organisations, national governments and individuals perceive and experience security.

First, the chapter asks how we might understand European security. We look at the debates about what constitutes 'Europe' and 'security'. Second, the chapter introduces readers to the relevance of the topic in the international relations curriculum. The chapter offers several areas of contemporary international relations strongly highlighted in European security. These areas are the important role of regional organisations, the role of the state and the role of the individual in international relations. Furthermore, we ask: what are the primary threats to European security today? What is the European security community/complex? What role should different regional organisations play in European security? What impact do states have on European security? How is European security challenged by non-state actors? How is European security affected by global security? Finally, the chapter details the structure of the book.

Unpacking European security

If we want to analyse European security we need to begin by considering what the term Europe actually means. As Delanty (1995, p. 1) argues: 'every age reinvented the idea of

Europe in the mirror of its own identity'. While, geographically, the conventional definition of Europe is delimited by the Ural Mountains and the river of the same name running into the Caspian Sea, this has often proved controversial. In particular, large geographical areas of Russia and Turkey are outside this boundary, but both have historical and political claims to be European, and both are important considerations in the question of European security, as we shall see in Chapter 7. Moreover, few would argue that the concept of Europe is purely geographical. Rather, over the centuries the word Europe has been associated with unifying concepts like the medieval Christendom or the Enlightenment. Importantly, such movements have been about fostering unity and inclusion on the one hand, but setting boundaries and, thus, exclusion on the other. The period this book covers is no different.

The Cold War divided the continent of Europe into two antagonistic blocs. As Chapter 2 outlines, both blocs developed mechanisms of security cooperation: in the West, the North Atlantic Treaty Organization (NATO) and the Western European Union, and, in the East, the Warsaw Pact. While some states remained neutral and non-aligned (Sweden, Finland, Switzerland, Austria and Ireland), security on the continent of Europe was a matter of mutual defence pacts and deep suspicion between the two blocs, rooted in the fear that the Cold War might turn into a hot military conflict (Hobsbawm, 1994). After the fall of the Berlin Wall in 1989, the collapse of communist regimes across Eastern Europe followed rapidly, and the constitutional reunification between East and West Germany was matched by rhetoric about the reunification of Europe.

The reunification of Europe took on a highly institutionalised format through the enlargement processes of both the EU and NATO (Schimmelfennig, 2003). Membership of both institutions was gradually extended to many of the former Warsaw Pact members. However, as German (2017) argues, it created new boundaries, new European frontiers – enlargement, while viewed as enhancing European security at the time, may, in fact, have led to new conflict. Moreover, it perpetuated an image of Fortress Europe – security within the bounds but insecurity outside. Russia was excluded and 'buffer zone' states like Georgia and Ukraine were left in the uncomfortable position of trying to placate both Russia and NATO/European Union (EU). The definition of what constitutes contemporary Europe in terms of military security has always struggled to accommodate Russia. More recently, too, Turkey, under Erdogan, despite being a long-standing member of NATO, has been in open disagreement with its allies, and increasingly, too, its European credentials are questioned. Finally, a core member of both NATO and the EU, the United Kingdom, has chosen to leave the EU; again this raises questions about what Europe means. Is it purely geographical, a question of institutional memberships, or a deeper sense of being a part of a joint political project?

If Europe is difficult to define, security is even more challenging. It is, perhaps, a myth that there was a clear understanding of what national security meant throughout the Cold War. Among both policymakers and academics, realism predominated as the explanatory framework for state behaviour, as Chapter 3 explains. Realism makes the assumption that states act rationally to maximise their interests while prioritising state survival, but, even during the Cold War, security decisions were made that were not based entirely on rational calculations of national interests. As Katzenstein (1996, p. 2) points out, the Cold War cannot be understood solely as a 'bipolar, ideological struggle'; nevertheless, it is true that there was a clear military threat evident during the Cold War and this took priority over any other security concerns for most European states. After the conflicts leading to decolonisation had ended, only where domestic terrorism was prolonged and serious was attention diverted from the main security concern of the East–West confrontation (Jongman, 1992).

The end of the Cold War meant that European states, for the first time in decades, had no immediate military threats to their physical integrity (with the major exception of the conflicts in the former Yugoslavia and former Soviet states – see Chapter 2). This opened up space to reconceptualise security in both academic and policy-making circles. As Chapter 3 explores in more depth, European academics were at the forefront of this discussion. Within this debate, two main strands were discernible: the broadening of the national security agenda to include non-military threats and the deepening of the security agenda to consider the security of individuals, not just states.

Ullman (1983) was one of the first to critique the concentration on external military threats, pointing out that this risked both ignoring non-military threats with the power to destabilise states and underestimating threats from within. This has led to much broader ideas about what might constitute security threats. The Copenhagen School, for example, identifies five general categories or sectors of security: military, environmental, economic, societal and political security (Buzan et al., 1998). Migration, international terrorism and environmental degradation have become standard chapters in security studies textbooks. However, the broadening of the security agenda is not without its critics. Some, like Ayoob (1997), argue that it is unhelpful to conflate problems of global management with international security. A more serious critique is outlined by proponents of securitisation theory; here, it is argued that by defining an issue as a security issue through speech acts, politicians can claim the need for extraordinary measures to block the threat, thus threatening human rights (Buzan et al., 1998).

At the same time, some security studies scholars and policy-makers focused on challenging the state as the referent object of security; that is, the thing to be secured – a debate known as the deepening agenda (see Chapter 8). The question they posed was whether entities other than the state should be able to claim security threats that need international action. Is the state always the best guarantor of its citizens' security? While authors have proposed moving upwards to the level of the international, and downwards to regional and societal levels, the argument that has gained most attention in the academic and practitioner worlds is that of human security: the security threats to the individual (UNDP, 1993). Similarly, as Chapter 9 shows, the place of women in peace and security began to attract concentrated scholarly attention. Both the broadening and deepening agendas challenged how Europeans thought about security, what they understood to be security threats and which institutions might be best placed to respond to such threats. The predominance of NATO and military security seemed threatened.

IR and contemporary European security

So far, we have discussed how the changes after the end of the Cold War influenced debates among academics and policy-makers about what European security actually means. We now need to situate those concerns within the wider discipline of International Relations (IR).

With the growth of the IR scholarship in the twentieth century, explaining conflict and its absence became a core object of attention. The search for answers surrounding security has been most pronounced in the realist paradigm of IR, which perceives the international system we live in today to be obsessed with security from others outside. As we shall see, this obsession lies at the level of the nation-state, although realists have their roots in realist philosophies of individual behaviour.

In the twentieth century, IR scholarship focused intensely on security in the Europe context. Europe as a subject of IR scholarship came about for two primary reasons. First, the twentieth century witnessed three major events that greatly shaped the way some explain international politics and, thus, security: the First World War, Second World War, and the Cold War. Each of these conflicts had its root in Europe, although all had a global impact. Even the space between the two world wars was of great interest, seeing as it was the case study in E. H. Carr's seminal work on the study of IR (Carr, 1946). Many scholars took the view that IR was about boom and bust; or, more appropriately, war and peace. In other words, peace failed when the status quo broke down and war ended when a new status quo was established (Kennedy, 1987). Second, the growth in IR scholarship came with the ascendency of the US academic system, which perpetuated a Euro-centric view of IR, for the reason mentioned above, in addition to the impact the European scholarly legacy has had on the US intellectual tradition (see Chapter 3 for more discussion). The good news, then, is that for students of European security, there is much to find out there in terms of academic literature, including theoretical and conceptual frameworks that were actually based on Europe in the beginning. The bad news may be that there is simply too much literature with which to come to terms. This is where this book fits in.

Our discussion of security begins with the question: 'Whose security?' We start by looking at three objects of security: states, individuals, and international organisations. Traditionally, IR scholarship has thought of security in terms of national security (Wolfers, 1952). And traditionalists have done this for good reasons: nations have a near monopoly on mass, organised violence. In other words, states have the ability to cause the most harm. At the same time, states have increasingly relied on alliances and international organisations to protect them and their allies. These institutions have become, at the least, mechanisms of national security and, at most, security actors within themselves. Yet, with the state and international organisations in mind, we think most often about our own security: the security of the individual. For example, we think about where we walk, at what time of day, and with whom. States, international organisations, and individuals are what 'security studies' refers to as the 'referent object': to what does this security refer? Since this book attempts to stress the role of each in our discussion of contemporary European security, we look at them in more detail.

As discussed, nation-states, or 'states', have been the traditional focus or 'referent object' in security studies. 'The academic study of international politics . . . continues to be motivated by and concerned with the two faces of Janus: war and peace between states' (Holsti, 1996, p. 6). There are two characteristics of states that make it the traditional focus of security studies. First, as a political community, a state has the responsibility to protect its people. As citizens and taxpayers, we expect our government to protect us, at the very least, from physical harm.

Second, a state tends to be large enough to maintain a capability to defend its population. In other words, ordinarily we do not expect city governments or wealthy individuals to protect us from physical harm. Instead, security is monitored and maintained at the highest level of political organisation: the state. The focus on national security has dominated security studies as a discipline but also dominates the way policy-makers determine what is and is not a threat. Finally, national security generally tends to be the way we (as citizens and taxpayers) think about security. It appears clear that the state is an important actor and object of security.

Yet, how does the 'state' fit into how we think about contemporary European security? For instance, the EU has offered European citizens the freedom to move and work across borders. At the same time, Europeanisation has encouraged greater sub-regional identification, such as being Breton first and French second. Today, someone living in Rennes may feel Breton, French and European (Luhmann, 2017). In this case, who needs to be secured? Who should be doing the securing? Perhaps this is where regional organisations fit. For instance, as we shall see in Chapter 6, the EU (or, more precisely, its member states) has made great progress in establishing mechanisms by which to maintain European security. At the same time, security has been a policy area where states remain unwilling to cede too much power or responsibility to the EU. Even in Europe, which has progressed so far in creating a regional political community, national security is primarily a lingering responsibility for states.

The 'pluralist' challenge to the traditional view of IR and, thus, security, argued that the focus on the state was at best misleading and at worst simply incorrect (Ullman, 1983). For instance, scholars of foreign policy could see that states do not act as a unitary actor tied to reacting to the international community. Rather, foreign policy analysis insisted that domestic factors played an important role in policy-makers' decisions. Issues of national security, as an aspect of foreign policy, are the responsibility of a select group of policy makers. This reinforces the focus on the state as the central agent and object of security. The next challenge to the state-centric approach to security looked beyond the state to established and formal interactions between states. In other words, security studies began to take account of international organisations as key agents of international security.

In contemporary international security, much of the responsibility to protect people from physical harm is borne by international organisations. The basis of international organisations is cooperation between two or more political communities. We can think of a defence alliance as a means of cooperation for the sake of mutual security. As this cooperation becomes more established, this multilateral relationship between states may become a political community within itself. This development has happened so much that today we talk about the 'United Nations (UN)' in the former Yugoslavia or 'NATO' in Afghanistan as agents of security. This transition of responsibilities from the state to international organisations occurs when decisions regarding those organisations', and, thus, member states', actions are taken at the level of multilateral decision making and enacted through previously established mechanisms to ensure security. These organisations, although dominated by more powerful states, may begin to take on an operational culture of their own, which differentiates their behaviour from any individual member state. In this way, international organisations become an additional focus of security studies and one of particular importance in Europe.

Institutionalising a security structure for Europe

Today, the three European security institutions under examination in this book have overlapping membership, which became more prominent following the post-Cold War enlargements. The EU, NATO and the Organization for Security and Co-operation in Europe (OSCE) share 22 member states out of 28, 29 and 57 countries, respectively, listed within Table 1.1. Of the seven non-EU NATO and OSCE European members, three NATO/OSCE

Table 1.1 Institutional membership

EU membership				
Austria	Belgium	Bulgaria	Croatia	Cyprus
Czechia	Denmark	Estonia	Finland	France
Germany	Greece	Hungary	Ireland	Italy
Latvia	Lithuania	Luxembourg	Malta	Netherlands
Poland	Portugal	Romania	Slovakia	Slovenia
Spain	Sweden	UK *		

NATO membership				
Albania	Belgium	Bulgaria	Canada	Croatia
Czechia	Denmark	Estonia	France	Germany
Greece	Hungary	Iceland	Italy	Latvia
Lithuania	Luxembourg	Montenegro	Netherlands	Norway
Poland	Portugal	Romania	Slovakia	Slovenia
Spain	Turkey	UK	USA	

OSCE membership				
Albania	Andorra	Armenia	Austria	Azerbaijan
Belarus	Belgium	Bosnia (BiH)	Bulgaria	Canada
Croatia	Cyprus	Czechia	Denmark	Estonia
Finland	France	Georgia	Germany	Greece
Holy See	Hungary	Iceland	Ireland	Italy
Kazakhstan	Kyrgyzstan	Latvia	Liechtenstein	Lithuania
Luxembourg	Malta	Moldova	Monaco	Mongolia
Montenegro	Netherlands	Norway	Poland	Portugal
Romania	Russia	San Marino	Serbia	Slovakia
Slovenia	Spain	Sweden	Switzerland	Tajikistan
FYROM	Turkey	Turkmenistan	Ukraine	UK
USA	Uzbekistan			

* At the time of writing this chapter, the United Kingdom is expected to leave the EU on 29 March 2019.

members and two OSCE members are EU candidate countries. This leads us to question what the role(s) of each institution are and how these have changed to address the post Cold War security environment. While each organisation was set up to carry out different tasks, the change in the meaning of security and how each has understood this has, in turn, affected how they have evolved. This has led to debates regarding burden sharing and duplication, particularly between the EU and NATO, as the former began to make incursions into the traditional area of defence, while the latter began to incorporate a civilian dimension into its crisis management activities.

The oldest of these organisations is NATO, which was founded on 4 April 1949 with the signing of the Washington Treaty. The aim of the organisation was to ensure security in the NATO area through nuclear deterrence and collective defence (Flockhart, 2011, p. 267). The latter is enshrined in Article Five, which underlines that an attack on one member is an attack on all members (NATO, 2018). However the article does not specify what action (if any) should be taken, leaving it to individual member states to decide on what 'appropriate action' means in practice. This would become important as discussions regarding NATO's role post Cold War materialised (see Chapter 2 and Chapter 4). While NATO sought to provide a defence alliance for its members, the EU's role contributed to security in a qualitatively different way. The underlying premise of the organisation, which started as the Economic Coal and Steel Community, before becoming the European Economic Community (EEC) on 1 January 1958, was to bring together the war machines of France and Germany. As such, the fundamental basis of the EEC was a political peace project conducted through economic reconstruction that brought together such themes as trust, reconciliation and interdependence (Manners and Murray, 2016, pp. 189–190). Finally, the OSCE was founded in 1975 as the Conference on Cooperation and Security in Europe. It sought to bring together countries on either side of the Iron Curtain and, in particular, the main protagonists – the USA and USSR. As Chapter 5 sets out, the organisation focused on a traditional politio-military approach to security but combined this with economic, environmental and human security dimensions. Thus, it occupied a position between the EEC and NATO in terms of its contribution to security while providing the only regional institutional platform for dialogue between the two sides.

The end of the Cold War and subsequent security events both within and outside of Europe were to have a significant impact on what kind of organisations the EU, NATO and the OSCE were. This led to key questions surrounding their development, and even existence, as security actors. The collapse of the USSR led to the creation of several new states which, in addition to the freeing of the captured east (i.e., those central and east European states which were under USSR tutelage), led to an expansion of all three organisations' memberships. Events in southern and Eastern Europe also meant that the EU, in particular, began to seek a security and defence role for itself, while, conversely, NATO sought to complement its traditional defence perspective with a cooperative security dimension focused on partnerships with non-NATO members, underscoring both organisations' ability to find new roles (Flockhart, 2011). Meanwhile, the CSCE, which became the OSCE in 1994, was hamstrung by the desire of the USA that it did not duplicate NATO's functions and of Russia, that wanted the OSCE to become the collective European security regional organisation of choice (Galbreath, 2007). Hence, the organisation, which at first sight seemed best equipped to fulfil a security agenda requiring a comprehensive approach, failed to meet this role. The EU's momentum towards a military actor accumulated in the Common Security and Defence Policy (CSDP) in 1999, while NATO expanded its remit to out of area operations in the Balkans. However, the post 9/11 environment was to test NATO's role as a military actor and lead it to seek to complement its traditional military security role with a civilian role, as underpinned by NATO's ISAF in Afghanistan (see Chapter 4).

Two key aspects precipitated this. First was a change in the security environment post Cold War and particularly post 9/11, which focused *inter alia* on international terrorism and the proliferation of weapons of mass destruction as core threat perceptions in the US and its European allies. Second was how these threats were to be addressed. In essence, the protection of Europe depended on the requirement to go out of area to meet the threat, as demonstrated by the then German Defence Minister Struck's comment that 'German defence will also be defended at the Hindu Kush' (Büchner, 2002, p. 2, translated for this edition), a mountain range in Afghanistan. This also highlighted a change in how war was to be conducted and peace achieved (or not), which involved a shift in security thinking and the transformation of American and European armed forces. While the Revolution in Military Affairs, involving rapid reaction forces and the advent of Network Centric Warfare was embraced by the US as its originator and, to a lesser degree, the UK and France, countries such as Germany were slower to react (Dyson, 2016). Theoretically, we can understand or explain this through alternative lenses – from differences in strategic culture to neo-classical realist insights into the role of domestic intervening factors, which affect the way in which a state can respond to the dictates of changes in the international environment (Dyson, 2016; Meyer, 2006).

None the less, winning the peace involves more than flexible armed forces, but a combination of military and civilian tools, underscored in the idea of a comprehensive approach to security, highlighted above. Moreover, the peace dividend that was supposed to materialise after the Cold War had resulted in European countries downsizing their armed forces and defence budgets (Howorth, 2014, p. 75), to the extent that the majority could not deploy significant military force unilaterally. Additionally, international law, underpinned by the dual components of legality and legitimacy, were gained through acquiring a UN Security Council Resolution for military action. This ensured that engagement in multilateral operations became the norm, although, as NATO's military action in Kosovo demonstrated, not always the rule (see below). However, this brings up the question as to whether international organisations act at the behest of their members or whether they acquire their own independent actorness as role theory would highlight, for example (Furness, 2013; Harnisch et al., 2011). It is important to note that states decide on whether to deploy their troops or put them on rotation in stand-by or very high readiness forces. That said, regional organisations have a role to play in presenting policy initiatives, which has been the case particularly in respect to the EU (see Chapter 6).

Hence, post Cold War, all three organisations were finding their role in the new security environment, which involved a certain amount of duplication between them. This has led to the burden-sharing debate – particularly between the EU and NATO. It should be noted, at this juncture, that there is no formal burden-sharing agreement between the two beyond the

Berlin Plus agreement (2002), which gives the EU recourse to NATO assets (Smith, 2011). Since the EU enlargement in 2004, however, the Berlin Plus agreement has become unusable due to the political stalemate surrounding the division of Cyprus (see Chapter 4). However, if we look at the Balkans in particular, we find that all three organisations were involved in security measures with separate but complementary roles (Smith, 2011). NATO's focus was obviously military, as its operations in Bosnia and Herzegovina (BiH), Kosovo and North Macedonia aptly demonstrated. Indeed, NATO was key to bringing the violence to an end, although its actions in Kosovo are controversial as it operated without a UN Security Council Resolution. The OSCE had a civilian role to play from the early 1990s, first in FYROM before providing a civilian focus to complement NATO's military operations in BiH and Kosovo. Hence, its focus was on border management, police reform, education and local elections (see Chapter 5). Finally, the EU as a security actor came later with the first civilian missions and military operations being deployed in 2003 in FYROM and BiH. Currently, the EU has EUFOR Althea in BiH (from 2004 to present), which took over from NATO's operation, and EULEX Kosovo (from 2008 to present), which provides the civilian dimension with NATO's KFOR providing the military protection – although coordination is, at times, challenging (Smith, 2011, pp. 253–256).

What does this tell us about the role of these three regional institutions? First, with over-lapping memberships, states can choose the institution that best fits the task they want carried out or which underpins their own security interests and/or strategic culture (Hofmann, 2011). This idea of forum shopping can be highlighted when looking at anti-piracy operations in the Gulf of Aden, for example, where the EU's Operation Atalanta and, until recently, NATO's Operation Ocean Shield were deployed. Second is that for all the discussion on the risk of unnecessary duplication between the EU and NATO, the former is not about to acquire an equivalent of Article Five. In other words, collective defence remains purely under the remit of NATO. More recently with the Ukraine crisis, NATO has been rediscovering its traditional collective defence role, which had been masked by its focus on crisis management operations, particularly in Afghanistan (see Ringsmose and Rynning, 2017). Meanwhile, the EU's and the OSCE's comprehensive approach means that they can fulfil civilian tasks which NATO cannot, even though NATO has been making moves in this direction, as the Provisional Reconstruction Teams demonstrate. However, the EU's military development separates it from the OSCE and, with a smaller membership without the two main military protagonists, can operate more easily. Hence, Europe's regional security architecture has developed in a way in which none of the three organisations fulfil identical tasks.

Contemporary European (in)securities

While debate about European security is conceptualised by its dense institutional architec-ture, the question remains whether this architecture actually secures Europe. At the time of writing, the key institutions have all been put under pressure and questions are being asked about whether they are fit for purpose. In the US, President Trump has directly questioned the collective security guarantee offered by NATO to its member states, bringing into question the transatlantic security relationship (see Chapter 4). The EU's ability to manage crises has been brought into question by the sovereign debt crisis, the refugee crisis, democratic backsliding by member states, resurgent nationalism and Brexit. Despite commitments to deeper internal security cooperation, European security has been rocked by repeated terrorism attacks (see Chapter 7). Meanwhile, a more aggressive Russia is creating insecurity in its neighbouring states by its interventions in both Ukraine and Georgia. This, in turn, seems to threaten the pan-European cooperation embodied by the OSCE (see Chapter 5). If the eastern neighbourhood feels threatening, Europe's southern neighbourhood is in open military conflict, destabilising many of Europe's neighbours (see Chapter 10).

In short, the threats to European security are multi-faceted and complex. Nor can they be simply be solved by military responses. As a result, whereas during the Cold War, security was something largely confined to ministries of defence, now multiple ministries are involved, making cooperation ever more complex. These threats also raise difficult questions for liberal democracies about the correct balance between civil liberties and security (see Chapter 7). Europe's security institutions are struggling to innovate in response to such wide-ranging and often hybrid threats. Security spending has not been a priority in recent decades and militaries have struggled to adapt and modernise (see Chapter 11). Frequently, they seem too immersed in their own institutional challenges. While concepts like women, peace and security (Chapter 9) and human security (Chapter 8) have been attractive to the institutions as they seek new narratives to explain their rationale, often they have not been able to meet these challenging objectives. At the same time, advances in military technology and the changing nature of warfare have demanded modernisation of both national armed forces and the European-level institutions that foster security cooperation.

In short, the current period seems to mark an end to the optimism embodied in the 1990s that European security was a question of the past. Rather as this book aims to do, we need to reconceptualise what security now means to European institutions, states and Europeans themselves. The challenges facing contemporary Europe are ones that force citizens, states and institutions to question what they understand security to mean, what the legitimate means to respond might be and why particular challenges are leading to feelings of insecurity, when previously they had not (Kinnvall et al., 2018).

Structure of the book

In order to address the key overarching themes in European security, this textbook looks at three research areas. The first, on framing European security, provides the historical and theoretical foundations to the book. Following on from this introductory chapter, the second chapter by Laura Chappell and Jocelyn Mawdsley introduces the reader to contemporary European security through a temporal review of key security innovations and events from the post-war settlement, through the Cold War and into the post Cold War period. Chapter 3, by André Barrinha and Sarah da Mota, provides an overview of the main theoretical approaches from the traditional realist and liberalist theories, to the constructivist turn in international relations and then to critical security studies. Hence, the chapter lays the foundation for a continual conceptual and theoretical conversation throughout the remaining part of the book.

The second area, on institutions of European security reviews the three primary security institutions in Europe: NATO, the OSCE and the EU. Chapter 4, by James Sperling, underscores the changing role of NATO from the Cold War to the present day and includes discussions on NATO's purpose, strategy and operations. Chapter 5, by David J. Galbreath, looks at the OSCE, which is particularly interesting for students of security given its focus on 'common and comprehensive security'. It highlights the changing functions of the OSCE and provides an overview of its missions as well as an emphasis on more recent political tensions. Chapter 6, by Laura Chappell and David J. Galbreath, analyses the increasing importance of security for the EU, focusing on the creation and development of the CSDP. It encompasses the key political and institutional innovations, underscoring the ongoing discussions on the role of the EU in defence as well as highlighting some of the main military operations and civilian missions.

The final area, on issues of European security, covers a range of important themes. We begin by introducing the challenges posed by soft security questions deliberately, because they have the most impact on the day-to-day lives of Europeans. Chapter 6 moves on to a discussion on resilience as a replacement, less interventionist concept in EU policy. The chapter by Raphael Bossong and Hendrik Hegemann looks at the ways in which internal security has become a matter for great concern for European societies and their security institutions and builds on the idea of securitisation. Topic areas include counter-terrorism, border control and the refugee crisis with a corresponding discussion on the trade-offs between privacy, civil rights and security. Chapter 8, by Jocelyn Mawdsley, expands the traditional discussion of European security to human security. It covers the introduction of the topic and explores how disillusionment has set in following the undermining of R2P in Afghanistan and Iraq. Broadening the scope beyond the military as traditionally conceived, Chapter 9, by Katharine A. M. Wright, underscores the importance of gender to European security. It compares and contrasts the gendered composition of two European security institutions, NATO and the EU's CSDP. In so doing, the chapter explores the role of structure, practice and performance in gendering European security and includes contemporary developments, particularly by introducing the Women, Peace and Security agenda encapsulated in UNSCR 1325.

The book then moves on to hard security questions. Chapter 10, by Peter Viggo Jakobsen, outlines the fundamental threats to Europe, highlighting 'the ring of fire' encompassing Europe from Russia through to the MENA region. The chapter examines European security institutions' responses and asks whether these new threats have empowered or undermined particular institutions. Chapter 11, by Simon J. Smith, examines the various ways defence forces in Europe have innovated to accommodate having to do more with fewer resources. It provides an insight into the varied and particular approaches to innovation that European militaries have incorporated to meet their material, ideational and operational challenges. The final chapter, by Laura Chappell, Jocelyn Mawdsley and David J. Galbreath, acts as a review of the key contributions within the chapters and sets out implications for the politics within the European security architecture. This includes what this means for how Europe might maintain regional peace and security.

Further reading

Galbreath, David J. (2007), *The Organization for Security and Co-operation in Europe (OSCE)*. Abingdon: Routledge.
Howorth, Jolyon (2014), *Security and Defence Policy in the European Union*. Basingstoke: Palgrave Macmillan.
Manners, Ian, and Murray, Philomena (2016), 'The End of a Noble Narrative? European Integration Narratives after the Nobel Peace Prize', *Journal of Common Market Studies*, 54 (1), 185–202.
Webber, Mark, and Hyde-Price, Adrian (eds) (2015), *Theorising NATO: New Perspectives on the Atlantic Alliance*. London: Routledge.

Weblinks

European Union: www.europa.eu
North Atlantic Treaty Organisation: www.nato.int
Organization for Security and Co-operation: www.osce.org
Stockholm International Peace Research Institute: www.sipri.org

References

Ayoob, Mohammed (1997), 'Defining Security: A Subaltern Realist Perspective', in Keith Krause and Michael Williams (eds), *Critical Security Studies: Concepts and Cases*. London: UCL Press, pp. 121–147.
Büchner, G. (2002), 'Neuer Auftrag für die Bundeswehr Struck: Wehrpflicht Bleibt', *Berliner Zeitung*, 5 December.
Buzan, Barry, Waever, Ole and de Wilde, Jaap (1998), *Security: A New Framework for Analysis*. Boulder, CO: Lynne Rienner.
Carr, Edward Hallett (1946), *The 20 Years' Crisis 1919–1939: An Introduction to the Study of International Relations* (2nd ed.). Basingstoke: Palgrave Macmillan.
Delanty, Gerard (1995), *Inventing Europe: Idea, Identity, Reality*. Basingstoke: Macmillan.
Dyson, Tom (2016), *Neoclassical Realism and Defence Reform in Post-Cold War Europe*. Basingstoke: Palgrave Macmillan.
Flockhart, Trine (2011), '"Me Tarzan – You Jane": The EU and NATO and the Reversal of Roles', *Perspectives on European Politics and Society*, 12 (3), 263–282.
Furness, Mark (2013), 'Who Controls the European External Action Service – Agent Autonomy in EU External Policy', *European Foreign Affairs Review*, 18 (1), 103–125.
Galbreath, David J. (2007), *The Organization for Security and Co-operation in Europe (OSCE)*. Abingdon: Routledge.
German, Tracey (2017), 'NATO and the Enlargement Debate: Enhancing Euro-Atlantic Security or Inciting Confrontation?', *International Affairs*, 93 (2), 291–308.
Harnisch, Sebastian, Frank, Cornelia, and Maull, Hans (2011), *Role Theory in International Relations: Approaches and Analyses*. Abingdon: Routledge.
Hobsbawm, Eric (1994), *The Age of Extremes: The Short Twentieth Century 1914–1991*. London: Abacus.
Hofmann, Stéphanie C. (2011), 'Why Institutional Overlap Matters: CSDP in the European Security Architecture', *Journal of Common Market Studies*, 49 (1), 101–112.

Holsti, Kal (1996), *The State, War and the State of War*. Cambridge: Cambridge University Press.

Howorth, Jolyon (2014), *Security and Defence Policy in the European Union*. Basingstoke: Palgrave Macmillan.

Jongman, Albert (1992), 'Trends in International and Domestic Terrorism in Western Europe, 1968–1988', *Terrorism and Political Violence*, 4 (4), 26–76.

Katzenstein, Peter (1996), 'Introduction', in Peter Katzenstein (ed), *The Culture of National Security: Norms and Identity in World Politics*. New York: Columbia University Press, pp. 1–32.

Kennedy, Paul (1987), *The Rise and Fall of the Great Powers: Economic and Military Conflict from 1500 to 2000*. New York: Random House.

Kinnvall, Catarina, Manners, Ian, and Mitzen, Jennifer (2018), 'Introduction to 2018 Special Issue of *European Security*: "Ontological (In)Security in the European Union"', *European Security*, 27 (3), 249–265.

Luhmann, Sybille (2017), 'A Multi-Level Approach to European Identity: Does Integration Foster Identity?', *Journal of Common Market Studies*, 55 (6), 1360–1379.

Manners, Ian, and Murray, Philomena (2016), 'The End of a Noble Narrative? European Integration Narratives after the Nobel Peace Prize', *Journal of Common Market Studies*, 54 (1), 185–202.

Meyer, Christoph (2006), *The Quest for a European Strategic Culture: Changing Norms on Security and Defence in the European Union*. New York: Palgrave Macmillan.

NATO (2018), *The North Atlantic Treaty*. Available at: www.nato.int/cps/ie/natohq/official_texts_17120.htm (accessed: 16 October 2018).

Ringsmose, Jens, and Rynning, Sten (2017), 'Now for the Hard Part: NATO's Strategic Adaptation to Russia', *Survival*, 59 (3), 129–146.

Schimmelfennig, Frank (2003), *The EU, NATO and the Integration of Europe: Rules and Rhetoric*. Cambridge: Cambridge University Press.

Smith, Simon J. (2011), 'EU–NATO Cooperation: A Case of Institutional Fatigue?', *European Security*, 20 (2), 243–264.

Ullman, Richard (1983), 'Redefining Security', *International Security*, 8 (1), 129–153.

UNDP (1993), *Human Development Report 1993: People's Participation*. Available at: http://hdr.undp.org/en/reports/global/hdr1993/ (accessed: 16 October 2018).

Wolfers, Arnold (1952), '"National Security" as an Ambiguous Symbol', *Political Quarterly*, 67 (4), 481–502.

From Cold War to European peace

2

Laura Chappell and Jocelyn Mawdsley

Introduction

It is impossible to understand contemporary European security without an appreciation of where its security institutions, practices and conventions come from. The aim of this chapter is to set the scene for the analysis that follows by tracing the historical developments that have shaped European understandings of security from the end of the Second World War to 1999. The devastation wreaked on the continent by the Second World War was quickly followed by the division of Europe into East and West; indeed, as Hobsbawm (1994) argued, the European demarcation lines had already been drawn in a series of summit meetings between the Soviets, British and Americans in the period of 1943–1945. The Cold War shaped the European security institutions of the twenty-first century, but also froze the multiple nationalist and ethnic tensions that had been such a feature of European security problems across the centuries. In some cases, this allowed reconciliation processes to take root, in others memories of past hatreds proved more resilient. The collapse of Communism in 1989, as Judt (2005) argues, was not just about the victory of capitalism; for many Europeans, particularly those in Central and Eastern Europe, it was about a return to Europe. Membership of Western European institutions offered an attainable set of political goals.

However, what might at first seem like a benign peace settlement to the once intractable ideological struggle between East and West has not been straightforward, nor has it been without its losers. The enlargement of the North Atlantic Treaty Organization (NATO) and the European Union (EU) has led to new borders, a new set of insiders and outsiders. The complex challenges of twenty-first century European security reflect some of the consequences of these decisions. Similarly, while the Cold War saw West European states lose their empires through the process of decolonisation, and instead focus on the European continent, the globalisation process means that, in the twenty-first century, European security problems demand a renewed global focus, something which some Europeans are uneasy about. But it is the history of the Cold War and its immediate aftermath that has shaped how contemporary Europeans organise security.

The first section of the chapter introduces the post-1945 settlement and the beginning of the Cold War. It focuses on the initial institutionalisation of European security, focusing on the North Atlantic Treaty and the Warsaw Pact. Second, the chapter examines how the Cold War unfolded in Europe. It highlights how the tension between the two superpowers, the United States and the Soviet Union, had an impact on both sides of the Iron Curtain. In particular, it looks at European responses to the Cold War, the policy of *détente* and the eventual end of the Cold War.

Third, the chapter looks at the continuities and changes in European security since the end of the Cold War. Hobsbawm (1994) argued that the Cold War had overshadowed the rivalries and conflicts that had previously shaped world politics, stabilising the provisional post-1945 borders. For Western Europe, the reconciliation process, particularly between France and West Germany, embedded in the European integration project, was strong enough to survive the potentially destabilising event of German reunification. As Griffiths (1993) argued, however, the end of the Cold War in Eastern Europe saw ethnic disputes re-emerge, most notably in the former Yugoslavia and the Soviet Union.

Finally, the chapter will address the recent history of four key European security institutions; NATO, the EU, the Organization for Security and Co-operation in Europe (OSCE), and the Council of Europe (CoE). Their respective histories and decisions on enlargement and boundaries since 1989 have shaped how security is understood in twenty-first century Europe. Hall (1996) pointed out the oddity of the post Cold War European order whereby old institutions persisted and evolved to deal with new realities. How these pre-existing institutions chose to respond to the end of the Cold War has both solved and created security problems. As Schimmelfennig and Sedelmeier predicted with respect to the EU, 'The future borders of the EU will replace the old East–West line of the Cold War as the central cleavage in the European system' (Schimmelfennig and Sedelmeier, 2002, p. 501). The Cold War entrenched the division of Europe; have decisions since 1989 merely moved the dividing line?

The division of Europe

A series of summits held by the allies from 1943–1945 had set some parameters for the post-war Europe. Now widely condemned as a cynical bargain, the idea of Soviet and Western spheres of influence was accepted, along with the partition of Germany into Soviet, American, British and French zones of occupation. Following the German surrender in May 1945, the partition of Europe effectively matched the military situation at this time. The advancing Soviet and American armies met at the Elbe. As Keylor (2011) argues, the two zones reflected the preferences of their liberating armies, as they re-established political systems and economic and foreign policies. This did not happen overnight: for several years after the war non-Communist parties took part in Central and Eastern European governments, while Communist parties were strong in many Western European states. However, Stalin was determined to establish pro-Soviet client states in the Soviet sphere of influence, and the political divisions began to harden.

By the end of the Second World War, the European continent was devastated. It was not just the physical destruction in terms of housing, communications, agricultural and industrial production, but also the human costs of large-scale displacements of people. This was not just the question of the repatriation or resettlement of Holocaust victims, refugees, forced labourers and prisoners-of-war, it was also about the movement of minority groups. As Judt (2005) points out, with the exception of Poland, which saw major border changes (losing territory to the East, but gaining territory in the West that had belonged to Germany), the post-1945 settlement saw the forced resettlement of national minorities, leaving states with much more homogenous populations. This was in comparison to the First World War peace settlement, which brought many border changes, but largely left people where they were.

The USA became deeply concerned with the vulnerability of Western European states to Soviet domination because of their inability to recover from the war economically. The US Secretary of State, George C. Marshall, in 1947 made an unprecedented offer of foreign economic aid to the states of Europe, including the Soviet Union and its satellites, in return for economic cooperation within Europe. This was considered but rejected by the Soviet Union and its allies. The 16 nations who agreed to take part drew up a four-year recovery plan, and, between 1948 and 1952, grants and credits worth $13.2 billion were disbursed (Keylor, 2011). The success of the Marshall Plan saw Western Europe embark on a period of rapid economic recovery and expansion, which further solidified the gap between the two blocs.

The search for a viable Western European security architecture design was already being discussed during the Second World War, with the British Foreign Office drawing up ideas about a Western European Security Group, based on a core Franco–British alliance (Greenwood, 1983). The Franco–British 1947 Treaty of Dunkirk established an alliance and mutual assistance guarantee. Both this treaty and the 1948 Brussels Pact, which extended the agreement to Belgium, Luxembourg and the Netherlands, were ostensibly to counter fears of any further German aggression (Germany is mentioned in both treaties). However, Greenwood (1983) and Trachtenberg (1999) both argue that declassified documents show that the fear was really about potential Soviet aggression, but that none of the signatories wanted to provoke the Soviets. Greenwood (1983) further states that the UK motivation for signing the Treaty of Dunkirk was to strengthen the French government and minimise the influence of the French Communist Party. For both London and Paris, the rapid post-war demobilisation of the American armed forces and the USA's domestic preference for a disengagement from Europe, were matters of real security concern. Paris was similarly concerned about how committed the UK was to the defence of mainland Europe. By 1947, however, the Greek civil war and Iranian and Turkish straits crises had shown the USA that the Soviet Union was committed to expansionism, and that the weakened British were unable to stop them. As a result, US President Truman announced that the USA was committed to bolstering friendly states on the periphery of the Soviet bloc if they were put under pressure, and duly sent assistance; a policy of containment that became known as the Truman Doctrine (Keylor, 2011).

Throughout 1947 and 1948, a gradual process of economic integration brought the three Western zones of occupation in Germany together, and, in June 1948, a common currency was launched. Moscow saw these developments as threatening, and began the Berlin blockade by halting surface deliveries of supplies to the enclave of West Berlin. This was countered by an American–British airlift, which delivered supplies until Stalin ended the blockade in May 1949. This incident did much to strengthen the process started by the Truman Doctrine, which was the conviction among the American political elite that their traditional isolationism was unsustainable and that they needed to offer a firm commitment to the defence of Western Europe (for more on US motivations, see Chapter 4).

Britain made two important proposals in the late 1940s. First, in 1946, Winston Churchill called for the creation of a Council of Europe. The CoE was founded by the Treaty of London in 1949. It is best known for the 1950 European Convention on Human Rights. The Convention created the European Court of Human Rights in Strasbourg, which remains an important adjudicator on human rights cases brought by citizens against member states. A further British proposal of linking the Brussels Pact states with the USA and Canada in the form of a North Atlantic security system was taken up by the US State Department, and negotiations began in July 1948. The Brussels Pact states, the USA and Canada were joined by Italy, Denmark, Norway, Iceland and Portugal in these negotiations and the North Atlantic Treaty, which contained a mutual defence clause (Article Five), was signed on 4 April 1949. Greece and Turkey would accede in 1952 and Spain in 1982, after the death of General Franco and its consequent return to democracy. The subsequent US military aid package to Western Europe formed the underpinnings of what became known as NATO. It is fair to say that NATO was sold in the various national capitals in different and not always coherent ways, and the eventual evolution of the institution was not immediately apparent. The first Secretary-General, Lord Ismay, is famously cited as claiming the purpose of NATO was 'to keep the Russians out, the Americans in and the Germans down' (Ismay, in Judt, 2005, p. 150), but this was already deceptive. The huge disparity in terms of ground forces meant the NATO allies were outnumbered 12–1 in Europe (Keylor, 2011). American military aid was helping to rearm and reform the NATO European armies, but it was clear that the USA's nuclear advantage would not form a sufficient defence and that West Germany would need to be rearmed, if NATO was to mount a credible defence of Western Europe.

Rearming West Germany, so soon after the disarmament process at the end of the Second World War, was decidedly politically unpalatable to many West European governments, but particularly to France. It was not universally popular in West Germany, either. There was also marked resistance to the idea from the West German population as a whole (Onslow, 1951) and from business and industry, which saw rearmament, and the industrial capacity that would be needed, as a threat to the civilian economic renaissance of the Federal Republic. Nevertheless, it took place, mainly because the government of Konrad Adenauer saw rearmament as a vital step towards its two prime foreign policy goals: regaining German sovereignty, and binding the Federal Republic more closely into Western Europe as a whole and the Western Alliance in particular (Schwarz, 1997). The French proposed two plans in 1950 to neutralise potential German power by enmeshing it into Western European structures: the Schumann plan and the Pleven plan. The Schuman plan would lead to the establishment of the European Coal and Steel Community (ECSC), the precursor to the EU, which put the member states' coal and steel production under a common high authority, thus preventing unilateral rearmament by West Germany, as increasing coal and steel production were vital to any rearmament process at that time. The 1957 Treaty of Rome would formally found the European Economic Community, which became the EU, and which would play a crucial role in the reconciliation process between Western European states by promoting increasing economic, and then political, cooperation. The Pleven plan would have created a European Defence Community (EDC – see Box 2.1).

Box 2.1 The European Defence Community (EDC)

In 1950, the then French Prime Minister, René Pleven, proposed a European Defence Community. The idea was to find a way in which West Germany could rearm, to contribute to Western defences, without their government having a sovereign armed force. It was to include France, Italy, West Germany and the Benelux countries. The EDC would have had a common budget, armaments procurement strategy and institutions, as well as having direct control over West German forces. Following negotiations, a treaty was signed on 27 May 1952, but the French National Assembly voted against ratification in 1954, meaning the EDC never came into being. French concerns centred around the threat to national sovereignty (especially while they were losing militarily in French Indochina) and the question of British commitment to Western European defence, as the UK would not join the EDC.

The demise of the EDC left all concerned in a difficult position. The British government, however, managed to propose a solution that was acceptable to all parties, which was the extension of the Brussels Pact to cover Italy and West Germany. This entailed a commitment on the part of the British to station troops in Europe (what became known as the British Army of the Rhine), thus placating French fears. In October 1954, the Brussels Pact five, plus West Germany and Italy, signed an agreement that created the Western European Union (WEU). Britain, the USA and France terminated the occupation of West Germany and allowed it to rearm (with the condition that it would not manufacture chemical, biological or atomic weapons on its territory), and, in 1955, West Germany joined NATO.

The Soviet Union had tried to stop these developments. The Stalin Note of March 1952 had proposed the reunification of a demilitarised Germany with no political or economic interference, but this was rejected by the West. Ten days after West Germany joined NATO and the military occupation came to an end in 1955, the Soviet Union announced the formation of the Warsaw Pact. This brought together Albania, Bulgaria, Czechoslovakia, Hungary, Poland, Romania and the Soviet Union in an alliance of cooperation and mutual assistance. Moscow also accepted the sovereignty of the German Democratic Republic, or East Germany, and brought it into the Pact (Judt, 2005). These developments institutionalised the security arrangements that would prevail until the end of the Cold War and solidified the division of Europe.

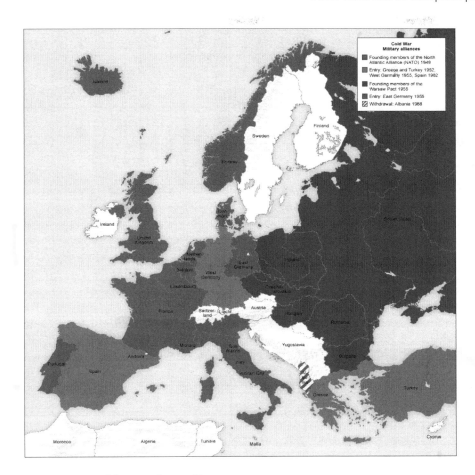

Figure 2.1   Cold War military alliances

Source: Wikimedia Commons (2006), 'Cold War Europe military alliances map', Available at: https://commons.wikimedia.org/wiki/File:Cold_war_europe_military_alliances_map_en.png (accessed: 19 January 2019).

Europe and the Cold War

For many Europeans, after the demarcation lines between East and West had been settled, the Cold War was a remarkably stable period, particularly in comparison with what had gone before. Once the Soviet Union had acquired an atomic bomb in 1949, the potential for outright war between the two sides receded, as it would have meant mutually assured destruction (MAD). Berlin had the potential to be a flashpoint, but after the construction of the Berlin Wall in 1961, when the city's division was made concrete, that danger faded. As Judt (2005) argued, the experience of the Cold War as a European was different to the experience of a Soviet or American citizen. Europeans, whether on the East or West of the Iron Curtain, understood that they could do little to influence either the United States or the Soviet Union, and so, despite Europe being the expected battleground if the Cold War turned hot, and where many of the nuclear weapons were targeted, it was a largely passive experience.

For the Warsaw Pact states, their impotence *vis-à-vis* the Soviet Union was made very clear early on. The 1956 Hungarian Uprising was quickly put down by Soviet troops, and the reformist government of Imre Nagy replaced. A period of liberalisation in Czechoslovakia under Alexander Dubček in 1968, known as the Prague Spring, was also quickly and brutally put down by the invasion of Soviet and other Warsaw Pact troops. When it came to negotiations between the two superpowers, the opinions of the Warsaw Pact states counted for little (Keylor, 2011). It also made a ground rule of the Cold War clear: the USA would not intervene in a Warsaw Pact state.

In the West, the rhetoric was of partnership, but the reality was that the West European states desperately needed the Americans to remain committed with ground troops in Europe. They were never entirely convinced of the USA's commitment and were still weakened by their wartime experiences, including the debts incurred. The period from the 1940s to the 1970s also saw the European colonial powers gradually accept the process of decolonisation, in some cases reluctantly following wars of attrition, and, along with it, accept that they were no longer global powers. Perhaps the final imperialist military mission was the Franco–British–Israeli attempt to regain Western control over the Suez Canal and depose the Egyptian President Nasser in 1956. The US Secretary of State, Dulles, and President Eisenhower made it clear that they did not support their allies, and that there would be consequences if the occupiers did not withdraw their troops, which they duly did, humiliated (Gaddis, 1997).

Similarly, popular opinion against the USA's nuclear weapons policies found little support from Western European governments, who largely went along with US decisions on NATO nuclear policy. In 1955, for example, a NATO war game, Exercise Carte Blanche, simulated a conflict with the Warsaw Pact involving tactical nuclear weapons. It concluded this would have meant the detonation of 355 nuclear weapons on French, Benelux and German soil, and calculated that 1.7 million people would die immediately and 3.5 million would be seriously injured. This was widely reported and caused civilian concern and led later to protests. This crystallised the West European security dilemma: they were dependent on the US nuclear deterrent to protect against conventional attack, where NATO remained outnumbered, but acutely vulnerable in the event of a nuclear war (Kamp, 1995).

Within NATO, there were often frustrations on the American side about the failure of the West Europeans to provide adequately for their own defences (see Chapter 4 for more detail). US levels of defence spending were simply politically unfeasible for West European electorates. At the same time, from the 1960s onwards, West European governments became increasingly concerned about the political consequences of dependence on US military technology and sought ways to retain some degree of doctrinal and technological autonomy, largely in the area of armaments cooperation, both bilaterally and institutionalised in NATO through the Independent European Programmes Group (IEPG). This quest for greater autonomy was particularly strong in France, which left NATO's integrated command structure in

1966, while still remaining a member. West Europeans feared a 'brain drain' of scientists and engineers to the USA and were acutely aware of the growing transatlantic science and technology gap, which was explained in large part by huge US spending on defence and space technology (Salomon, 1977). This fear reached its peak in the 1980s, when President Reagan launched his Strategic Defence Initiative, known as the Star Wars programme, which aimed to produce a missile defence system to protect the USA, which would have undermined NATO's nuclear deterrence doctrine and was thought to heighten the risk of conventional war. These small-scale efforts by the Europeans did, though, provide them with the institutional beginnings for enhancing cooperation following the end of the Cold War.

But perhaps the greatest instability for Europeans on both sides of the Iron Curtain, but particularly in the West, was the fear that their interests were not being taken into account as the two superpowers negotiated the parameters of their nuclear-armed coexistence. Paradoxically, these fears were at their greatest when relations between the Soviet Union and the United States improved. As Garaud (1985) points out, during the years of *détente* (generally deemed to be the period between the late 1960s and late 1970s, although efforts began following the Cuban missile crisis of 1962), and even before, the American administration sought to limit the risks the USA took in defence of Western Europe. There were proposals to limit numbers of US ground forces in Europe, while statesmen such as Kennan and McNamara urged that the USA repudiate nuclear first use if its European allies were attacked. While the disarmament talks led to treaties limiting the number of nuclear weapons, and, in 1975, to the Helsinki Accords, improving overall relations between West and East, which were to play a role in ending the Cold War (see Chapter 5), the West Europeans were aware that the Americans were making calculations about whether relations with their allies or *détente* with the Soviet Union was more important (Schulman, 1967). This is not to say that Europeans were opposed to *détente*: West German Chancellor Willy Brandt's Ostpolitik, which, between 1969 and 1974, gradually normalised relations between West Germany and East Germany, and thus other Warsaw Pact states, made a powerful contribution to the enabling of the Helsinki Accords, which brought about the creation of the Conference on Security and Co-operation in Europe (CSCE).

The Soviet invasion of Afghanistan in 1979 and the election of Ronald Reagan in the USA in 1980, with his campaign against the 'Evil Empire', marked the end of *détente*. Worsening economic conditions in the Soviet Union, though, led the newly appointed General Secretary of the Soviet Communist Party, Mikhail Gorbachev, in 1985, to launch domestic reforms under the headings of *glasnost* (openness) and *perestroika* (restructuring). Gorbachev's willingness to improve relations with the West was met warmly, and ultimately it was his refusal for the Soviet Union to intervene against protests in Warsaw Pact countries that led to the fall of the Berlin Wall in 1989, the collapse of Communism, and, ultimately, the end of the Cold War and the dissolution of the Soviet Union. The decades of relative stability during the Cold War and the decolonisation process had meant many of the old rivalries among West European states had become irrelevant, particularly in the context of the European integration process (Hobsbawm, 1994). As the 1990s were to show, this was not always the case in the East.

Europe and the end of the Cold War

The 1990s European security situation was to be marked by the contrasting fortunes of Central and Eastern Europe on the one hand, and the former Yugoslavia and the ex-Soviet republics on the other. The former had largely peaceful revolutions, with the exception of Romania, and the 1990s saw them placed on the path towards EU and NATO membership, although economic hardship did ensue on the way to functioning market economies. It also paved the way for the reunification of Germany on 3 October 1990 and the 'velvet divorce' in Czechoslovakia on 1 January 1993 to create two independent countries: the Czech Republic (now Czechia) and Slovakia. The latter group of countries, however, suffered war, massacre and devastation as the frozen and semi-frozen situation in the former Union of Soviet Socialist Republics (USSR) and the Balkans, respectively, erupted. Indeed, Lawrence (1994, p. 227) notes that 'the conflicts concern efforts to redraw political boundaries on ethnic criteria'. These successes and failures shaped the institutional architecture in Europe with the evolution of NATO's purpose and the creation within the EU of a European Security and Defence Policy which brought about the eventual demise of the Western European Union (WEU). These institutions also operated within the context of the change in the international system with one Superpower – the USA – remaining, although it is important to note that Russia continued to consider its neighbourhood to be under its sphere of influence despite a number of these countries gaining independence.

None the less, the end of East–West confrontation was to bring about a supposed 'peace dividend' which resulted in the downsizing of West European countries' armed forces. Additionally, Soviet forces stationed in Central and Eastern Europe were being withdrawn, although this process took a number of years. In Poland, for instance, the last Soviet troops left in September 1993 (Kuźniar, 2001, p. 34). The end of the Cold War also left a space for the broadening of the security agenda, although the transition from territorial defence thinking towards out of area operations, including crisis management and conflict prevention, took until 9/11 to fully evolve. Indeed as Hobsbawm (1994, p. 560) notes, 'the global danger of war had not disappeared. It had merely changed'. This was clear prior to the Balkan wars with the first Gulf War in 1991, in which West European countries joined their American allies either militarily or, in the case of Germany, economically through 'chequebook diplomacy'. However, the slow reaction of Western Europe to realise this and the subsequent reliance on the USA for hard power when the peace dividend failed to last had implications for Europe's role as an exclusive civilian, or soft, power. Europeans were expected to take up their share of the burden.

The new security environment also expanded to include issues of democracy, human rights, the environment, organised crime as well as post conflict stabilisation. Hence, it was not just the EU that had a role to play but also the Council for Europe and the CSCE, which was to become the OSCE in 1994. The former expanded at the beginning of the 1990s to include not just the newly independent countries of central and Eastern Europe, but also Russia in 1996. The latter, which already included Russia, also enlarged, due to the number of newly independent countries, making it 'a truly pan-European institution' (Baylis, 1998, p. 18). Thereafter, both organisations incorporated West and East Europe.

The 'return to Europe' – integration of the Central and Eastern European countries (CEECs)

The existence – let alone the enlargement – of Europe's security architecture was not a foregone conclusion. This was particularly the case with NATO, as the collapse of the USSR and the disbanding of the Warsaw Pact led to questions regarding the organisation's purpose following the end of the Cold War. In essence, NATO gradually developed two additional roles in the 1990s, beyond collective defence. The first was a crisis management role, as highlighted in respect to the Balkan conflicts, which is discussed extensively in Chapter 4 (Yost, 2010). The second, following on from the idea of NATO as a security community, was as a socialisation agent including the promotion of liberal norms (Flockhart, 2011, pp. 102–103). Hence, this partnership purpose included the Partnership for Peace (PfP) programme, among others, which originally was set up as an alternative to membership (Yost, 2010).

The reaction from the EU and NATO in respect to enlargement was one of reluctance, with the former offering aid and trade and cooperation agreements instead. This position evolved over the course of the 1990s. One of the most prominent supporters of EU and NATO enlargement was the newly unified Germany, itself the subject of suspicion. The unification of Germany was not initially supported by either the UK or France, due to concerns regarding German intentions, particularly whether the Germans would acquire a military strength commensurate to its economic and political power. Germany's independent recognition of Slovenia and Croatia in 1991 did little to dampen these concerns. The European Commission's (EC) initial reaction to German unification was the development of a political element to what became the Maastricht Treaty (1992), which introduced a Common Foreign and Security Policy (CFSP) as well as initiatives in Justice and Home Affairs. From this point onwards, the EC became known as the EU.

In the context of the destabilisation of the Balkans (see below) the EU was the first to offer a membership perspective with the creation of the Copenhagen Criteria in 1993, as they feared the instability would spread. This stipulated that a country could join if it was European, met a range of political and economic criteria and adopted the *acquis communautaire*, which is the body of EU law (European Commission, 2012). Accession negotiations were subsequently opened with Poland, Czech Republic, Hungary, Slovenia, Estonia, as well as Cyprus in 1998. Slovakia, Lithuania, Latvia, Malta, Romania and Bulgaria followed in 1999. In the case of the latter two, the conflict in Kosovo provided an important catalyst for ensuring their inclusion. At this stage, there was no decision on when these countries would finally accede to the EU. None the less, the growing possibility of EU enlargement met these countries' demand for a return to Europe. For the EU, enlargement can be understood through the desire to stabilise the continent, the EU's 'kin-based duty' to enlarge to countries who shared a European identity (Sjursen, 2002) or, as Schimmelfennig (2001) argues, because the EU was trapped by its own rhetoric as the membership rules created this obligation. In other words, the adoption of the EU's norms and values by the CEECs ensured their validity and failing to enlarge would have undermined the EU's integration process (Schimmelfennig, 2003, p. 74).

NATO was slower to accept enlargement, as NATO was focused on a 'Russia-first' policy and Russia was unsurprisingly anti enlargement. However, the PfP programme did little to meet the CEECs demands for accession, particularly considering NATO's Article Five guarantee, underwritten by the Americans. By the mid-1990s, however, the anti-enlargement element in NATO began to lose ground. First, a study was carried out on enlargement in 1995 (see Chapter 4). Then, in 1996, Bill Clinton's re-election campaign in the USA supported the idea. Russia, for its part, extracted concessions, including support for accession to the World Trade Organization and G-7, and enlargement therefore went ahead. Poland, the Czech Republic and Hungary joined in 1999 with the other CEECs following in 2004. This led to disillusionment in respect to the EU due to NATO's much speedier process. However, enlargement of both the EU and NATO to the CEECs left the question as to whether a new iron curtain further East had replaced the old one.

Disintegration in South East and Eastern Europe and the rise of conflict

While the CEECs were consolidating their democracies, helped along by the promise of EU and NATO membership, elsewhere in Europe 'the spectre of chaos' haunted some of the newly independent states of the USSR (Lawrence, 1994, p. 219), as well as the Balkans. A rush for independence by the Soviet Republics occurred at the beginning of the 1990s, when Yeltsin suggested that the republics' borders may be renegotiated (Hobsbawm, 1994, p. 495). None the less, a number of these newly independent countries contained sizable minorities and previously autonomous provinces. As Lawrence (1994, p. 227) notes,

> in the former USSR there were 104 nationalities of which 89 had no republic. In addition, 64 million people lived in states where they were not the ethnic majority, and of the 23 inter-republic borders only 3 were not contested.

While conflict was successfully averted in the Crimea as well as in the Baltics, as Latvia, Lithuania and Estonia, which had Russian minorities (see Chapter 5), eventually gained an EU and NATO accession perspective, this was not the case elsewhere.

Although the collapse of the USSR was certainly a catalyst for conflicts in the Caucasus (including those in Chechnya and between North Ossetia and Ingushetia, all within Russia), Moldova and the Central Asian post-Soviet states, the causes and longevity of them also reflect other interrelated factors. First was the ethnic mix and historical legacies of the newly independent countries. Particularly in respect to the Caucasus, Soviet nationalist policies which included 'cynical cartography' and 'large scale population transfers' under Stalin ensured that rival groups claimed particular territories as their own 'on the basis of historical rights or injustices' (Hunter, 2006, p. 113). A second factor was state building in these newly independent states. As Hughes and Sasse (2001, p. 3) point out, this was 'in the main inherited from the Soviet ethno-federal state architecture'. These led to a number of what became known as 'frozen conflicts'.

Two of these conflicts were within Georgia and relate to the regions of Abkhazia (originally a USSR republic in the 1920s), which wanted self-determination, and South Ossetia, which wanted to join with Russia. Both engaged in war with Georgia, in the Abkhazia case potentially with assistance from Moscow, when their autonomous powers were annulled. In the case of the former, since 1993 ceasefires have been agreed, implemented and then broken down again. The latter agreed a ceasefire in 1992. Both conflicts had frozen by the end of the 1990s, although they were to erupt again in 2008 through the Russian–Georgian war. Meanwhile, Armenia and Azerbaijan contested the region of Nagorno-Karabakh, which was primarily made up of Armenians but had been given to Azerbaijan. A ceasefire was agreed in 1994 after four years of conflict, which Armenia won, and remained 'frozen' for the remainder of the 1990s, despite efforts from the OSCE's Minsk Group to resolve the conflict. The unresolved nature of this erupted yet again in 2016. Finally, the region of Transnistria within Moldova constituted the fourth frozen conflict as accommodation between the two sides proved impossible due to linguistic, economic and political concerns. Alongside the UN, the only European based institution active within the region in the 1990s was the OSCE and, as Chapter 5 demonstrates, the outcome has been mixed. Moreover, Russia considers the Caucasus, along with Ukraine and Belarus, as part of its sphere of influence and, as the 2000s were to prove, Russia will defend those interests if necessary through the use of force to prevent their orientation to the West.

In contrast to the lack of European institutional interest in the conflicts in the former USSR beyond the OSCE, the collapse of the former Yugoslavia led to an influx of international and regional organisations. Towards the beginning of the conflict in the Balkans in 1991, Jacques Poos, the Luxembourg Foreign Minister declared, 'this is the hour of Europe' (Judt, 2005, p. 676). However, EC diplomacy failed and instead the USA had to be relied upon to eventually provide for Europe's security.

Yugoslavia had risen from the disintegration of the Ottoman and Hapsburg Empires and comprised six republics: Serbia, Bosnia and Herzegovina, Slovenia, Croatia, Macedonia and Montenegro, although in reality it was under Serbian domination. While the Second World War was marked by conflict between Croats and Serbs, under Tito nationalist tendencies had been frozen. Beyond these historical issues other reasons lay behind the collapse of the former Yugoslavia. In 1974, a new constitution was created to prepare for post-Tito federalism, which led to rotating leadership. As Lawrence (1994, p. 230) notes, this 'paralysed the centre and pushed power to regional leaders', leading to division between the component republics. It also led to Serbian grievances and a rise in nationalism as the constitution effectively granted Kosovo and Vojvodina *de facto* independence (Griffiths, 1993, p. 41). When Tito died in 1980, a power vacuum ensued and this enabled nationalist tendencies to rise. In the late 1980s and in the context of an economic crisis, the leaders of the different republics advanced alternative economic and political solutions which were incompatible, particularly those of Slovenia and Croatia on the one hand and Serbia on the other, which had been under the leadership of Milosevic since 1987 (see Lawrence, 1994). Although Slovenia and Croatia proposed that Yugoslavia should become an alliance of federal states in 1990, this was unacceptable to Milosevic. Hence, in 1991, Slovenia and Croatia declared independence. The former had no sizable Serbian population and so its claim for independence was eventually accepted after approximately ten days of war.

Croatia, however, was a different matter as Serbian minorities resided in Croatia as well as Bosnia and Herzegovina and Kosovo. Hence, Serbia moved quickly and took one third of Croatia, which brought about international sympathy for the latter. The EC held a peace conference in the autumn of 1991; however, it was the UN which negotiated a ceasefire between the two sides, as well as agreeing to deploy a UN operation (Griffiths, 1993, p. 49). In addition to diplomatic efforts, an embargo on delivering arms to any part of the former Yugoslavia was implemented by the UN in 1991, although the USA pulled out in 1994 due to its desire to re-arm the Bosnian government. The EU and the UN also imposed economic sanctions in 1992. While North Macedonia's declaration of independence was eventually accepted and it largely escaped major conflict, partly due to the international community's conflict prevention efforts through the UN and the C/OSCE, none of these steps was to prevent the atrocities that occurred in Bosnia Herzegovina. The country declared independence in 1992, following a referendum in which the Serb minority had not participated (Griffiths, 1993, p. 53). The massacre of Bosnian Muslims at Srebrenica, one of the UN's six 'safe areas', in 1995, following the withdrawal of Dutch UN peacekeepers, represented the failure of the international community, in addition to European security organisations, to prevent such atrocities. Following a USA-led NATO air campaign (see Chapter 4), the USA negotiated the Dayton Agreement, which brought the war to an end, demonstrating Europe's continued reliance on US hard power. The Dayton Agreement was followed by NATO's Implementation Force (IFOR), which, a year later, was replaced by a subsequent Stabilisation Force (SFOR).

However, descent into war was to follow in respect of Kosovo, which was considered to be the birthplace of the Serbian nation. Serbia sent in its military as a response to the Kosovo Liberation Army's guerrilla activities, targeting the Albanian community. With international concerns regarding potential ethnic cleansing, NATO intervened without a UN Security Council Resolution, using air strikes on Serbia. Serbia eventually withdrew and NATO, the OSCE and, eventually, the EU sent in peacekeeping missions. Kosovo declared independence in 2008, although this has not been recognised by five EU member states (Spain, Greece, Cyprus, Romania and Slovakia), following that of Montenegro in 2006.

The collapse of the USSR and Yugoslavia revealed the inability of Europe's then security architecture to provide for security on the continent, as the slow and ineffective response to these crises showed. However, as Baev (1999, p. 31) notes, the decade also saw more peace operations deployed in Europe than any other region in the world. Indeed, the UN, NATO, the OSCE and the CoE deployed peacekeeping and field missions to the former Yugoslavia, followed in the subsequent decade by the EU as the European Security and Defence Policy (ESDP) became active (see Chapter 6). This underscores the different roles that each organisation has played in conflict prevention, crisis management and post-conflict stabilisation within the same region. It also emphasises how unprepared Europe's security architecture was for the change in security situations following the end of the Cold War.

Europe's regional security architecture: continuity and change

Undoubtedly, the experiences of the 1990s had an impact on Europe's regional security architecture. At the beginning of the decade, these institutions were still orientated towards Cold War security tasks rather than to the challenges created by the break-up of the USSR and Yugoslavia. Indeed, Griffiths (1993, p. 91) notes that 'the response resembled a process not dissimilar to putting "square pegs in round holes"'. The beginning of the 1990s saw a debate between different proposals for the development of European security architecture following the end of the Cold War. According to Croft (2000, p. 5), these included:

1. Developing collective security through the C/OSCE (German–Czech view).
2. Developing a separate defence identity through the EU (Franco-Belgian view).
3. Creating a concert of powers through a European security council by modifying the C/OSCE (Russian view).
4. Preserving NATO primacy (US–UK view).

Neither of the ideas centred on the OSCE were taken up. Russia's proposal was, unsurprisingly, not supported by either the major NATO countries or the newly independent CEECS. The idea of collective security through the OSCE also fell victim to the preference for NATO, particularly by the CEECs. Instead, as outlined in Chapter 5, the institution built upon its 'common and comprehensive' security focus, particularly in respect to conflict prevention and post-conflict stabilisation as demonstrated in OSCE field missions in FYROM, Bosnia and Kosovo, as well as in the former USSR. It also developed its human security focus to include human rights, gender, and minority rights. This emphasis on the principles of democracy, human rights and the rule of law was also at the core of the CoE, which focused more on the legal elements, underpinned by the European Court on Human Rights. Indeed, the implementation of democratic security was at the heart of the CoE's work from the early 1990s. However, neither organisation would be at the forefront of Europe's new security architecture.

Instead, the focus turned to NATO and the EU. NATO evolved from an organisation focusing on collective defence to one that engaged in crisis management, as witnessed in the Balkans. Hence, the collapse of the former Yugoslavia had an impact on NATO's tasks, as it became the only European based security institution that had the capability to deploy hard power. However, the balance between collective defence and crisis management was to become the focus of a debate regarding NATO's evolution as an institution following 9/11 and the deployment of ISAF in Afghanistan. The EU also reacted to its inability to provide for security in its own neighbourhood. US calls for European burden sharing, the Kosovan war in 1999, along with changes in UK domestic politics and the EU's increasing international role, created conditions for the EU to desire a greater security and defence role (see Chapter 6). This manifested itself not in the European Strategic and Defence Identity (ESDI), which had been created to provide for the European pillar in NATO, but, rather, through the formation of the ESDP in 1999, which seeks to complement, rather than compete with, NATO. Nevertheless, despite EU member states' desire to close the capability–expectations gap (Hill, 1993), divisions regarding when, where and how these countries used military force remained.

Conclusion: themes and issues

Understanding how and why contemporary European security institutions and practices are as they are is important for understanding European security. The legacy of the Cold War still matters and, indeed, as antagonism between Russia and the West has worsened, some believe that its structures and practices remain relevant. While, for most of Europe, the period post 1989 has been one of rapid change followed by comparative peace and stability, it is important to recognise that there are still unresolved conflicts and that the institutional settlements that emerged created winners and losers, insiders and outsiders.

In tracing the development of European security from 1945 to 1999, the chapter has high-lighted a number of themes. The first is that the USA has played, and continues to play, a crucial role in securing much of Europe. However, Europeans have not always agreed with some US policies and actions and so they have sought to achieve greater autonomy. In the 1990s, in particular, Europeans began to develop more independence but also had to face up to their military reliance on the USA. However, as the subsequent chapters demonstrate, this has proved challenging. Those who, in the early 1990s, predicted the demise of NATO have been proved wrong. There is still not an accepted division of labour on security tasks between NATO, the EU, the OSCE and the CoE.

Moreover, the idea that the West 'won' the Cold War has had implications in respect of Russia; particularly regarding the West's inability to recognise that Russia has a sphere of influence that it will defend. Conflict has not disappeared. While some conflicts were resolved or 'frozen', the 2000s demonstrated that war had not disappeared from the European security agenda, as European forces went out of area engaging in both peacekeeping and major military interventions. More recently, the continent became engulfed in a ring of fire rather than the ring of peace that it had envisaged.

Further reading

Gaddis, John Lewis (1997), *We Now Know: Rethinking Cold War History*. New York: Oxford University Press.
Hobsbawm, Eric (1994), *The Age of Extremes: The Short Twentieth Century 1914–1991*. London: Abacus.
Judt, Tony (2005), *Postwar: A History of Europe Since 1945*. London: Heinemann.
Schimmelfennig, Frank (2003), *The EU, NATO and the Integration of Europe: Rules and Rhetoric*. Cambridge: Cambridge University Press.

Weblinks

For an overview of the history of the EU, see: https://europa.eu/european-union/about-eu/history_en
For an overview of the history of NATO, see: www.nato.int/cps/ie/natohq/declassified_139339.htm
For an overview of the history of the OSCE, see: www.osce.org/history

References

Baev, Pavel (1999), 'External Interventions in Secessionist Conflicts in Europe in the 1990s', *European Security*, 8 (2), 22–51.

Baylis, John (1998), 'European Security in the Post-Cold War Era: The Continuing Struggle Between Realism and Utopianism', *European Security*, 7 (3), 14–27.

Croft, Stuart (2000), 'The EU, NATO and Europeanisation: The Return of Architectural Debate', *European Security*, 9 (3), 1–20.

European Commission (2012), *Accession Criteria*. Available at: http://ec.europa.eu/enlargement/policy/glossary/terms/accession-criteria_en.htm (accessed: 16 October 2018).

Flockhart, Trine (2011), 'NATO and the (Re)Constitution of Roles: "Self," "We," and "Other"?', in Sebastian Harnisch, Cornelia Frank, and Hanns W. Maull (eds), *Role Theory in International Relations*. Abingdon: Routledge, pp. 95–112.

Gaddis, John Lewis (1997), *We Now Know: Rethinking Cold War History*. New York: Oxford University Press.

Garaud, Marie-France (1985), 'Foreign Perspectives on the SDI', *Daedalus*, 114 (3), 307–313.

Greenwood, Sean (1983), 'Return to Dunkirk: The Origins of the Anglo–French Treaty of March 1947', *Journal of Strategic Studies*, 6 (4), 49–65.

Griffiths, Stephen (1993), *Nationalism and Ethnic Conflict: Threats to European Security*. Oxford: Oxford University Press.

Hall, John (1996), *International Orders*. Cambridge: Cambridge University Press.

Hill, Christopher (1993), 'The Capability–Expectation Gap, or Conceptualising Europe's International Role', *Journal of Common Market Studies*, 31 (3), 305–328.

Hobsbawm, Eric (1994), *The Age of Extremes: The Short Twentieth Century 1914–1991*. London: Abacus.

Hughes, James, and Sasse, Gwendolyn (2001), 'Comparing Regional and Ethnic Conflicts in Post-Soviet Transition States', *Regional and Federal Studies*, 11 (3), 1–35.

Hunter, Shireen (2006), 'Borders, Conflict, and Security in the Caucasus: The Legacy of the Past', *SAIS Review*, 26 (1), 111–125.

Judt, Tony (2005), *Postwar: A History of Europe since 1945*. London: Heinemann.

Kamp, Karl-Heinz (1995), 'Germany and the Future of Nuclear Weapons in Europe', *Security Dialogue*, 26 (3), 277–292.

Keylor, William (2011), *The Twentieth-Century World and Beyond: An International History since 1900* (6th ed.). Oxford: Oxford University Press.

Kuźniar, Roman (2001), *Poland's Security Policy 1989–2000*. Warsaw: Scholar.

Lawrence, Philip (1994), 'European Security: From Euphoria to Confusion', *European Security*, 3 (2), 217–235.

Onslow, C. G. D. (1951), 'West German Rearmament', *World Politics*, 3 (4), 450–485.

Salomon, Jean-Jacques (1977), 'Science Policy Studies and the Development of Science Policy', in Ina Spiegel-Rösing and Derek de Solla Price (eds), *Science, Technology and Society: A Cross-Disciplinary Perspective*. Beverly Hills: Sage, pp. 43–70.

Schimmelfennig, Frank (2001), 'The Community Trap: Liberal Norms, Rhetorical Action, and the Eastern Enlargement of the European Union', *International Organization*, 55 (1), 47–80.

Schimmelfennig, Frank (2003), *The EU, NATO and the Integration of Europe: Rules and Rhetoric*. Cambridge: Cambridge University Press.

Schimmelfennig, Frank, and Ulrich Sedelmeier (2002), 'Theorizing EU Enlargement: Research Focus, Hypotheses, and the State of Research', *Journal of European Public Policy*, 9 (4), 500–528.

Schulman, Marshall (1967), 'Europe versus "Détente"?', *Foreign Affairs*, 45 (3), 389–403.

Schwarz, Hans-Peter (1997), *Konrad Adenauer: A German Politician and Statesman in a Period of War, Revolution and Reconstruction. Vol. 2: The Statesman: 1952–1967*. Providence, RI: Berghahn Books.

Sjursen, Helene (2002), 'Why Expand? The Question of Legitimacy and Justification in the EU's Enlargement Policy', *Journal of Conservation and Museum Studies*, 40 (3), 491–513.

Trachtenberg, Marc (1999), *A Constructed Peace: The Making of the European Settlement, 1945–1963*. Princeton, NJ: Princeton University Press.

Yost, David S. (2010), 'NATO's Evolving Purposes and the Next Strategic Concept', *International Affairs*, 86 (2), 489–522.

Contesting approaches to European security

3

André Barrinha and Sarah da Mota

Introduction

The study of security emerged after the Second World War as a sub-field of International Relations, or IR (Wæver, 2004, p. 2), analysing the ways in which states were threatened by other states through the main theories of IR. In the USA, this happened in a period in which the country was reforming its security apparatus and affirming itself as the new main power of the international system. National Security Studies became part of university curricula in the US, while in Europe the same contents were taught under the 'Strategic Studies' label (Wyn Jones, 1999), in a social and political context marked by the trauma of the war, the progressive end of Europe's superiority over the world, and Western European projects of cooperation and integration. Despite the different starting points, both sides of the Atlantic quickly converged on a common geopolitical priority: the Cold War. Security was seen back then in a restricted way, mainly as a military issue.

In the late 1970s and early 1980s, in a context of increasing disillusionment with power politics, and dominant socio-economic models (O'Hagan, 2002, p. 112), the social resistance to war and armament grew stronger (Armitage and Virilio, 1999, p. 37), and security progressively became more than conflict and warfare (or the possibility of). Richard Ullman's work on environmental security (1983), and Barry Buzan's *People, States and Fear* (1983) opened the widening *versus* deepening debate, in which both the extent and meaning of security were open for discussion – security became a *contested* concept.

In the post Cold War context, the idea of European security emerged and developed along with both the progression of European integration and as a counter-positioning to US theories, perceptions and dominance of international security. Europe became a hub for the development of new theoretical approaches and the object of study on which those approaches were applied; a similar dynamic to what we have nowadays, albeit with less focus on school development and inter-school debates.

Since IR opened up to reflectivist[1] readings of the world during the latter stages of the Cold War, most key concepts in the discipline – order, sovereignty, peace – became contestable.

There is nothing new in this regard about European security, one could say. The interesting aspect about this concept, we would argue, is that it contains not one, but two, contestable terms within it: 'European' and 'security'. The idea of European security reveals an ambivalence that implies both a constant multiplicity of security approaches, but also the projection of a unitary security identity to the rest of the world, either through NATO or the EU. This means that when saying or writing European security, there is a subjacent understanding – out of many different possibilities – of what Europe means, but also, of what security is.

This chapter is about how these two terms have been coupled together by different authors since the end of the Cold War. It is set out in a way that enables the constant 'dialogue' between the course of theoretical development and the concrete evolution of European security. It is not explicitly focused on a particular concept of security, or of Europe, for that matter. Its interest is in showing the multiple ways in which the concept has been debated. By doing so, it also highlights the priorities of the political agenda of the time. Some authors and periods were more concerned with the relations between the US and European states; others more focused on the evolution of the EU as a security actor. What they said matters, but also when and why.

Theories do not happen out of the blue; they are developed in articulation with previous works, but also in reaction to the politics of the time. In this sense, the way European security has come to be studied should be understood within a wider social, political and intellectual context – that is, as a *history* of the theories on European security, particularly of those that allow us to better contextualise Europe in IR.[2]

In terms of structure, this chapter starts by looking at some of the major works developed within the rationalist framework (mostly realism and liberal approaches), followed by the cultural turn that connected identity and discourse to issues of security. It then discusses the rise of Critical Security Studies and how they have shaped our understanding of European security.

Rationalist views

Rationalist approaches in Security Studies are defined by the assumption that states are rational actors whose behaviour is possible to predict. Doing so involves the adoption of a series of methodological tools 'rooted in material and empirically verifiable factors' (Buzan and Hansen, 2009, p. 30). Realism, particularly in its 'neo' version, has been the dominant representative of the rationalist voice in Security Studies. The language of security during the Cold War was, to a large extent, characterised by the realist principles of containment, deterrence and strategic advantage. Security was a game of chess in which, more often than not, one state's gains would be another's losses. As we will have the opportunity to see later in the chapter, that dominance was only significantly questioned with the emergence of constructivist voices in the discipline, combined with the progressive development of Critical Security Studies, both of which could be situated firmly in the reflectivist camp.

In the 1980s, the eventual expansion of security as a concept to other areas of social and political life – food security, environmental security – was seen as concerning by some leading realist authors, such as Stephen Walt. If security could be applied to any aspect of social and political life, then nothing was security (Walt, 1991; Hyde-Price, 2007). In Walt's view, an expanded understanding of the concept that took on broad issues such as economic recession or pollution 'would destroy its intellectual coherence and make it more difficult to devise solutions to any of these important problems' (Walt, 1991, p. 213). This rather orthodox view of security has been applied to European security by other American thinkers, most famously by John Mearsheimer.

Writing during the twilight of the Cold War, Mearsheimer (1990), a leading offensive realist, argued that the end of the bipolar confrontation was bad news for Europe. The stability generated by the distribution of military capability along two main poles of power – the Soviet Union and the USA – the balance between the two, and the nuclear dimension of their arsenals were the reasons why war had been absent from Europe since 1945. The end of the Cold War would lead to a situation of multipolarity, with a subsequently higher propensity for instability (Mearsheimer, 1990, p. 7).

Two decades letter, in a keynote lecture to the annual ECPR conference, Mearsheimer was unrepentant in his position. He now added that three key issues would determine the possibility of peace in Europe: the future of out of area missions, the USA's pivot to Asia (and subsequent reduction in its European presence) and, rather prophetically, the future of Russia–Ukraine relations. Ultimately, however, Europe's fate remains, in Mearsheimer's view, in the hands of the American 'pacifier' (Mearsheimer, 2010). From this perspective, European security is only meaningful in relation to the American hegemonic power; as a 'rational response to systemic pressures' (Cladi and Locatelli, 2017, p. 19).

Despite the vastly different geopolitical context – post 9/11 and post theIraq invasion – other neorealist authors followed this same type of approach in their analyses of European security (Art, 2004; Hyde-Price, 2007; Posen, 2006). Under this perspective, Europe oscillates between a position of balancing[3] (soft for Robert Art, and hard for Barry Posen) and bandwagoning[4] (Cladi and Locatelli, 2012), and the US is the ultimate guarantor of its security – a view that seems increasingly problematic in 2018. Europe itself revolves around a constant balance of power, in which its actors need to assess constantly their options regarding each other, but also regarding the main forces in European security – the US, Russia and Germany (Art, 2004). If anything, the end of the Cold War seems to have intensified the debate around the balance of power in Europe (Howorth and Menon, 2009, p. 729). This view has led to two main consequences in terms of the study of European security. First, it meant that the realist contribution was limited by what they understood to be the fundamental issues of war and conflict, having little to say about other security dynamics taking place in Europe. Second, it also meant that realism was partially sidelined in Europe, making it a somewhat peripheral approach to the study of European security as we entered the 2000s.

Neo-classical realism has attempted to rejuvenate the links between this school of thought and the study of security in Europe by bridging this neorealist version with the more normative and nuanced classical approach of the mid-twentieth century (Table 3.1). According to Tom Dyson, neoclassical realism offers a combination between 'neorealism's emphasis on the "survival" motivation of states, with classical realism's focus on the dependence of political leaders on domestic society for material resources and support for foreign and

Table 3.1 Realism and its multiple shades

Approach	Period	Focus	Key authors
Classical realism	Mid-twentieth century	Power as the defining concept in international politics	Hans Morgenthau, E. H. Carr, Reinhold Niebuhr, John Herz
Neo-realism	1970s–1980s	Anarchical structure of the international system	Kenneth Waltz
Defensive realism	1980s–1990s	States as security maximisers	Stephen Walt, Jack Snyder
Offensive realism	1980s–2000s	States as power maximisers	John Mearsheimer
Neo-classical realism	1990s–2000s	Domestic factors influence states' decision making	Fareed Zakaria, Randall Schweller, Gideon Rose, William Wohlforth

defence policy goals' (2010, p. 120). The inclusion of domestic factors in the analysis of states' international behaviour changes how we observe and explain IR. Randall Schweller (2004) compares interwar Britain and France, and concludes that their reticence in engaging in war with Germany (and, therefore, 'underbalance') was based on domestic factors and not in the nature of the balance of power. Schweller criticises the balance of power theory, and looks 'inside' Europe, taking a more nuanced approach to its security. However, he is ultimately trying to answer the same sort of questions set by neorealism, which leads to a similar understanding of what European security ultimately is (see Rynning, 2011 for a more thorough critique of neo-classical realism).

The liberal alternative

Liberalism has traditionally been seen as the counter-balance to realist approaches to IR. Given the centrality of regional organisations in European security – including NATO, the EU and OSCE – it is not surprising that an approach that places its emphasis on the possibility of cooperation in international politics always had something to say about it (Dover, 2007; Menon, 2011).[5] However, two caveats should be introduced when discussing the liberal contribution to the European security debate. First, these are not security theories, but, rather, IR approaches applied to the European case. Second, for all their differences, they share many of realism's core tenets, such as state-centrism and the belief in the anarchical nature of the international system (Kolodziej, 2005).

When it comes to European security, rather than analysing it from the perspective of balancing or bandwagoning *vis-à-vis* the US, they focused on the dynamics of cooperation between European states. Liberal intergovernmentalists argue that states will decide when and how to cooperate based on the potential for outcome maximisation. National preferences are defined based, not only on governments' positions, but also on the views of a series of stakeholders, including public opinion, bureaucrats and private companies. These approaches look at the role of constitutional constraints, political parties and the bargaining dynamics that take place domestically and internationally. Robert Dover's (2007) work on the Europeanisation of British defence is a good example of this.

Neoliberal institutionalists, on the other hand, focus on the benefits of cooperation and the fact that institutions create incentives and commitments that lead to further cooperation and make it costly for states to abandon them, including in the security and defence sphere. Simply put: in IR, the costs of cooperation are usually lower than the costs of not cooperating (North, 1990). Neoliberal institutionalism became particularly useful to explain the evolution of the EU's defence component since the late 1990s. As Anand Menon argues,

> [i]nstitutionalism offers the analytical tools to allow us not only to explain its development over time, but also the impact of how policies are made on the policies pursued, and, more broadly, both the potential and limits of the Union's security and defence policies.
>
> (2011, p. 84)

Although framed with a liberal approach, Stephanie Hoffman argues that, when looking at European defence, particularly its Common Security and Defence Policy (CSDP), the relations and ties between bureaucrats and national representative based in Brussels also play an important role in determining the orientation of this policy field (Hoffman, 2011, p. 43). Resorting to the typology employed by Robert Keohane and Joseph Nye in the 1970s, Hoffman argues that, in addition to intergovernmental relations, we should also consider the importance of transgovernmental actors when studying decision-making

Table 3.2 Differences between rationalism and reflectivism in security studies

Rationalist assumptions	Reflectivist assumptions
• Anarchy in the international system taken for given • States as the primary actors in IR • State identity and interests are given. Exogenous to theory/process • States are rational actors • All actors seek to maximise their utility defined in material terms as power, security and wealth • Explanation is the aim of theory and research	• Identity and interests of states are not given • States produce and reproduce interests in a continuous process • Interests are shaped by identity and norms as much as materially • Understanding/interpretation is the aim of theory and research
Examples: realism, liberalism	Examples: constructivism, critical Security Studies

Adapted from Wæver (2004).

process in this field. Such an approach touches on ideas of socialisation that are rather predominant in constructivist takes on European security.

The cultural 'turn'

It is not particularly contentious to say that constructivism became the dominant approach to IR in Europe, and also to how its security is studied. In the late 1980s, authors such as Nicholas Onuf (1989), Friedrich Kratochwil (1989) and Alexander Wendt (1992) brought the works of Peter Berger and Thomas Luckman (1966), John Searle (1995) and Anthony Giddens (1984) to the study of international politics and, subsequently, international security. At its most basic level, constructivism understands IR as the result of social interactions. Therefore, structures do not determine IR; at most, they act as a mediator between human agency and social dynamics. Most importantly, constructivism brings to the fore issues of identity, culture and the power of ideas, which were always seen, within a rationalist framework, as a negligible or secondary factor in explaining how the world works.

After the Cold War, the revival of culture appears as a critical factor defining the field of security studies, especially in Europe, where newly constructed identities, new nation-states in the Balkans and in the Baltics and new regional projects enhanced the significance of territory and identity (Tunander, 2008, p. 165). Constructivist approaches to European security were to develop alongside two 'real world' dynamics: the enlargement processes of NATO and the EU, and the development of myriad bilateral and multilateral agreements between European states in order to further collaborate on security and defence matters, mostly within the context of NATO and the EU. The two parallel enlargement processes were seen as particularly revealing of the centrality of identities, norms and ideas in IR, or 'cultural transformation' (Delanty, 2003, p. 10), in a manifest renegotiation of how differences could be accommodated within the same political organisation. In this sense, both NATO and the EU 'developed a specific western identity that was embedded in the construction of shared democratic norms' (Fierke and Wiener, 1999, p. 723).

These processes drew attention to something else: the power of attraction of these organisations. This capacity for attraction, or symbolic power (Williams, 2007; Williams and Neumann, 2000), meant their existence was not solely defined by their primary functions – defence of the Atlantic space in the case of NATO; promotion of the single market in the case of the EU – but they had a normative quasi-civilisational role to play in Europe and beyond. In the case of NATO, enlargement implied expanding the security community to new members from different cultures and traditions, bringing issues of identity, behaviour and belonging to the fore (Adler, 2008; da Mota, 2018, pp. 157–159).

Indeed, in Michael C. Williams' view, security was no longer simply about material capabilities. Rather, 'the field of security was transformed into one where cultural and symbolic forms of power become vital' (2007, p. 3). This had an external dimension to it, but also an internal one, particularly in terms of the EU. By the late 1990s, the EU was arguably the most important security actor in Europe, not because of its security and defence policy – rather incipient at the time – but because of its integration process and how it contributed to removing security as a primary concern for European states when dealing with each other (Wæver, 2000, p. 264).

Ironically, culture, and the concept of strategic culture in particular, was brought into the study of security much earlier by Jack Snyder (1977), an author more commonly associated with rationalism. In a report written for RAND Corporation on Soviet nuclear strategy, culture was helpful in explaining the behaviour of strategic actors when all the other rational explanations failed (Krause, 1998). Other rational approaches attempting to integrate culture in a rationalist framework developed in the following years (see Johnston, 1995; Klein, 1988). Peter Katzenstein's *The Culture of National Security* was a marker in terms of placing culture at the centre of the security debate from a sociological perspective. He argued that 'security interests are defined by actors who respond to cultural factors' (Katzenstein, 1996, p. 2), whereas culture was to be understood as

> both a set of evaluative standards (such as norms and values) and a set of cognitive standards (such as rules and models) that define which social actors exist in a system, how they operate and how they relate to one another.
>
> (1996, p. 6)

As mentioned earlier, the 2000s saw in Europe the approval of a raft of measures and policies that were leading to the redefinition of its security architecture. Failing to explain these dynamics on rationalist grounds, the concept of strategic culture started to emerge as a leading concept in the problematisation of these new dynamics. The controversy around the European participation in the Iraq war and the approval of the European Security Strategy in 2003 gave a renewed impetus to those researching these topics. Finally, there was a 'nascent strategic narrative, and a readily observable social mechanism through which an EU strategic culture reveals itself' (Norheim-Martinsen, 2011, p. 518). Whereas strategic culture became the most common concept in the literature, security culture was also brought to the debate, a concept that provided 'decision-makers with a frame of core assumptions, beliefs and values about how security challenges can and should be dealt with' (Monteleone, 2017, p. 85). For some authors (Barrinha and Rosa, 2013; Edwards, 2006), security culture is a more encompassing concept than strategic culture, more suitable to security priorities that sit outside traditional IR.

Overall, this cultural turn contributed to move the centre of the debate from a firmly established rationalist perspective to a more reflectivist understanding of the world – and, in this case, of European security – enmeshing identities and social processes. But, more decisively, it was the affirmation of Critical Security Studies that tilted the discussion towards reflectivism, especially in Europe.

Critical European security

As mentioned earlier, the 1990s witnessed the emergence of theoretical approaches that questioned the rationalist assumptions prevalent until then in the study of security. These dynamics were particularly visible in Europe, where reflectivist takes on security assumed multiple dimensions, from the introduction of the Frankfurt School's Critical Theory to anti-foundational approaches influenced by continental thinkers such as Jacques Derrida and Michel Foucault. At the core of these new approaches was the 'recognition of the idea that *security is essentially a derivative concept*; this means, simply, that contending theories about world politics produce different conceptualizations of what security is all about in world politics' (Booth, 2005, p. 13). Europe became both a hub for the development of new theoretical approaches and the object of study to which those approaches were applied. That dynamic continues to this day, albeit with less focus on school development and inter-school debates.

Critical Security Studies do not derive from a unitary set of theories, and are, rather, composed of various approaches with different intellectual origins that are fundamentally European at their core. Originally, Critical Security Studies emerged in the late 1980s–early 1990s as an aspiration to the transcendence of traditional precepts typical of the Cold War period, and not as an exclusive theoretical school. Their emergence and development cannot be dissociated from the newly established multipolar world, where generalised optimism went hand in hand with the search for new paradigms, epistemologies, and methodologies that reflected the post Cold War drive to make sense of a new world order (Hyde-Price, 2007, p. 19). There are three distinct influences that can, none the less, be identified within the *critical* study of security: the Welsh school of Aberystwyth, which reclaims the 'critical' label to itself; the Copenhagen school, which usually denies that label; and post-structuralism, often considered acritical and globally rejected as a critical current (Mutimer, 2007). In all, 'critical security' as such can be seen as an essential quest for the ontology of security, but also for the interconnected possibility of social change, for the inclusion of difference, for overcoming the status quo, mirroring the unknowns, the stakes and the challenges of the post Cold War international conjuncture.

Box 3.1   The Aberystwyth School

Key authors: Richard Wyn Jones; Ken Booth; Robert Cox
    Key points:

- Inspired by the Frankfurt School and post-Marxism
- Connects the conception of security to a loose concept of emancipation, whereby one can only meaningfully exist with the other
- Rejection of the Realist paradigm of security, which is state focused, to prioritise the security of individuals
- Critique of the domination by superpowers and proposal of counter-hegemonic forces
- Focus on the insecurities of individuals and vulnerable groups

Generally, the critical tradition of Aberystwyth prioritises the intrinsic humanity of security objects and subjects, and values individual lives as the ultimate end of politics (Booth, 2007, p. 326). For instance, another author of this school of thought, Robert Cox, contended as early as 1987 that international order was failing to value in equal terms the interests of the socially weak and marginalised. As he never stood for an order dominated by superpowers, Cox preferred to focus on the insecurities of individuals and vulnerable groups, seeking counter-hegemonic forces that would be able to oppose prevailing security discourses. This somewhat radical new way of apprehending security is not really revealing of a renewed interest in European security *per se*, but, rather, can be seen as a broader move towards the expansion of the international security agenda to *foci* that had remained outside the bipolar logic of the world during the previous decades. After the Cold War, a 'new ontology of world order' (Cox, 2002, p. 77) opened the door for those concerned with power, world order, counter-hegemony and, at the same time, with individuals, which denounces the unknown character of the 1990s' multipolarity as a source of unbalance when pondering the new international security architecture, and also the overcoming of states as the sole referent objects of security.

There is often confusion between the Critical Security Studies that developed in Aberystwyth and the broader family of critical approaches to security that started to gain shape after a conference on the topic in 1994 at York University (Canada). This event would be the basis for *Critical Security Studies: Concepts and Cases*, edited by Keith Krause and Michael C. Williams (1997), in which many of these critical approaches were congregated.

From all the new early 1990s Security Studies theories that flourished in Europe, the one developed by a group of researchers from the Copenhagen Peace Research Institute (COPRI), including Barry Buzan and Ole Wæver, was arguably the most ground-breaking[6] and controversial[7] one. The Centre for Peace and Conflict Research, eventually renamed Conflict and Peace Research Institute (COPRI) set up in 1985 had as one of its projects, 'Non-military Aspects of European Security'. That is where the Copenhagen School was born. According to Jef Huysmans, 'the Copenhagen project . . . emerged within a typically European security landscape which has given its work an explicitly European flavour' (1998, p. 480). Among other works, Barry Buzan, Ole Wæver, and Jaap de Wilde's *Security: A New Framework for Analysis* (1998) celebrates the idea that security is socially constructed and that it is by looking at how the processes of construction – securitisation processes – unfold that it is possible to understand how an issue becomes a security issue. In Copenhagen, the notion of securitisation as a 'speech act' was also developed around the idea that security may also materialise as language and, thus, be *performed*; accordingly, a speech act sets a determined event or question as a security issue (Wæver, 1995). With Copenhagen, the broadening move of the security agenda happening in the 1990s continued deepening towards the questioning of the ontology of security processes, or the phenomenology of security policies.

Box 3.2 The Copenhagen School

Key points:

- Barry Buzan, Ole Wæver, and Jaap de Wilde's *Security: A New Framework for Analysis* (1998).
- Security is sectoral: political, military, economic, societal, environmental.

- The notion of 'securitisation as a speech act' is the School's cornerstone; it also calls for the distinction between securitising actors and referent objects of security.
- Regional security complexes as the analytic concept that enables the application of securitisation theory to international relations. The world is divided into security regions.

These trends, which reveal a new epistemology of security, need to be framed within a context in which identity conflicts arising during the 1990s, both inside Europe (Balkans), and at its borders (Caucasus, Middle East), suddenly presented a new set of more diffuse and interdependent features, typically of a transnational nature. Along with the crescent media exposure of those conflicts, they entailed a new *visibility* of security, to which discourse and culture became central. For European security in particular, this trend was all the more explicit with Bosnia and Kosovo.

After several decades without war in Europe, these two conflicts in the Balkans critically influenced the literature on security with impactful contributions not only for the Copenhagen School, as for post-structuralist approaches to security. David Campbell (1998) offers a post-structuralist analysis of the Bosnian war that shows how the violence of the war was determined by the assumption that a political community should be a perfectly aligned entity in terms of its territory, identity and state, leading to the desire for a homogenous community. Another important work at the time was Lene Hansen's (2006) discourse analysis of the Bosnian war, in which she dissects how the different discourses surrounding the conflict defined the very trajectory and outcome of the war along ethno-political features.[8]

Mainly associated with French intellectuals such as Jean Baudrillard, Jacques Derrida, Michel Foucault, Jacques Lacan, and Jean-François Lyotard, post-structuralism can be defined as 'a fragmentary assemblage of diverse social, political, and philosophical thought that engages with, but also calls into question, the "structuralist" tradition'. It is rooted in the artistic, architectural and cultural movement that emerged in the West during the 1950s and 1960s, and especially focuses on 'how claims about "the world" are dependent upon certain forms of knowledge' (Peoples and Vaughan-Williams, 2010, p. 63).

Post-structuralism is, together with the international political sociological strand coming from Pierre Bourdieu, a strong influence on the philosophical basis of the so-called Paris School, the label given to the work on European internal security (and its externalisation) conducted by Dider Bigo (2000) and his associates, based at Sciences Po in Paris. The emphasis of post-structuralist thought on language, practices, deconstruction, truth, power and biopolitics has been all the more meaningful since 9/11, denouncing the logic of exceptionalism and the illiberal character of the practices of security entailed by the global war on terror, such as ethnic profiling, the language of risk and securitisation (Amoore and de Goede, 2008; Bigo and Tsoukala, 2008; Dillon and Lobo-Guerrero, 2008).

Box 3.3   Keeping pace with the academic debate: the EU in the early 2000s

In parallel, the evolution of the EU's approach to international security reflects the widening (new security threats) and deepening (new referent objects of security) of the international security agenda (Williams, 2008, pp. 7–9), as well as the abovementioned issues highlighted by the different critical approaches. The European Security Strategy (ESS), namely, is a document drafted by the former High Representative Javier Solana and approved by the European Council in 2003 that draws on a broad understanding of security, by considering both traditional and new threats, internal and external realms, and the importance of prevention:

> Our traditional concept of self-defense – up to and including the Cold War – was based on the threat of invasion. With the new threats, the first line of defence will often be abroad. The new threats are dynamic. The risks of proliferation grow over time; left alone, terrorist networks will become ever more dangerous. State failure and organized crime spread if they are neglected – as we have seen in West Africa. This implies that we should be ready to act before a crisis occurs. Conflict prevention and threat prevention cannot start too early.
>
> (Council of the European Union, 2003, p. 9)

The agenda of European security has normally accompanied the global trends developing within the context of the broadening move of security, in particular human security, humanitarianism, and the security development nexus. The 2004 Barcelona Report of the Study Group on Europe's Security Capabilities discussed in what way the ESS may be implemented, suggesting a Human Security Doctrine for the European Union and the establishment of a 'Human Security Response Force' as well as a new legal framework 'to govern both the decision to intervene and operations on the ground' (Glasius and Kaldor, 2005, p. 5). To Kamil Zwolski, human security has been precisely the pivotal security concept that has underpinned 'the EU's commitment to link security objectives with development policy' (2012, p. 71), thereby intertwining security considerations into its development policy, and development issues into security strategies (see Chapter 8 for more detail).

Amid Europe's identity crisis, other approaches have stimulated new insights on the implications of 'doing European security', deeply questioning the sense of European agency. Postcolonialism has contributed significantly to the critique of the role of old colonial powers in moulding interventions outside Europe, tying security to a development agenda that is drawn on liberal interventionism, to the disputed notion of historic responsibility and to biopolitical concerns of containment of non-European populations (Ayoob, 2002; Darby, 2009; Duffield, 2005). Within Security Studies, postcolonial perspectives especially inform the critique of the Eurocentric character of the historic and geographic givens that, since the Second World War, have systematically misrepresented the role of the global South in security relations (Barkawi and Laffey, 2006, p. 329).

These considerations can be seen as part of the call for a paradigm shift to decentre the study and practice of Europe's IR, in order to reconstitute European agency in face of the non-European world (Onar and Nicolaïdis, 2013). Accordingly, a postcolonial lens such as Onar and Nicolaïdis' foretells that only by acknowledging the colonial component within the EU project itself can the EU overcome its existential crisis – sense of decline, crisis of European identity and multiculturalism – reinvent its normative power and hope for a renewed European agency in a non-European world (2013, pp. 285–288). Profound reflexivity, thus, seems to be needed in the conception and materialisation of European security, which includes calling into question the assumptions underlying the conceptions of boundary, territory, community and ethno-cultural belonging in the constitution of Europe, according to Catarina Kinvall (2016). Considering the recent waves of immigration as a 'postcolonial move into Europe', Kinvall argues for a discussion of Europe as 'postcolonial space' that comprehends the dynamics of power, imperialism and globalism underpinning the idea of Europe that 'was transferred to postcolonial societies', so as to understand that 'colonialism never left Europe unaffected and is part of European reality' (2016, p. 153).

This reflexive move can be seen in gender approaches as well (see Chapter 9). For example, Maria Stern's discourse analysis of the ESS uncovers the gendered and racialised features of Europe's conception of its own security as a global security actor. She explores how the text of the ESS displays 'multiple notions of feminity and masculinity, enmeshed in colonial logics and racialised associations . . . in the construction of a "Europe" as a subject that can be secured' (Stern, 2011, p. 31), to ultimately show that a masculinised and colonial Europe has violently represented and excluded Otherness as both feminised and subordinate.

Conclusion

The 1990s and early 2000s were extraordinary times in terms of European security and in its concrete, 'real life' dynamics. There was a unique intellectual fervour that led to the creation of multiple schools and approaches and theories: from Aberystwyth to Paris, the debates and the ideas unfolded at a pace that radically changed how we understand European Security. But 'on the ground', the devastating identity conflicts in Europe and outside, the enlargement of NATO and the EU, and the transformation of these two organisations in terms of their respective security structures, also shifted our understanding of European security away from the pure state-centred rational actor approaches. But, as we came to realise, some of these ideas have become problematic. For example, Stefano Guzzini argues that this idea of a Western identity is closely linked to the recent return of geopolitical thought, as '[a]n answer to, or an easy fix for, the sense of dis-orientation and foreign policy identity crises which followed 1989', fostering the politics of representation of 'an exclusionary Fortress West' (2015, p. 5).

The migration crisis, the potential de-Europeanisation of the UK from Europe, the societal security concerns in some Central and Eastern European countries, the overall changing power dynamics in international order, and the impact of technology on security, suggest there is much to theorise in the coming years. From all these issues, technology is, arguably, the area that has most to develop (see Andersson, 2016; Bellanova and Duez, 2012). Cyberspace, artificial intelligence, robotics, space and bio-sciences will change the face of European Security in the coming decades, and, with it, how we study it.

Notes

1 In his now famous ISA Presidential speech, Robert Keohane argues that reflectivist approaches understand the individual and states as 'affected by institutional arrangements, by prevailing norms, and by historically contingent discourse among people seeking to pursue their purposes and solve their self-defined problems' (1988, p. 382). In common they have the fact they 'emphasize the importance of human reflection for the nature of institutions and ultimately for the character of world politics' (Keohane, 1988, p. 382). This includes most constructivist approaches, but also Critical Security Studies, as we will further explore in the next section. His definition is a broad church that includes "interpretive" scholars, but also 'strongly materialist historical-sociological approaches indebted to Marxism, or political-theoretical arguments emphasizing classical political philosophy or international law' (Keohane, 1988, p. 382).
2 This means theories that were developed exclusively to address internal security concerns are not discussed in this chapter.
3 One aspect most realists agree on is that states tend to interact according to a balancing logic, that is, they tend to react to changes in the international system by allying with other states in order to balance the power of another, more powerful, state or group of states. For some realists, this balancing mechanism happens only when states feel threatened. In that case, we have a balance of threat and not a balance of power (see Walt, 1987).
4 Bandwagoning is when a state sides with the superior power, rather than balancing against it.
5 A good exception to this is Seth Jones' work on security cooperation in Europe. In any case, his conclusion follows the same line of previous realist takes on the subject: European states cooperate in the security realm in order to 'increase Europe's ability to project power abroad and to decrease reliance on the United States' (2007, p. 222).
6 By incorporating researchers from different theoretical backgrounds in IR, the Copenhagen School ended up creating a theory appealing enough to different sectors of IR and Security academia, especially within Europe.
7 The debate in the *Review of International Studies* (1997–1998) and many other supportive and critical articles that followed have been fundamental in the redefinition of Security Studies.
8 After free elections were held in 1990 in all republics of the Yugoslav Federation, confrontation arose and escalated from 1992 among a multicultural population composed of Bosniaks, Serbs and Croats, as the republic of Bosnia Herzegovina became the object of territorial claims from the neighbouring republics of Croatia and Serbia.

Further reading

Booth, Ken (2007), *Theory of World Security*. Cambridge: Cambridge University Press.
CASE Collective (2006), 'Critical Approaches to Security in Europe: A Networked Manifesto', *Security Dialogue*, 37 (4), 443–487.

Cladi, Lorenzo, and Locatelli, Andrea (2017), *International Relations Theory and European Security: We Thought We Knew*. London: Routledge.

Huysmans, Jef (2006), *The Politics of Insecurity: Fear, Migration and Asylum in the EU*. London: Routledge.

Weblinks

Open University podcasts on IR theory: www.youtube.com/results?search_query=international+relations

Two useful IR blogs are:

Duck of Minerva: http://duckofminerva.com/

E-IR: www.e-ir.info/

References

Adler, Emmanuel (2008), 'The Spread of Security Communities: Communities of Practice, Self-Restraint, and NATO's Post-Cold War Transformation', *European Journal of International Relations*, 14 (2), 195–230.

Amoore, Louise, and de Goede, Marieke (2008), 'Transactions After 9/11: The Banal Face of the Preemptive Strike', *Transactions*, 33 (2), 173–185.

Andersson, Ruben (2016), 'Hardwiring the Frontier? The Politics of Security Technology in Europe's "fight against illegal migration"', *Security Dialogue*, 47 (1), 22–39.

Armitage, John, and Virilio, Paul (1999), 'From Modernism to Hypermodernism and Beyond: An Interview with Paul Virilio', *Theory, Culture & Society*, 16 (5–6), 25–55.

Art, Robert (2004), 'Europe Hedges Its Security Bets', in T. V. Paul, J. Wirtz, and M. Fortmann (eds), *Balance of Power Revisited: Theory and Practice in the 21st Century*. Stanford: Stanford University Press, pp. 179–213.

Ayoob, Mohammed (2002), 'Humanitarian Intervention and State Sovereignty', *International Journal of Human Rights*, 6 (1), 81–102.

Barrinha, André, and Rosa, Marco (2013), 'Translating Europe's Security Culture', *Critical Studies on Security*, 1 (1), 101–115.

Barkawi, Tarak, and Laffey, Mark (2006), 'The Postcolonial Moment in Security Studies', *Review of International Studies*, 32 (2), 329–352.

Bellanova, Rocco, and Duez, Denis (2012), 'A Different View on the "Making" of European Security: The EU Passenger Name Record System as a Socio-Technical Assemblage', *European Foreign Affairs Review*, 17 (2), 109–124.

Berger, Peter L., and Luckmann, Thomas (1966), *The Social Construction of Reality*. New York: Anchor Books.

Bigo, Didier (2000), 'When Two Become One: Internal and External Securitisations in Europe', in Morten Kelstrup and Michael C. Williams (eds), *International Relations Theory and the Politics of European Integration: Power, Security and Community*. London: Routledge, pp. 171–204.

Bigo, Didier, and Tsoukala, Anastassia (2008), 'Understanding (In)Security', in Didier Bigo and Tsoukala, Anastassia (eds), *Terror, Insecurity and Liberty: Illiberal Practices of Liberal Regimes After 9/11*. Abingdon: Routledge, pp. 1–9.

Booth, Ken (2005), 'Critical Explorations', in Ken Booth (ed), *Critical Security Studies and World Politics*. London: Lynne Rienner, pp. 1–18.

Booth, Ken (2007), *Theory of World Security*. Cambridge: Cambridge University Press.

Buzan, Barry (1983), *People, States and Fear: The National Security Problem in International Relations*. London: Wheatsheaf.

Buzan, Barry, and Hansen, Lene (2009), *The Evolution of International Security Studies*. Cambridge: Cambridge University Press.

Buzan, Barry, Wæver, Ole, and de Wilde, Jaap (1998), *Security: A New Framework for Analysis*. Boulder, CO: Lynne Rienner.

Campbell, David (1998) *National Deconstruction: Violence, Identity, and Justice in Bosnia*. Minneapolis, MN: University of Minnesota Press.

Cladi, Lorenzo, and Locatelli, Andrea (2012), 'Bandwagoning, Not Balancing: Why Europe Confounds Realism', *Contemporary Security Policy*, 33 (2), 264–288.

Cladi, Lorenzo, and Locatelli, Andrea (2017), 'Structural Realism: Balancing, Bandwagoning or What?', in Lorenzo Cladi and Andrea Locatelli (eds), *International Relations Theory and European Security: We Thought We Knew*. London: Routledge, pp. 11–27.

Council of the European Union (2003), *A Secure Europe in a Better World: European Security Strategy* 15895/03, 8 December 2003. Brussels: Council of the European Union. Available at: http://data.consilium.europa.eu/doc/document/ST-15895-2003-INIT/en/pdf (accessed: 13 January 2019).

Cox, Robert W. (1987) *Production, Power, and World Order: Social Forces in the Making of History*. New York: Columbia University Press.

Cox, Robert W., with Schechter, Michael G. (2002), *The Political Economy of a Plural World: Critical Reflections on Power, Morals and Civilization*. London: Routledge.

Da Mota, Sarah (2018), *NATO, Civilisation and Individuals. The Unconscious Dimension of International Security*. London: Palgrave.

Darby, Phillip (2009), 'Rolling Back the Frontiers of Empire: Practising the Postcolonial', *International Peacekeeping*, 16 (5), 699–716.

Delanty, Gerard (2003), 'The Making of a Post-Western Europe: A Civilizational Analysis', *Thesis Eleven*, 72 (1), 8–25.

Dillon, Michael, and Lobo-Guerrero, Luis (2008), 'Biopolitics of Security in the 21st Century: An Introduction', *Review of International Studies*, 34 (2), 265–292.

Dover, Robert (2007), *Europeanization of British Defence Policy*. London: Routledge.

Duffield, Mark (2005), 'Getting Savages to Fight Barbarians: Development, Security and the Colonial Present', *Conflict, Security & Development*, 5 (2), 141–159.

Dyson, Tom (2010), *Neoclassical Realism and Defence Reform in Post-Cold War Europe*. Basingstoke: Palgrave Macmillan.

Edwards, Geoffrey (2006), 'Is There a Security Culture in the Enlarged European Union?', *The International Spectator*, 41 (3), 7–23.

Fierke, Karin, and Wiener, Antje (1999), 'Constructing Institutional Interests: EU and NATO Enlargement', *Journal of European Public Policy*, 6 (5), 721–741.

Glasius, Marlies, and Kaldor, Mary (2005), 'Individuals First: A Human Security Doctrine for the European Union', *Internationale Politik und Gesellschaft*, 1/2005, 62–82.

Giddens, Anthony (1984), *The Constitution of Society*. Berkeley, CA: University of California Press.

Guzzini, Stefano (2015), 'Foreign Policy Identity Crises and Uses of the "West"', *Danish Institute for International Studies Working Paper 5*, 4–24.

Hansen, Lene (2006), *Security as Practice: Discourse Analysis and the Bosnian War*. London: Routledge.

Hoffman, Stephanie (2011), 'CSDP: Approaching Transgovernmentalism?, in Xymena Kurowska and Fabian Breuer (eds), *Explaining the EU's Common Security and Defence Policy: Theory in Action*. London: Palgrave, pp. 41–62.

Howorth, Jolyon, and Anand, Menon (2009), 'Still Not Pushing Back: Why the European Union Is Not Balancing the United States', *Journal of Conflict Resolution*, 53 (5), 727–744.

Huysmans, Jef (1998), 'Revisiting Copenhagen: Or, on the Creative Development of Security Studies Agenda in Europe', *European Journal of International Relations*, 4 (4), 479–505.

Hyde-Price, Adrian (2007), *European Security in the Twenty-first Century: The Challenge of Multipolarity*. Abingdon: Routledge.

Jones, Seth G. (2007), *The Rise of European Security Cooperation*. Cambridge: Cambridge University Press.

Johnston, Alastair Ian (1995), 'Thinking About Strategic Culture', *International Security*, 19 (4), 32–64.

Katzenstein, Peter J. (1996), 'Introduction: Alternative Perspectives on National Security', in Peter J. Katzenstein (ed), *The Culture of National Security: Norms, and Identity in World Politics*. New York: Columbia University Press, pp. 1–6.

Keohane, Robert (1988), 'International Institutions: Two Approaches', *International Studies Quarterly*, 32 (4), 379–396.

Kinvall, Catarina (2016), 'The Postcolonial Has Moved into Europe: Bordering, Security and Ethno-Cultural Belonging', *Journal of Common Market Studies*, 54 (1), 152–168.

Klein, Bradley S. (1988), 'Hegemony and Strategic Culture: American Power Projection and Alliance Defence Politics', *Review of International Studies*, 14 (2), 133–148.

Kolodziej, Edward A. (2005), *Security and International Relations*. Cambridge: Cambridge University Press.

Kratochwil, Friedrich (1989), *Rules, Norms, and Decisions*. Cambridge: Cambridge University Press.

Krause, Keith (1998), 'Critical Theory and Security Studies: The Research Programme of "Critical Security Studies"', *Cooperation and Conflict*, 33 (3), 298–333.

Krause, Keith, and Williams, Michael (1997), *Critical Security Studies: Concepts and Cases*. Minneapolis, MN: University of Minnesota Press.

Mearsheimer, John (1990), 'Back to the Future: Instability in Europe after the Cold War', *International Security*, 15 (1), 5–56.

Mearsheimer, John (2010) 'Why Is Europe Peaceful Today?', *European Political Science*, 9 (3), 387–397.

Menon, Anand (2011), 'Power, Institutions and the CSDP: The Promise of Institutionalist Theory', *Journal of Common Market Studies*, 49 (1), 83–100.

Monteleone, Carla (2017), 'Beyond Material Factors? Identity, Culture and the Foreign and Security Policy of the EU', in Lorenzo Cladi and Andrea Locatelli (eds), *International Relations Theory and European Security: We Thought We Knew*. London: Routledge, pp. 83–99.

Mutimer, David (2007), 'Critical Security Studies: A Schismatic History', in Alan Collins (ed), *Contemporary Security Studies*. New York: Oxford University Press, pp. 53–73.

Norheim-Martinsen, Per M. (2011), 'EU Strategic Culture: When the Means Become the Ends', *Contemporary Security Policy*, 32 (3), 517–534.

North, Douglass C. (1990), *Institutions, Institutional Change and Economic Performance*. Cambridge: Cambridge University Press.

O'Hagan, Jacinta (2002), *Conceptualizing the West in IR*. Basingstoke: Palgrave Macmillan.

Onar, Nora, and Nicolaïdis, Kalypso (2013), 'The Decentring Agenda: Europe as Post-Colonial Power', *Cooperation and Conflict*, 48 (2), 283–303.

Onuf, Nicholas (1989), *World of Our Making*. Columbia, SC: University of South Carolina Press.

Peoples, Columba, and Vaughan-Williams, Nick (2010), *Critical Security Studies: An Introduction*. London: Routledge.

Posen, Barry R. (2006), 'European Union Security and Defense Policy: Response to Unipolarity?', *Security Studies*, 15 (2), 149–186.

Rynning, Sten (2011), 'Realism and the Common Security and Defence Policy', *Journal of Common Market Studies*, 49 (1), 23–42.

Schweller, Randall L. (2004), 'Unanswered Threats. A Neoclassical Realist Theory of Underbalancing', *International Security*, 29 (2), 159–201.

Searle, John (1995), *The Construction of Social Reality*. New York: Free Press.

Snyder, Jack (1977), *The Soviet Strategic Culture: Implications for Limited Nuclear Operations*. Santa Monica, CA: RAND.

Stern, Maria (2011), 'Gender and Race in the European Security Strategy: Europe as "Force for Good"?', *Journal of International Relations and Development*, 14 (1), 28–59.

Tunander, Ola (2008), 'Geopolitics of the North: *Geopolitik* of the Weak: A Post-Cold War Return to Rudolf Kjellen', *Cooperation and Conflict*, 43 (2), 164–184.

Ullman, Richard H. (1983), 'Redefining Security', *International Security*, 8 (1), 129–153.

Wæver, Ole (1995), 'Securitization and Desecuritization', in Ronny D. Lipschutz (ed), *On Security*. New York: Columbia University Press, pp. 48–86.

Wæver, Ole (2000), 'The EU as a Security Actor: Reflections from a Pessimistic Constructivist on Post-Sovereign Security Orders', in Morten Kelstrup and Michael C. Williams (eds), *International Relations and the Politics of European Integration: Power, Security and Community*. London: Routledge, pp. 250–294.

Wæver, Ole (2004), 'Aberystwyth, Paris, Copenhagen: New "Schools" in Security Theory and Their Origin Between Core and Periphery', International Studies Association Annual Convention, Montreal, 17–20 March.

Walt, Stephen (1987), *The Origins of Alliances*. Ithaca, NY: Cornell University Press.

Walt, Stephen (1991), 'The Renaissance of Security Studies', *International Studies Quarterly*, 35 (2), 211–239.

Wendt, Alexander (1992), 'Anarchy Is What States Make of It: The Social Construction of Power Politics', *International Organization*, 46 (2), 391–425.

Williams, Michael C. (2007), *Culture and Security: Symbolic Power and the Politics of International Security*. Oxford: Routledge.

Williams, Michael C., and Neumann, Iver (2000), 'From Alliance to Security Community: NATO, Russia and the Power of Identity', *Millennium – Journal of International Studies*, 29 (2), 357–387.

Wyn Jones, Richard (1999), *Security, Strategy, and Critical Theory*. London: Lynne Rienner.

Zwolski, Kamil (2012), 'The EU as an International Security Actor after Lisbon: Finally a Green Light for a Holistic Approach?', *Cooperation and Conflict*, 47 (1), 68–87.

NATO and the transatlantic community, 1949–2019

4

James Sperling

Introduction

The North Atlantic Treaty (1949) forged an unbreakable security bond between Western Europe and North America. The Treaty marked a historic departure in US diplomacy. President Harry S. Truman, in committing the US to the defence of Europe, ignored President George Washington's admonition that the United States should not enter into any 'entangling alliances'. The transatlantic alliance, and its eventual institutionalisation as the North Atlantic Treaty Organization (NATO), was not only the essential component of the US grand strategy of containment, but also represented a unilateral American security guarantee that made possible the post-war political and economic recovery of Western Europe, legitimised the long-term stationing of American military forces on European soil, and provided a material foundation for US leadership of the West.

The creation of NATO, its ability to sustain a transatlantic consensus on common geopolitical interests and aspirational foreign policy goals, and the creation of a transatlantic community of like-minded states, was not foreordained. In fact, NATO was beset during the Cold War (1947–1990) by serial crises of confidence over the credibility of the American nuclear guarantee, episodic fears of abandonment or entrapment by Europeans and Americans alike, and an inability to strike a balance between American leadership and the European desire for greater equality within the alliance (see Thies, 2009).

With the end of the Cold War and dissolution of the Soviet Union, tensions within the Atlantic Alliance became, if anything, more pronounced. The sudden absence of an existential threat left the alliance bereft of purpose. NATO, a compulsory alliance during the Cold War without the option of exit for Europeans or North Americans, became, in 1990, a voluntary alliance with one. It meant that the European risk of resisting US leadership lessened just as the ability of the US to wring concessions from its allies was impaired. The Balkan wars of the 1990s, the need to prevent a power vacuum in central Europe, and the transition to democracy and the market in the former Warsaw Pact states soon provided an alternative rationale for NATO in the absence of a direct threat from a known adversary. None the less, the task of collective defence remained NATO's *raison d'être*. This continuity of core purpose, however, is often overshadowed by the profound adaptation of NATO after 1990. Security threats and the range of malign actors have also multiplied since 1990, affected the member states asymmetrically, and present security vulnerabilities not particularly amenable to a military response.

This chapter charts the trajectory of NATO between from 1949 and 2019. Three major themes emerge in the analysis of NATO during the Cold War (1949–1990): the difficulty of maintaining the credibility of the unilateral American security guarantee; the mutual economic recriminations that rent the fabric of the transatlantic bargain struck in the 1950s and threatened the cohesion of the Atlantic Alliance in the 1970s; and periods of strategic alienation when the particularistic national interests of the major member states clashed with those of the alliance. NATO after the Cold War (1990–2019) has faced a very different set of challenges: redefining its purpose in successive strategic concepts in order to align NATO capabilities and purposes with the putative threats facing its member states; assimilating its former adversaries into the Western system of security governance; managing the internal adaptation of the alliance to meet the challenges of low intensity and expeditionary warfare; and minimising conflicts within the alliance that arose from burden- and risk-sharing in NATO operations, as well as a recalibration of the limits of American leadership and the European willingness to follow.

The conclusion addresses the potential impact of the Trump presidency on NATO. As a candidate, Trump cast into question the necessity of NATO and its relevance to US security. His foreign policy rhetoric has been expressed in the idiom of 'America first' just as his worldview has been nakedly transactional. The election of Donald Trump to the US presidency may represent an aberration, or mark a permanent return to the discredited foreign policy strategies of the interwar period; it may mean that NATO can no longer be considered an inviolable covenant, but as a contract nearing its expiration date.

NATO and the Cold War: 1949–1990

The deterioration in Soviet–American relations in the immediate post-war period ensured that the United Nations would not emerge as an effective collective security organisation. Washington and Moscow were locked in a geostrategic competition, the object of which was hegemony in Europe. The Americans also faced a strategic conundrum within their sphere of influence: they needed to allay the western European concern that the Second World War did not solve the 'German problem'. Thus, the North Atlantic Treaty effectively achieved the hat-trick, described by Lord Ismay, NATO's first Security General, of 'keep[ing] the Soviet Union out, the Americans in, and the Germans down'.

The Truman Doctrine, which committed the US to 'support free peoples who are resisting attempted subjugation by armed minorities or by outside pressures', provided the logic for the North Atlantic Treaty. The Treaty contains a mere 14 articles and designated the North Atlantic Council as the decision-making forum. In Article Five (the mutual defence clause), the signatory states agreed that 'an armed attack against one or more of them in Europe or

North America shall be considered an attack against them all . . .'. Article Four, the collective security clause of the Treaty, played a minor role in the Alliance prior to 1990, but became the legal foundation for addressing the proliferation of security threats that did not meet the Article Five threshold. Article Six delineated the geopolitical space covered by the Treaty (the Atlantic region north of the Tropic of Cancer), which became relevant in the post Cold War era when the US, particularly, insisted that NATO had to 'go out of area or go out of business' (Lugar, 1993). Article Three has provided a Treaty-based justification for American complaints about burden sharing; it committed the member states to 'maintain and develop their individual and collective capacity to resist armed attack'. The US effectively redefined Articles Three and Six after 1990: the allies were expected to acquire force projection capabilities incidental to collective defence and expanded NATO's geopolitical scope far beyond that specified in Article Six. And Article Ten, the so-called 'open door' provision of the Treaty, provided the basis and criteria for allowing Greece and Turkey to join the Alliance in 1951, Germany in 1954, and Spain in 1982. It also facilitated the post Cold War serial enlargements into eastern and central Europe.

Article Two codified what many NATO scholars have referred to as the 'transatlantic bargain' struck between the US and the Europeans (Sloan, 2016): in exchange for the unilateral American security guarantee (which is what Article Five in fact represented in 1949) and Marshall Plan economic aid, the European states would 'eliminate conflict in their international economic policies and will encourage economic collaboration between any or all of them'. Americans expected the Europeans to promote greater economic cooperation with each other, thereby creating a firm foundation for a unified (western) Europe that could eventually evolve into a co-equal pillar of the Alliance. The North Atlantic Treaty thus provided the security enabling the western Europeans to rebuild their economies, consolidate democracy, and eventually contribute to the costs of maintaining a liberal international economic order. The Marshall Plan and North Atlantic Treaty together constructed the transatlantic community and legitimised American leadership of it.

The first step towards creating the 'O' in NATO occurred in 1950, when General Dwight D. Eisenhower was named Supreme Allied Commander Europe. Between 1950 and 1952, the command structure was established (Supreme Headquarters Allied Powers Europe and Supreme Allied Commander Atlantic) and the integrated military commands put in place (Allied Command Europe and Allied Command Atlantic) (see Kaplan, 2014). The outbreak of the Korean War facilitated NATO's institutionalisation, but also led to the alliance's first 'crisis'. The US viewed the war as an intentional Soviet feint in Asia to distract the US, leaving Europe vulnerable to a Soviet attack. Although the Korean War turned out to be a parochial affair, it generated American demands that the Europeans accelerate rearmament to compensate for the diversion of US troops to the Korean peninsula. The Europeans failed to do so. That failure was exacerbated by the French National Assembly's non-ratification of the treaty establishing the European Defence Community (EDC).

These two episodes foreshadowed what would become chronic conflicts within NATO. The European inability (or unwillingness) to meet the 1952 Lisbon force goals generated US accusations of European free-riding, while the Europeans sought to ensure that rearmament did not undercut the US extended nuclear deterrent. The US strategy of 'massive retaliation' – that the US would respond to a Soviet provocation with nuclear weapons 'at places and with means of our own choosing' – would be maximally credible from the European perspective if the only possible American response to a Soviet attack on Western Europe were nuclear rather than conventional. The US considered the stillborn EDC as the institutional vessel for effectively aggregating European forces within an institutional structure subordinate to NATO. The EDC was also viewed as the perfect mechanism for rearming Germany and reintegrating Germany into the transatlantic community. American frustration over the EDC led Secretary of State John Foster Dulles to muse that the US would undertake an 'agonizing reappraisal' of its security commitment to Europe (see Duchin, 2007). Although an empty threat, it facilitated German membership of NATO, the restoration of German sovereignty in 1955, and the legal foundation for German rearmament.

Similarly, the British and French were dismayed when the Eisenhower administration failed to support their effort to reclaim the Suez Canal during the second Arab–Israeli War in 1956. Concurrently, the American policy of 'rollback' – a promise that the US would actively support the liberation of the Warsaw Pact countries – was discredited when the US failed to support the Hungarian Revolution. These two events weakened NATO's internal cohesion: the French concluded that the Americans could not be trusted, the British concluded that it could not act without American approval, and Europeans belatedly understood that American abandonment was not impossible in the event of a Soviet military provocation in Europe. The successful launching of Sputnik in 1957 only intensified those concerns, since it made inoperable the doctrine of massive retaliation: the Soviets now possessed the capability to launch a retaliatory nuclear strike on the US. Massive retaliation already lacked plausibility because it left the US with two equally unpalatable options: acquiescence or nuclear war. The absence of credible military responses to a Soviet challenge falling short of a direct threat to US territory generated a new military doctrine, the 'New Look'. This doctrine introduced tactical nuclear weapons into the war-fighting equation to compensate for conventional shortfalls. The doctrinal transition to limited nuclear war after an initial conventional engagement (or what the Kennedy administration called 'flexible response') may have bolstered the credibility of the extended American deterrent. But it did so at the cost of ensuring that, in the event of war, Europe would require 'liberation' by allied forces and be the first victim of any nuclear exchange. The European aversion to 'flexible response' ensured that it only became official NATO military doctrine in 1967 as the military complement to the 1967 Harmel Report, which charted a less confrontational strategy towards the Soviet Union (see below).

The seeds of distrust sown in 1956 accelerated the French and British determination to acquire an independent nuclear deterrent.[1] The UK deterrent was designed to function as a 'trigger' ensuring the USA's participation in a European war, while the French deterrent was conceived as a means for separating itself strategically from the US while deterring a Soviet attack on France (see Freedman, 2003, pp. 298–327). Efforts were made during this period to provide Europeans with some control over the (non-)use of nuclear weapons in the European theatre. The multilateral force (MLF) proposal was conceived as a seaborne nuclear deterrent under NATO command with multinational crews. Of the major allies, only Germany was interested in that arrangement, despite its questionable utility as an effective deterrent. After the Johnson administration unceremoniously dropped the MLF proposal, the Nuclear Planning Group was created to 'establish a consultative process on nuclear doctrine within NATO' (North Atlantic Treaty Organization, 2018).

The Kennedy administration's articulated goal that the Atlantic alliance evolve into two equal pillars found favour in the Johnson and Nixon administrations, but both administrations expected the Europeans to follow the American lead without significant resistance. The European pillar did not materialise; the allies lacked a common strategic vision and were unwilling to aggregate their military capabilities meaningfully. Moreover, the range of European attitudes toward American leadership fell along a continuum marked at one end by the British position (fidelity and deference to American preference) and at the other by the French position (the necessity of European independence and equidistance from US policy outside Europe).

The economic component of the transatlantic bargain was no less subject to contention. The shared Euro–American preference for an economically integrated Europe was realised with the signing of the Treaty of Rome in 1957, which established the European Economic Community that eventually evolved into the European Union. But strains on the economic component of the transatlantic compact emerged in the late 1950s, when chronic American balance of payments deficits, which had financed post-war Europe's economic recovery and growth, were recognised to be unsustainable. The outflow of dollars during the 1950s was not problematic so long as the dollar remained the only (or virtually only) transaction and investment currency. Once European currencies became convertible, the dollar shortage of the 1950s turned into the dollar glut of the 1960s (Calleo, 1970). The dollar glut had consequences for the alliance. First, Americans demanded significant offset payments (primarily from Germany) to cover the cost of stationing of US troops in Europe. Second, by financing the war in Vietnam with deficit spending, the US abused its role as the guardian of the key currency in the international economy and engendered endless transatlantic recriminations over macroeconomic policy. American dissatisfaction with Europeans was expressed in a series of Mansfield Amendments, beginning in 1966, to reduce the number of troops in Europe.[2] The nexus between the strains on the Bretton Woods international economic system and the ambiguities of the American unilateral security guarantee became a permanent feature of the transatlantic relations until the end of the Cold War.

The most extreme manifestation of this transatlantic discord was French President Charles de Gaulle's decision to withdraw France from NATO's integrated military command structure in 1966. The French withdrawal did not fundamentally alter the ability of the alliance to deter the Soviet Union (Hunt, 1966). It did, however, cause a rupture within the alliance owing to the signal it sent; France, like many others, including Germany, believed that constructive engagement with the Soviet Union would not only minimise the prospect of war in Europe but also increase European autonomy and independence from an American foreign policy viewed as indifferent to European interests.

NATO adopted the Harmel Doctrine in 1967, a dual-track strategy of deterrence and *détente* to lessen the intensity of the Cold War. It reflected changes in the geostrategic landscape: the approach of nuclear parity between the US and the Soviet Union, the French desire for a more balanced relationship with the two superpowers, and West Germany's desire to lessen tensions with East Germany. The suppression of the 1968 Prague Spring was paradoxically (in retrospect) constructive in so far as NATO inaction assured the Soviet Union that the West accepted its hegemonic position in Eastern Europe, as did the mutual recognition of the two post-war German states in 1972. These two developments settled two outstanding issues of the post-war settlement: the international status of the two Germanys, and the contested diplomatic and military–strategic demarcation of NATO's eastern boundary.

Although the Cold War transitioned into a stable crisis – neither the United States nor the Soviet Union had an interest in disturbing the *status quo* – the Atlantic community was riven by internal conflicts that reflected a loss of political and economic cohesion. Three events placed the transatlantic bargain into question: the Nixon Doctrine (1968), the progressive dismantling of the marquee feature of the Bretton Woods monetary system – a fixed exchange rate regime underpinned by the dollar – between 1971 and 1973, and the differentiated allied responses to the 1973 Arab–Israeli war and oil crisis.

The Nixon Doctrine signified the American 'retreat from empire' (Osgood, 1973). Although directed primarily at regional surrogates outside Europe, it none the less unnerved the NATO allies, particularly the Germans (Kaltefleiter, 1973). The American retreat was more marked in response to the unrelenting pressure on the dollar and the American inability to credibly support the Bretton Woods fixed exchange regime absent a coordinated revaluation of the major international currencies against the dollar. That revaluation was not forthcoming until the Nixon administration announced, in August 1971, that the US would no longer exchange foreign reserves held in dollars into gold and then managed to extract a net 10% devaluation of the dollar against the world's major currencies in December 1971. It proved to be too little, too late. The international monetary system transitioned abruptly to a system of floating exchange rates in February 1973. Floating exchange rates did not end macroeconomic acrimony within the transatlantic community and an unstable dollar complicated efforts to create a European monetary system.

Thus, the transatlantic bargain began the process of unravelling in 1966, when France withdrew from NATO's integrated military command and finally came unstuck in 1973 when the United States unilaterally revalued the dollar and, thereby, repudiated its legal obligation to preserve the value of the dollar (Cohen, 1974). These macroeconomic developments were a harbinger of the conflicts that arose when the United States accommodated the impact of the four-fold oil price rise in 1974 with inflation, whereas the Germans and others in Europe implemented restrictive macroeconomic policies intended to adjust to the price rise. By the mid-1970s, the only elements of the initial transatlantic bargain that remained were the American security guarantee and European economic integration, although the former was suspect, while the latter was increasingly seen in Washington as in opposition to, rather than in partnership with, the US.

After President Nixon's resignation in 1974, President Ford ushered in a brief period of inter-alliance comity and facilitated macroeconomic coordination within the G-7. The Carter Presidency, however, reinjected enmity into transatlantic relations, particularly with his administration's responses to the invasion of Afghanistan and the growing Euro-strategic nuclear imbalance. Germany's Chancellor, Helmut Schmidt, and President Jimmy Carter had a troubled relationship, and was the clearest manifestation of the growing strategic alienation within the alliance. The Carter administration first placed American credibility into doubt with the leaked 'Presidential Memorandum 10', which revealed an administration uncertain it could defend Europe in the event of a conventional war (Burt, 1978). Two months later, Carter then decided against deploying the neutron bomb in Europe after having announced that the US would do so in order to redress a perceived Euro-strategic nuclear imbalance. These decisions resurrected concerns over the credibility of Article Five and set the stage for intense conflicts over the NATO Intermediate-Range Nuclear Forces (INF) modernisation and deployments into the early 1980s.

In order to avoid the costs of modernising NATO's theatre nuclear weapons and making tactical nuclear war less difficult technically, German Chancellor Schmidt championed a 'two-track' proposal to restore the strategic balance in Europe. NATO would forgo INF modernisation in exchange for the withdrawal of already deployed Soviet INF. In the absence of such a bargain, NATO would deploy Pershing II and cruise missiles in Europe. NATO adopted Schmidt's proposal, but it required the US to enter into good-faith negotiations with the Soviet Union, something the Reagan administration did not do. Moreover, the Reagan administration in fact favoured deploying modernised INF in Europe. Chancellor Schmidt concluded that US behaviour voided any obligation to deploy modernised INF on German soil. Other European governments, excepting the UK, drew a not dissimilar conclusion. In the end, those NATO states and Germany eventually agreed to the deployment of modernised Pershing and cruise missiles.

The subsequent Soviet–American double-zero agreement in 1988 effected not only the withdrawal of the Pershing IIs stationed in Europe, but required the Germans to surrender the Pershing IAs under their control. This American *volte face* on nuclear weapons deepened existing suspicions that the American security guarantee was hedged, and stoked fears of singularisation: a nuclear war in Europe would be restricted to German territory. Yet, President Ronald Reagan's more circumspect and constructive diplomacy in his second term hastened the end of the Cold War, the dissolution of the Soviet Union, and the unification of Germany – an outcome embraced in Washington and Bonn if nowhere else.

NATO after the Cold War: 1991–2019

The end of the Cold War occasioned an unarticulated change in the balance of power *within* the alliance that required the US to accommodate the European demand for greater defence autonomy, equality, and sensitivity to European interests. NATO faced the task of successfully assimilating the former Warsaw Pact states into an institutionalised security framework, a critical requirement for any stable security order. This goal was eventually realised by extending NATO membership to the majority of the central and eastern European states. The alliance also sought to institutionalise a 'special relationship' with the Russian Federation as well as ensure that the remaining successor states of the former Soviet Union became stakeholders in the Western system of security governance. A second task required NATO to redefine its remit and responsibilities for regional order (and eventually global order after the events of 11 September 2001). The concept of out-of-area operations was progressively redefined: in Senator Richard Lugar's initial formulation, 'out of area' expanded the longitudinal, but not the latitudinal, remit of the alliance (see Lugar, 1993). After 11 September, NATO expanded operational responsibilities longitudinally and latitudinally; it eventually encompassed the geopolitical space spanning the Straits of Gibraltar to the Straits of Malacca and from Saharan Africa to the Arctic Circle. The expansion of NATO's defence perimeter created a new set of pathologies plaguing the alliance: the American demand that European armed forces undergo a major transformation in order to wage expeditionary warfare, unproductive debates about burden- and risk-sharing within the Alliance, and European fears of entrapment sparked by the short-lived American preference that NATO 'go global'.

The end of the Cold War paradoxically enhanced NATO's role *vis-à-vis* the member states as a political and military actor (Sperling and Webber, 2018). In the early 1990s, there were initially serious discussions about the continued necessity of NATO and the need for an alternative, comprehensive security framework encompassing the Eurasian geopolitical space. The Bush administration spoke of a 'new world order' while Europeans stuck to the concept of a common European house, neither of which meant the same thing to principals on either side of the Atlantic. Washington, however, insisted that the US retain the 'pivotal responsibility for ensuring the stability of the international balance' and that NATO remain the foundation of any post Cold War security order (President of the United States, 1990, p. 2). The US refused to jettison NATO for an alternate security institution, particularly if it threatened American leadership prerogatives. But it was also understood that a stable peace was contingent upon the integration of the Warsaw Pact states and the successor states of the former Soviet Union into a NATO-governed order.

NATO's first institutional innovation was the creation of the North Atlantic Cooperation Council (NACC). The NACC provided non-NATO European states with an institutional home within NATO; it was conceived as a mechanism for providing those states a 'voice' in shaping a new security order. NACC was also intended to spread the NATO norms of democracy and civilian control of the military. The NACC was no substitute for NATO membership, however. The Eastern European states sought NATO membership as insurance against a renascent Russia. At the same time, Russia insisted that NATO not enter into its traditional sphere of influence. The NATO solution was the Partnership for Peace (PfP). The PfP programme achieved a number of objectives; it facilitated the creation of closer bilateral relationships between NACC states and NATO, committed NATO to enlargement without a timetable for doing so, enabled NATO to monitor the willingness and ability of states to join NATO, and offered states the prerogative of Article Four consultations.[3]

The PfP did not dampen the demand for NATO membership. Moreover, many NATO members, particularly Germany and the US, believed that Article Ten of the Washington Treaty compelled the alliance to accept any European state that met the minimum normative criteria for membership and the ability to contribute to the common defence. The NATO Study on Enlargement (1995) and the subsequent Membership Action Plan (MAP) (see North Atlantic Treaty Organization, 1999a) jointly enumerated the political and military criteria for accession. The key political qualifications for membership were domestic democratic governance, respect for individual liberty, and adherence to the rule of law. The military criteria required that an aspirant state would reinforce alliance cohesion, contribute to the common defence, and demonstrate the will and capability to contribute to out-of-area military operations. Aspirants were also expected, post-accession, to adhere to the obligations of the Washington Treaty, particularly a willingness to honour Article Ten.

The preparatory stage of the enlargement process required aspirant states, *inter alia*, to promote internal stability and economic well-being and to settle any outstanding ethnic, territorial, or international disputes that could subsequently draw the alliance into a militarised conflict. It also enumerated a set of behavioural expectations: aspirant states would refrain from the threat or use of force, make a good faith effort to build a consensus on all issues confronting the alliance, and engage at all levels of alliance decision making, from the North Atlantic Council to the PfP (North Atlantic Treaty Organization, 1999a, § I, pars. 2 and 3).

NATO's first post Cold War enlargement took place in 1999. The accession of Poland, the Czech Republic, and Hungary was relatively noncontroversial. The second NATO enlargement – the so-called 'Big Bang' enlargement – was finalised at the 2002 Prague Summit. It included Slovenia, Slovakia, Romania, the three Baltic States (Latvia, Lithuania, and Estonia), and Bulgaria. Not all of these countries fully met the accession criteria, but all enjoyed the patronage of at least one major EU state and could rely upon US insistence that the Article Ten 'Open Door' principle be respected. Subsequently Albania, Croatia, and Macedonia declared, in March 2002, their interest in joining NATO; Albania and Croatia entered the alliance in April 2009, and Macedonian membership is imminent now that Greece has lifted its objection to membership. Montenegro, the most recent accession state, joined in 2017.

Georgia and Ukraine were identified at the 2008 NATO Bucharest Summit as candidates for eventual NATO membership. Both initially enjoyed vigorous American support for the transition to MAP membership status, prior to the Russo–Georgian War of 2008 and the Russian annexation of Crimea and the loss of the Donbass region to Russian-supported separatists in 2014. The major European allies never shared the American enthusiasm for either state's accession, owing to both nations' unsettled territorial disputes with Russia and a rediscovered sensitivity to the Russian need for a sphere of influence along its western border.

The much heralded 'peace dividend' at the end of the Cold War had two consequences. First, it required the reconsideration of NATO's purpose and initiated strategic adaptation to a new geopolitical context. Second, it made plausible the creation of a militarily capable European pillar of the alliance, which in turn would bestow upon the Europeans responsibility for regional stability short of an Article Five contingency. A militarily and diplomatically capable Europe could reduce the cost of NATO for the US without forgoing the benefit of American leadership, while the Europeans could acquire greater autonomy from the US without forgoing the American deterrent.

The profound shift in NATO's strategic environment after 1990 initiated a wide-ranging and continuous debate on the alliance's purpose and role. The London Declaration (1990) foresaw NATO as an 'agent of change' that would transform its former adversaries into partners. Yet, the alliance was not so naïve as to discount the residual threat the Soviet Union still presented. The 1991 New Strategic Concept enumerated the new security threats confronting the alliance (e.g., the proliferation of weapons of mass destruction, supply disruptions of raw materials, terrorism) and the potential risks attending a political, social or economic collapse in Central and Eastern Europe. It concluded that NATO not only had to preserve its collective defence capability, but also had to acquire military capabilities for crisis management along NATO's periphery. Events in Europe compelled additional adaptations. The crisis in Bosnia led NATO to accept the peacekeeping role in support of United Nations Security Council (UNSC) Resolutions or responding to a UN request to act regionally. By 1997, NATO recognised that the challenge of 'regional crisis and conflict management' stood alongside the 'core function of collective defence' (North Atlantic Treaty Organization, 1997, para. 3; 1999b, para. 10).

NATO altered its military doctrine in order to reflect the shift from static territorial defence against an explicit Soviet threat to the amorphous threats and civil disorder in failing states after 1992. Americans subsequently insisted that the European allies not only acquire the capability to conduct operations along the entire conflict spectrum (from peacekeeping to high-intensity warfare), but also to acquire interoperable force projection capabilities that would enable NATO to act 'out of area'. The 1999 Strategic Concept stipulated that NATO forces would be capable of not only providing the minimum level of military capabilities necessary to meet an (unlikely) Article Five contingency, but also acquire force projection capabilities for executing non-Article Five expeditionary operations beyond the periphery of the Alliance (North Atlantic Treaty Organization, 1999b, pars 20 and 24).

The NATO allies lacked those force projection capabilities in 1999. Towards alleviating that deficiency and keeping track of national efforts, NATO produced four catalogues of European capabilities deficiencies between 1999 and 2010: the April 1999 Defense Capabilities Initiative identified 58 capabilities shortfalls; the June 2001 North Atlantic Council Defence Minister's report emphasised Europe's need to acquire intelligence, surveillance, target acquisition, and reconnaissance capabilities; the June 2002 Prague Capabilities Commitment focused on primary force and strategic lift shortfalls; and the 2006 Comprehensive Political Guidance responded to shortfalls arising from the experience of coalition warfare in Afghanistan. The 2010 Strategic Concept singled out two areas in need of urgent improvement: an increased number of deployable and sustainable forces; and enhanced information systems and cyber security consistent with the growing dependence upon network-enabled capabilities (North Atlantic Treaty Organization, 2010a, pars 12, 19, 25 and 37). The persistent European failure to meet these capability goals was aggravated by declining defence expenditures and a disproportionately high share of defence expenditures devoted to personnel costs.

The Europeans desired greater operational independence from the US, just as the US wished the Europeans to assume responsibility for low intensity military operations in the European neighbourhood. Washington favoured a European Security and Defence Identity (ESDI) nested within NATO in order to create a more capable European pillar within the Atlantic Alliance without ceding autonomy to the Europeans at the expense of American leadership. The Europeans largely accepted the American blueprint for the ESDI, but the poor European showing during the Kosovo intervention led the Europeans to seek instead an autonomous military capability outside NATO. France and the UK, in their 1998 Saint Malo Agreement, recognised that Europe required guaranteed access to military capabilities 'pre-designated within NATO's European pillar' but should also acquire 'national or multinational European means *outside* the NATO framework' (Saint Malo Summit, 1998, para 3). This desire for autonomy captured American attention. The US Secretary of State, Madeleine Albright, laid down the marker for American acquiescence to European autonomy outside NATO in the language of the '3 D's': no EU duplication of NATO structures, no EU delinking from NATO's core mission, and no discrimination against European allies that were not members of the EU.

The 1999 Cologne European Council Declaration substituted the EU embedded European Security and Defence Policy (ESDP) for the NATO embedded ESDI. Although Europeans desired an autonomous planning capability to meet European-specific contingencies, they could not forgo access to the existing NATO command infrastructure. The Europeans and the US reached a mutual accommodation with the Berlin-plus agreement that reassured 'Alliance member states that Europe's autonomous efforts would be compatible and complementary to NATO's strategic and military orientations' (Kucheida, 2005, p. 10). Berlin-plus enabled the EU to undertake autonomous missions while relying upon NATO's operational infrastructure without precluding an autonomous EU planning capability in the future. However, the agreement did little more than extend to the EU those prerogatives previously ceded to the Western European Union in the early 1990s, but it left the US (or Turkey) with a potential veto over the use of certain categories of NATO assets, a caveat potentially limiting the EU's operational autonomy.

These institutional adaptations were less important than the change in NATO's operational purpose. Between mid-1992 and 2003, NATO executed 17 military operations in the region: seven in Bosnia, four in Macedonia, three in Kosovo and three naval deployments in the eastern Mediterranean. Only two of those 17 operations remain active: Operation Joint Guard (Kosovo) and Operation Active Endeavour (OAE) (a maritime mission in the Mediterranean). Those operations fulfilled a range of security objectives, from sanctions monitoring to no-fly zone enforcement to humanitarian interventions to the protection of EU, OSCE and UN personnel. The operations in Bosnia and Kosovo were critical to NATO's expeditionary evolution. The three operations in Bosnia – Operation Deliberate Force (1995), IFOR (1995–1996) and SFOR (1996–2005) – drew heavily on NATO resources and tested NATO capabilities. Operation Deliberate Force was a sustained air campaign against Serb forces in Bosnia threatening UN peacekeeping troops. IFOR provided the first major test of the Allied Rapid Reaction Corps (ARRC), a 60,000 strong NATO force established in 1992 to conduct, *inter alia*, peace-making operations. The ARRC deployment relieved the embattled UN peacekeeping force (UNPROFOR) and paved the way for the Dayton Peace Accords. SFOR was a follow-on 31,000 strong peacekeeping force that eventually handed off its responsibilities in 2005 to the European Union's ongoing EUFOR Althea mission. The NATO response to the 1999 Kosovo crisis, Operation Allied Force (OAF), took the form of a bombing campaign that brought about a cessation of hostilities between Serbs and Kosovars. NATO then dispatched the 50,000 strong KFOR for peacekeeping purposes. These military operations in the Balkans provided the crucible for allied cooperation in expeditionary warfare further afield.

The NATO allies invoked Article Five for the first time in response to the 11 September 2001 terrorist attacks. That show of allied solidarity demonstrated that NATO meant something more to Europeans than a unilateral US security guarantee. The multifaceted threat of 'global terrorism' required a rethinking of NATO strategy, particularly with respect to the balance between the military and non-military means to combat it. The 2002 Allied Joint Doctrine amended the 1999 Strategic Concept in critical respects, particularly with respect to the fundamental change in the conception and source of insecurity. It held that non-Article Five expeditionary operations could be conducted 'in any part of the world' (North Atlantic Treaty Organization, 2010b, p. 1). Just as important, terrorism was identified as an existential threat that required an enhanced NATO role in anti-terrorism, counter-terrorism, diplomatic consultation and coordination, and policy strategies for enhancing allied resilience to successful terrorist attacks in theatre or on NATO territory. The 2006 Comprehensive Political Guidance (CPG), the first comprehensive statement on NATO strategy after 2001, stated the obvious: terrorism and the proliferation of weapons of mass destruction (WMD) posed the principal threats to allied security. Greater prominence was given to Article Four contingencies arising from the negative security externalities of failing states as well as a broadening of the potential Article Five contingencies to include 'unconventional forms of armed assault', subsequently subsumed under the label of hybrid warfare (North Atlantic Treaty Organization, 2006, pars 5–7). The 2010 Strategic Concept recast crisis management operations far 'beyond NATO's borders' as a strategy for preventing a possible 'direct threat to the security of Alliance territory and populations' (North Atlantic Treaty Organization, 2010a, para 20). These documents jointly reflected an allied consensus that a parochial definition of security *and* NATO's responsibilities outlined in the 1949 North Atlantic Treaty were inadequate if NATO were to keep its member states secure. NATO's operational geopolitical ambit correspondingly expanded. NATO undertook maritime missions combating piracy in the Gulf of Aden and Horn of Africa (2008 to the present), logistical support for African Union operations in Darfur (2002) and Somalia (2005), humanitarian aid after natural disasters in Haiti (2010) and Pakistan (2005–2006), a training mission in Iraq (2004–2011), and a UN mandated air campaign in Libya (2011).

The major NATO operation between 2003 and 2014 was the International Security and Assistance Force (ISAF) in Afghanistan. The original UNSC Resolution mandated that NATO stabilise and secure Kabul in the aftermath of the American-led invasion of Afghanistan to drive the Taliban out of power and deny Al Qaeda a safe sanctuary. The UN progressively enlarged the territorial responsibility of ISAF and, in 2008, the UNSC expanded the ISAF mission 'to address the threat posed by the Taliban, Al-Qaida and other extremist groups' (United Nations Security Council, 2008). Until that time, the US (and some NATO allies) conducted Operation Enduring Freedom (OEF) in Afghanistan. OEF remained outside ISAF owing to the potential pitfalls of coalition warfare, particularly when some allies were unwilling to engage in high intensity warfare. The number of allied troops in Afghanistan (OEF and ISAF combined) was 52,784 in 2002, and peaked at 132,000 in 2011 with the Obama administration's surge. After ISAF and OEF ended in 2014, NATO launched its Resolute Support Mission (RSM) in 2015. RSM has a troop strength of 16,000 and is tasked with training Afghan security forces.

NATO also conducted operations within the geopolitical space identified in Article Six. Turkey requested an Article Four consultation owing to the destabilisation of Syria and the threat of missile attacks from contested Syrian territory. In December 2012, NATO agreed to Operation Anatolian Protector/Active Fence, which augmented Turkish air defences in December 2012 with PATRIOT air and missile defence batteries supplied by Germany, Italy, Spain, the Netherlands, and the US. NATO has also conducted maritime operations in the Aegean Sea since 2016 to control the influx of illegal migration from Syria, as well as the introduction of Operation Sea Guardian to cover 'the full range of maritime security tasks' in the Mediterranean (NATO, 2016). NATO also initiated air policing missions in the Baltics, Slovenia, and Albania to ensure that the airspace of the entire alliance would be monitored. Baltic air policing was enhanced as part of the Readiness Action Programme (RAP) after the Russian annexation of Crimea in 2014, while a parallel southern air policing mission to protect NATO airspace in the Black Sea region was initiated in 2017.

Recriminations over burden- and risk-sharing remerged after 2001. Burden sharing became particularly divisive owing to an American insistence that 'Europeans' were not making a proportional contribution to NATO missions, a perception reinforced by asymmetrical risk sharing that obscured the actual contributions made by risk-averse allies. Then Secretary of Defense, Robert Gates, expressed American grievances, when he claimed that NATO was divided '[be]tween those willing and able to pay the price and bear the burdens of alliance commitments, and those who enjoy the benefits of NATO membership . . . but don't want to share the risks and the costs' (Gates, 2011). Similarly, President Barack Obama suggested in his 2016 *Atlantic* interview that an important US foreign policy goal was arresting the European unwillingness to assume a proportionate share of the burden and risk in NATO-mandated military operations (Goldberg, 2016; see also Chollet and Kiel, 2016, pp. 9–10; de Hoop Scheffer et al., 2015, pp. 2–3).

These claims are as misleading as they are unproductive. Despite the low level of defence expenditures by the NATO allies,[4] the Europeans and Canadians contributed a proportional number of military personnel to combined NATO operations relative to their share of NATO GDP. There are significant variations in regional presence: the United States has been over-represented in operations *outside* of Europe, while the Europeans and Canadians have been over-represented *within* Europe. There is also a marked asymmetry of effort *among* the European member states. The post Cold War accession states over-contributed to NATO operations both inside *and* outside Europe. But a similar blanket claim cannot be made for the Cold War states: only Denmark, France, Italy, Portugal, and the UK made proportionate or disproportionately large contributions to NATO operations. Post-Afghanistan, the US contributions to NATO-led air and sea operations have generally fallen below those of the major European allies (Sperling and Webber, 2018).

Selective risk avoidance became deeply divisive once NATO forces engaged in high intensity warfare. It has not pitted the US against the rest, but instead – like burden sharing – divides the alliance. Canada, Denmark, the Netherlands, and the UK, for example, were publicly critical of the European allies avoiding combat operations or imposing debilitating caveats on their armed forces in Afghanistan (Cook, 2008). Although British, Canadian, and American armed forces accounted for approximately 88% of the 3,348 combat-related deaths in Afghanistan, there was a stark intra-European division between those accepting risk and shirking it: British, Canadian, Danish, Estonian, French, and Norwegian forces absorbed

74% of non-US NATO combat deaths, but only accounted for 47% of non-US NATO troops deployed. Operation Unified Protector (OUP) in Libya elevated the pattern of risk acceptance, shirking and avoidance to a new level. Only eight NATO allies accepted a combat role (Belgium, Canada, Denmark, France, Italy, the Netherlands, the UK, and the US), and five others made a direct military contribution only (Bulgaria, Spain, Greece, Romania, and Turkey). The German government not only cast an abstention on the UNSC resolution authorising OUP, but withdrew German warships from OAE and German crews from AWACS patrols in the Mediterranean (see Sperling, 2016).

The unattributed assertion that the US was leading OUP 'from behind' in April 2011, and Secretary of State Clinton's assertion in *Foreign Policy* that a US 'pivot' to Asia was necessary, rekindled allied concerns about an American retrenchment at Europe's expense, the prospect of an eventual disengagement from Europe, and NATO's potential irrelevance if it did not make a parallel shift to the Pacific (Clinton, 2011; Lizza, 2011). Clinton's logic was unassailable in 2011: the most likely peer competitors of the US were located in the Indo-Pacific region and America's economic future was more likely than not to be shaped by its commercial and financial relations with Asian nations. Consequently, there was a greater need for an American investment in underdeveloped multilateral security and economic institutions in the Indo-Pacific, since Europe was at peace. Moreover, as President Obama made clear in his *Atlantic* interview, he believed it was time for the Europeans to assume greater responsibility for Europe, given its economic and military capacity *and* the American frustration with Europe's inability to emerge as a global actor commensurate with the capabilities (Goldberg, 2016).

It is not entirely clear that there has been, in fact, a rebalancing to Asia. Between 2011 and 2017, the number of US forces stationed in Asia declined from 83,000 to 74,000 (an 11% decline), while US forces stationed in NATO Europe declined from 67,700 to 65,000 (a 4% decline). If the forces stationed in the US earmarked for Armed Forces Europe (35,000) and Armed Forces Pacific (51,000) are added to those stationed abroad, the US maintains a larger presence in Asia than Europe. None the less, the 'pivot' or 'rebalancing' to Asia might be best considered an exercise in signalling rather than a major shift in the deployment of US forces. It may have placed the Europeans on notice that they would have to do more militarily and diplomatically to cope with second and third order regional threats, but it did not call NATO or the continuing strategic importance of Europe into question.

The Russian annexation of Crimea and support of secessionist factions in eastern Ukraine in 2014 renewed NATO's original purpose and accelerated NATO's 'return' to Europe. It would be difficult to overestimate the diplomatic shock of Russia's actions. Just as the allies were anticipating a military strategic respite from the decade-long war in Afghanistan, developments in Ukraine reanimated suppressed suspicions about Russian intentions along NATO's eastern frontier. It caused the lamentable resurrection of Russia as a clear and present danger to NATO member states, underscored (for those who had forgotten) the continued importance of the Article Five guarantee, and shifted the allied focus from expeditionary warfare to deterrence and collective defence (North Atlantic Treaty Organization, 2015a, para 8).

The 2014 Wales Summit Declaration and Wales Declaration on the Transatlantic Relationship sought to avoid aggravating the rupture in NATO–Russian relations, while taking sufficiently robust measures to dissuade Russia from seeking to undermine the constitutional order in NATO allies with large ethnic Russian populations. The alliance threaded that needle with the Readiness Action Program (RAP). The RAP implemented several measures, including tripling in size of the NATO Response Force (NRF) to 40,000, enhancing standing naval forces, creating a 'spearhead force' – the Very High Readiness Joint Task Force – within the NATO Response Force to respond quickly and effectively to any violation of the Baltic states territorial integrity, enhancing allied air policing of Estonia, Latvian, and Lithuanian airspace, and conducting allied military exercises on a par with those undertaken during the Cold War (North Atlantic Treaty Organization, 2015b). The Russian incursion into Ukraine also offered the NATO frontier states a golden opportunity to renew their call for the permanent stationing of NATO troops on their territory. The alliance agreed at the 2016 Warsaw Summit to provide an 'enhanced forward presence' in the Baltic states and Poland. The allies agreed to station a rotating multilateral battalion in each of those countries. The alliance thereby reassured those allies that the collective defence guarantee is credible and bolstered conventional deterrence in northeast Europe without violating the NATO pledge that it would not permanently station allied troops in the new member states.

Conclusion

This new-found equilibrium within NATO – a clear purpose, a defined adversary, and an established set of instruments to deter and defend against that threat – was upended with the election of Donald Trump to the presidency of the United States. The new president immediately placed into question the long-term cohesion of the transatlantic relationship with musings about NATO's obsolescence and lack of relevancy. Despite the best efforts of then Secretary of Defense James Mattis to reassure the NATO allies that the US remained committed to Europe and NATO, the continuing lack of policy coherence, the rapid cycling of national security-related personnel, and the constant stream of foreign policy 'Twitter bombs' have left analysts and policy makers alike disorientated, if not unnerved. Trump, in tweet and policy, has seemingly sought to fundamentally renegotiate – if not nullify – the transatlantic bargain.

Trump pushed the long-standing transatlantic bargain to its illogical extreme. Whereas the transactional demand for greater burden sharing within NATO had long served as a tactical diplomatic gambit to ensure its military viability, Trump elevated burden sharing into a strategic principle that makes the US defence guarantee – and, by extension, fidelity to NATO – dependent on Europeans meeting US-defined defence spending minima, and that Europeans willingly accept that 'America knows best'. Trump believes that European defence spending shortfalls represent a burden on the American taxpayer, that the NATO spending benchmark should be 4% of GDP rather than 2%, and that NATO is a one-sided bargain favouring Europe (North Atlantic Treaty Organization, 2018, pp. 2–3). He has, however, abandoned the most corrosive claims made in 2015 and 2016, namely, that NATO is obsolete and that the Article 5 guarantee is contingent upon Europeans paying 'what they owe' to the US. Successive policy documents – the 2017 National Security Strategy (President of the United States, 2017, p. 48), the National Defense Security Review (Department of Defense, 2018a, p. 11) and 2018 Nuclear Posture Review (Department of Defense 2018b, pp. 59–60) – have been generally consistent with Obama-era policy statements: NATO is essential to US security and the Russian Federation poses a palpable military threat to *all* NATO member states.

Yet, Trump's unscripted remarks suggest that he continues to believe otherwise (Brands, 2018, pp. 16–17). Such remarks, in tone and content, in conjunction with unilateral withdrawals from the Paris Climate Accord and the nuclear deal with Iran, as well as the decision to move the US embassy from Tel Aviv to Jerusalem, have perhaps inflicted irreversible damage to American leadership. These decisions have been made even worse with threats that secondary sanctions will be levied on European companies that do business with Iran, and the opening of a Section 232 investigation to justify (on national security grounds) higher tariffs on German automobiles (Agence France Presse, 2018; McAuley, 2018). Moreover, Trump's penchant for toying with his counterparts in Europe, as was the case with French President Macron prior to the suspension of US participation in the Iranian nuclear agreement in 2018, has engendered a loss of faith in American leadership and laid bare the relative futility of negotiating with a president who takes pride in his unpredictability and ignorance in equal measure. These traits led German Chancellor Angela Merkel to conclude in 2017 that Germany (and Europe) could no longer depend on the US (Henley, 2017); European Council President Donald Tusk to observe that 'with a friends like [Trump], who needs enemies' (Khan, 2018); and French President Macron similarly to conclude that Europeans can no longer rely on the US for their security (Young, 2018).

The difficulty for NATO into the near future revolves around the different nature of the conflicts within the transatlantic alliance. The Obama foreign policy (and those of his predecessors), when in conflict with those of Europe, were at the margins of the alliance rather than at its core. Obama and his predecessors understood that diffuse reciprocity made the Atlantic Alliance a beneficial, if sometimes asymmetrical, bargain for Americans and Europeans alike. The Trump administration, however, has proved itself to be reactive (nullify Obama's foreign policy successes), impetuous (Twitter rants against allies and enemies alike), and myopically transactional (*cui bono?*). Yet, NATO is likely to survive the Trump presidency because a renascent and revisionist Russian Federation provides the glue binding the alliance. The collateral damage inflicted on the transatlantic community by the Trump administration's broader diplomatic and trade gambits, however, may be irreversible.

Notes

1 European concerns were both alleviated and deepened with the adoption of 'mutually assured destruction' during the Kennedy administration. While it stabilised the strategic nuclear balance of terror, it also deepened the concern that a conventional and nuclear war would be restricted to Europe.

2 Efforts to reduce the number of US troops in Europe continued into the 1970s and 1980s with the 1973 Jackson–Nunn Amendment, the 1982 Stevens Amendment, and the 1984 Nunn Amendment. None passed.

3 The NACC was replaced by the Euro-Atlantic Partnership Council in 1997.

4 The expected 'peace dividend' led to precipitous declines in NATO states' defence budgets as a share of GDP in the 1990s. US defence budgets averaged 4.0% of GDP, while the figures for the Europeans were even lower: 3.3% for the UK, 3.15% for France, 1.85% for Germany, and 2.0% for Italy. Despite high intensity combat operations in Afghanistan, European defence budgets rose only marginally as a share of GDP and remained below the NATO benchmark of 2% of GDP. At the 2014 Wales Summit, the allies pledged to meet the 2% goal for overall defence spending within a decade, as well as the 20% benchmark on procurement (North Atlantic Treaty Organization, 2014, para 14).

Further reading

Cottey, Andrew (2013), 'The European Neutrals and NATO: Ambiguous Partnership', *Contemporary Security Policy*, 34 (3), 446–472.

Larrabee, F. Stephen (ed) (2012), *NATO and the Challenges of Austerity*. Santa Monica, CA: RAND.

Sandler, Todd, and Hirofumi Shimizu (2014), 'NATO Burden Sharing 1999–2010: An Altered Alliance', *Foreign Policy Analysis*, 10 (1), 43–60.

Von Hlatky, Stéfanie (2014), 'Transatlantic Cooperation, Alliance Politics and Extended Deterrence: European Perceptions of Nuclear Weapons', *European Security*, 23 (1), 1–14.

Webber, Mark, Sperling, James, and Smith, Martin A. (2012), *NATO's Post-Cold War Trajectory: Decline or Regeneration?* Basingstoke: Palgrave Macmillan.

Weblinks

Council on Foreign Relations NATO Review: www.cfr.org/backgrounder/north-atlantic-treaty-organization-nato

NATO Official Website: www.nato.int/

NATO YouTube Feed: www.youtube.com/channel/UCHlEaKbepQ_S9iIoZPKVQew *Independent* NATO newsfeed: https://www.independent.co.uk/topic/Nato

References

Agence France Presse (2018), 'German Carmakers Dismayed as US Weighs Auto Tariffs', *Local*, 24 May. Available at: www.thelocal.de/20180524/german-carmakers-dismayed-as-us-weighs-auto-tariffs (accessed: 20 October 2018).

Albright, Madeleine (1998), 'Statement to the North Atlantic Council', Statement to the North Atlantic Council as released by the Office of the Spokesman, U.S. Department of State, Brussels, 8 December. Available at: https://1997–2001.state.gov/statements/1998/981208.html (accessed: 30 October 2018).

Bluth, Christoph (1995), *Britain, Germany and Western Nuclear Strategy*. Oxford: Oxford University Press.

Brands, Hal (2018), 'The Unexceptional Superpower: American Grand Strategy in the Age of Trump', *Survival*, 59 (6), 7–40.

Burt, Richard (1978), 'US Doubts Ability to Defend Europe in Conventional War', *New York Times*, 6 January. Available at: www.nytimes.com/1978/01/06/archives/us-doubts-ability-to-defend-europe-in-conventional-war-confident-of.html (accessed: 30 October 2018).

Calleo, David (1970), *The Atlantic Fantasy: The U.S., NATO and Europe*. Baltimore, MD: Johns Hopkins University Press.

Chollet, Derek, and Kiel, Steven (2016), 'United States: All About the Burdens', *Transatlantic Take*, 123, 1–3. Available at: www.gmfus.org/sites/default/files/publications/pdf/NATOSummitCollection_July5_.pdf (accessed: 30 October 2018).

Clinton, Hillary (2011), 'America's Pacific Century', *Foreign Policy*, 11 October. Available at: http://foreignpolicy.com/2011/10/11/americas-pacific-century/ (accessed: 30 October 2018).

Cohen, Benjamin J. (1974), 'The Revolution in Atlantic Economic Relations: A Bargain Comes Unstuck', in Wolfram F. Hanrieder (ed), *The United States and Western Europe: Political, Economic and Strategic Perspectives*. Cambridge: Winthrop, pp. 106–133.

Cook, Frank (2008), 'NATO Operations: Current Priorities and Lessons Learned', *NATO Parliamentary Assembly Committee Report*. Brussels: NATO Parliamentary Assembly.

De Hoop Scheffer, Alexandra, Quencez, Martin, and Michelot, Martin (2015), 'The Five Most Contentious Issues on the Road to Warsaw', *German Marshall Fund of the United States Policy Brief*. Available at: www.gmfus.org/publications/five-most-contentious-issues-road-warsaw (accessed: 30 October 2018).

Department of Defense (2018a), *The National Defense Strategy of the United States of America: Sharpening the American Military's Competitive Edge*. Washington, D.C.: Department of Defense.

Department of Defense (2018b), *Nuclear Posture Review*. Washington, DC: Department of Defense.

Duchin, Brian R. (2007), 'The "Agonizing Reappraisal": Eisenhower, Dulles, and the European Defense Community', *Diplomatic History*, 16 (2), 201–221.

Freedman, Lawrence (2003), *The Evolution of Nuclear Strategy*. Basingstoke: Palgrave.

Gates, Robert M. (2011), 'The Security and Defense Agenda (Future of NATO)', Speech by US Secretary of Defense, Brussels, 10 June. Available at: http://archive.defense.gov/Speeches/Speech.aspx?SpeechID=1581 (accessed: 30 October 2018).

Goldberg, Jeffery (2016), 'The Obama Doctrine', *Atlantic*, April. Available at: http://www.theatlantic.com/magazine/archive/2016/04/the-obama-doctrine/471525/ (accessed: 30 October 2018).

Henley, Jon (2017), 'Angela Merkel: EU Cannot Completely Rely on US and Britain Any More', *Guardian*, 28 May. Available at: www.theguardian.com/world/2017/may/28/merkel-says-eu-cannot-completely-rely-on-us-and-britain-any-more-g7-talks (accessed: 30 October 2018).

Hunt, Brigadier K. (1966), 'NATO Without France: The Military Implications', *Adelphi Paper 32*. London: Institute for Strategic Studies.

Kaltefleiter, Werner (1973), 'Europe and the Nixon Doctrine: A German Point of View', *Orbis*, 17 (1), 75–95.

Kaplan, Lawrence S. (2014), *The United States and NATO: The Formative Years*. Lexington, KY: University of Kentucky Press.

Khan, Mehreen (2018), 'EU's Tusk: "With Friends Like Trump, Who Needs Enemies?"' *Financial Times*, 16 May. Available at: www.ft.com/content/c3002464–5907–11e8-b8b2-d6ceb45fa9d0 (accessed: 30 October 2018).

Kucheida, J.-P. (2005), 'Cooperation in the Operational Area Between the EU and NATO: Reply to the Annual Report of the Council', European Parliament Document A/1918, Brussels, 7 December.

Lizza, Ryan (2011), 'Leading from Behind', *New Yorker*, 26 April. Available at: www.newyorker.com/news/news-desk/leading-from-behind (accessed: 30 October 2018).

Lugar, Richard G. (1993), 'NATO: Out of Area or Out of Business: A Call for U.S. Leadership to Revive and Redefine the Alliance', Remarks Delivered to the Open Forum of the U.S. State Department, 2 August.

McAuley, James (2018), 'Europeans Scramble to Save Iran Nuclear Deal, But Face New Concerns over U.S. Sanctions', *Washington Post*, 9 May. Available at: www.washingtonpost.com/world/europe/europeans-scramble-to-save-iran-nuclear-deal-but-face-new-concerns-over-us-sanctions/2018/05/09/39937066–536f-11e8-abd8–265bd07a9859_story.html?utm_term=.546874dd0d44 (accessed: 30 October 2018).

North Atlantic Treaty Organization (1997), 'Madrid Declaration on Euro-Atlantic Security and Cooperation', Press Release M-1 (97)81, Madrid, 8 July. Available at: www.nato.int/docu/pr/1997/p97–081e.htm (accessed: 30 October 2018).

North Atlantic Treaty Organization (1999a), 'Membership Action Programme', Press Release NAC-S(99)066, 24 April. Available at: www.nato.int/cps/en/natohq/official_texts_27444.htm (accessed: 30 October 2018).

North Atlantic Treaty Organization (1999b), 'The Alliance's Strategic Concept', Press Release NAC-S(99)65, Washington, DC, 24 April. Available at: www.nato.int/docu/pr/1999/p99–065e.htm (accessed: 30 October 2018).

North Atlantic Treaty Organization (2006),'Comprehensive Political Guidance Endorsed by NATO Heads of State and Government', NATO document, 29 November. Available at: www.nato.int/cps/on/natohq/official_texts_56425.htm (accessed: 30 October 2018).

North Atlantic Treaty Organization (2010a), 'Active Engagement, Modern Defence: Strategic Concept for the Defence and Security of the Members of the North Atlantic Treaty Organization', NATO document, 19 November. Available at: www.nato.int/cps/ua/natohq/official_texts_68580.htm (accessed: 30 October 2018).

North Atlantic Treaty Organization (2010b), *AJP-3.4(a): Allied Joint Doctrine for Non-Article 5 Crisis Response Operations*. Brussels: NATO Standardisation Agency.

North Atlantic Treaty Organization (2014), 'Wales Summit Declaration', Press Release (2014) 120, 5 September. Available at: www.nato.int/cps/ic/natohq/official_texts_112964.htm (accessed: 30 October 2018).

North Atlantic Treaty Organization (2015a), 'Statement by NATO Defence Ministers', Press Release (2015)094, 25 June. Available at: www.nato.int/cps/en/natohq/news_121133.htm?selectedLocale=en (accessed: 30 October 2018).

North Atlantic Treaty Organization (2015b), 'NATO's Readiness Action Plan', NATO Fact Sheet, October. Available at: www.nato.int/nato_static_fl2014/assets/pdf/pdf_2015_10/20151007_1510-factsheet_rap_en.pdf (accessed: 30 October 2018).

North Atlantic Treaty Organization (2016), 'Operation Active Endeavour (Archived)', NATO website. Available at: www.nato.int/cps/ua/natohq/topics_7932.htm (accessed: 30 October 2018).

North Atlantic Treaty Organization (2018), 'Statements by NATO Secretary General Jens Stoltenberg and US President Donald Trump in the Cabinet Room at the White House', Transcript, 17 May. Available at: www.nato.int/cps/en/natohq/opinions_154819.htm (accessed: 30 October 2018).

Osgood, Robert E. (1973), 'Introduction: The Nixon Doctrine and Strategy', in Robert E. Osgood (ed), *Retreat From Empire: The First Nixon Administration*. Baltimore, MD: Johns Hopkins University Press.

President of the United States (1990), *National Security Strategy of the United States*. Washington, DC: White House. Available at: http://nssarchive.us/NSSR/1990.pdf (accessed: 30 October 2018).

President of the United States (2017), *National Security Strategy of the United States*. Washington, DC: White House. Available at: www.whitehouse.gov/wp-content/uploads/2017/12/NSS-Final-12–18–2017–0905.pdf (accessed: 30 October 2018).

Saint Malo Summit (1998), 'Joint Declaration on European Defence Issued at the British-French Summit', Saint-Malo, 4 December. Available at: www.cvce.eu/content/publication/2008/3/31/f3cd16fb-fc37–4d52–936f-c8e9bc80f24f/publishable_en.pdf (accessed: 30 October 2018).

Sloan, Stanley (2016), *Defense of the West: NATO, the European Union and the Transatlantic Bargain.* Manchester: Manchester University Press.

Sperling, James (2016), 'Neorealism and Alliance Politics', in Mark Webber and Adrian Hyde-Price (eds), *Theorizing NATO: New Perspectives on the Atlantic Alliance.* Basingstoke: Palgrave, pp. 61–92.

Sperling, James, and Webber, Mark (2018), 'NATO Operations', in Hugo Meijer and Marco Wyss (eds), *The Handbook of European Defence Policies and Armed Forces.* Oxford: Oxford University Press, pp. 888–914.

Thies, Wallace J. (2009), *Why NATO Endures.* Cambridge: Cambridge University Press.

United Nations Security Council (2008), 'Resolution 1833', Document S/RES/1833, 22 September. Available at: www.un.org/en/ga/search/view_doc.asp?symbol=S/RES/1833(2008) (accessed: 30 October 2018).

Young, Zachary (2018), 'Macron: Europe Can't Depend on US for Security: French President Sets Out His Diplomatic Vision for the Year Ahead', *Politico*, 27 August. Available at: www.politico.eu/article/europe-defense-macron-cant-depend-on-us-for-security/ (accessed: 30 October 2018).

The Organization for Security and Co-operation in Europe

5

David J. Galbreath

Introduction

On the 'contact line' in Eastern Ukraine, the current war in the Donbas still rages. At the centre of this is the Organization for Security and Co-operation in Europe (OSCE), which has come to the fore as observers, rapporteurs and peace-builders in the conflict. The OSCE, as it is today, was born out of the Conference on Co-operation and Security in Europe (CSCE) founded in 1975. Since then, the Conference and then the Organization saw Europe go from *Détente* and Cold Peace to state breakdown and ethno-nationalist conflict. Unlike either NATO or the EU, the CSCE transformed into the OSCE as a direct result of the changes in European security that followed the Cold War. The result was to give the European security architecture an organisation that included among its participating states both the USA and the Russian Federation, not to mention all of the former Warsaw Pact and NATO member states. This breadth of inclusion was matched by the OSCE's innovative approach to security. As we shall see in this chapter, the OSCE provides an alternative approach to European security, which has only recently been adopted by the EU. As much as the CSCE was born out of a certain period of the Cold War known as *détente*, the OSCE came to represent the complex and delicate nature of the post Cold War European security architecture.

We see in this chapter how the OSCE offers a different approach to European security that has only recently been shared by other international organisations. In particular, the OSCE focuses on 'common and comprehensive' security, as mandated by the founding Helsinki Final Act. By common consensus, CSCE participating states agreed that a threat to any one country's national security was a threat to the regional stability as a whole and, thus, a threat to each and every other state. This common approach to security is shared in the United Nations Charter, but is not as explicit or pointed in terms of the UN's primary goal as it is in the OSCE. By being comprehensive, the Final Act represents an understanding among states that security comes not only at the end of a gun, as one state attacks another state, but can be what we call today 'societal', environmental, economic or even political security. This 'common and comprehensive' approach to security further added to confidence and security-building measures (CSBMs) that sought not only to respond to conflict, but to prevent it from the outset. This focus on conflict prevention through the perspective of 'common and comprehensive' security gave the OSCE a unique role to play in the European security architecture.

In this chapter, we look at the development and contribution of the CSCE and the OSCE to European Security. The chapter begins with a discussion of how the Cold War changed in the era known as *détente*. This section focuses on the political moves towards the agreement of the founding Helsinki Final Act and Decalogue, as well as the challenges to the fledgling CSCE as the Cold War once again turned hot with the Soviet invasion of Afghanistan in 1979. The following section looks at how the changes in European security following the Cold War combined with the comprehensive approach to produce an organisation unique to the European security architecture. We pay particular attention to the creation of the institutions of the OSCE and how they relate to Europe's security challenges. Next, the chapter turns to look at the OSCE's presence in the field. Unlike any other security organisation in Europe, the OSCE has had a large-scale field presence through its missions, offices, centres and institutional investigations. The final section concentrates on the unresolved tensions that exist within the OSCE, which have brought it to crisis point.

Out of *Détente*

The Cold War became increasingly warm as the tensions over Berlin, Korea, Berlin (again) and eventually Cuba threatened to bring the world and life as we know it to a nuclear end. The Berlin stalemate and the near cataclysmic war over Cuba forced a relative degree of rethink in both the USA and the Soviet Union. In short order, although for different reasons and different endings, both of the Cuban Missile Crisis's 'Cold Warriors' lost office (John F. Kennedy, assassinated, and Khrushchev, deposed). As the USA became trapped in an unwinnable war in Vietnam, and the Soviet Union became more sedentary in terms of leadership, both countries sought ways to improve confidence and reduce uncertainty between the super-powers. The first such confidence building measure was the set of negotiations comprising the first Strategic Arms Limitations Treaty agreement (SALT I) from 1969 until 1972. This was followed by SALT II and, eventually, the START series of strategic arms reduction agreements.

A major shift also came from the change in foreign policy in West Germany. Since the Second World War, successive Christian Democrat governments had sought existential defence against the Soviet Union and its German protégé, East Germany, as it did when it joined NATO in 1954 (with the establishment of the Warsaw Pact following). With the West German election in 1966, the Social Democrats were elected to power and Willy Brandt became foreign minister. As foreign minister and eventual Chancellor, Brandt pushed a policy referred to as 'Ostpolitik', which sought to change West Germany's relationship with the Soviet Union and its Warsaw Pact allies. The policy was born out of the West German fear that a third world war would be fought in and across Germany, and, more importantly, the status of Berlin might well have been the very spark that would set off such a conflict. Ostpolitik sought to normalise the relationship with the Soviet Union, or at least open lines of communication between West Germany and the Eastern Bloc. The Soviet Union recognised it as rapprochement. The United States was cautious and sceptical. East Germany, on the other hand, was outright hostile. As a result, the Soviet Union signed a cooperative agreement with West Germany in 1968 without the consent of East Germany. This confidence building measure between West Germany and the Soviet Union paved the way to better relations between the United States and the Soviet Union, with the SALT I negotiations following.

Successful strategic arms limitation talks between the two super powers paved the way for other efforts to establish CSBMs. Having perceived a perpetual challenge in Europe, the Soviet Union had a clear goal to seek confirmation of its control over Central and Eastern Europe. The European NATO allies and non-aligned states also sought an agreement that would lay the foundation for long-term CSBMs. The USA (and East Germany) was brought reluctantly to the negotiating table. By 1972, the USA and its NATO allies and the Soviet Union and its Warsaw Pact allies, along with Europe's non-aligned states, found themselves in Helsinki negotiating the form of a permanent agreement between state parties. This negotiation would be referred to as the Helsinki Process and would result in the Helsinki Final Act.

In his reflection on the Helsinki negotiations (which, incidentally, was a series of three meetings in Helsinki and Paris), Fall (1977) identifies several groups of states with particular agendas at the negotiations. The majority of the European NATO states, perhaps best represented by West Germany, sought a constructive, progressive peace treaty. Such was the view of the European community in general. The second group of states was the European non-aligned states, arguably best represented by Yugoslavia, Sweden and Finland. These states sought the end of hostilities between East and West, but also threats to themselves specifically, such as Soviet displeasure over Yugoslavia. The third group was the Soviet Union and its Warsaw Pact allies. As stated, the Soviet Union sought an end to hostilities, but, more importantly, recognition of its dominance in Central and Eastern Europe. Of this group, East Germany was the most resistant to any long-term agreement, as they saw a closer relationship between East and West as a threat to the survival of the East German state (which history tells us they were right to think). The final group of states was led by the USA, and included stalwart Cold War allies such as the UK. For the USA, the key was the use of the Helsinki negotiations as a way to raise claims on the states of Central and Eastern Europe. In other words, in as much as the Soviet Union was keen to use the negotiations to confirm their hegemony over the Eastern Bloc, the USA sought to challenge it through peaceful means, given that Hungary in 1956 and Czechoslovakia in 1968 indicated armed resistance to Soviet domination would not work.

The Helsinki negotiations were as much about language as they were about the underlying principles. The four groups of states each received something from the resulting Final Act. The USA and the Soviet Union both got an agreement to prevent further intervention in Central and Eastern Europe. While the USA saw this as a preventative measure against the so-called Brezhnev doctrine of Soviet intervention, the Soviet Union saw the principle of non-interference as a confirmation of the *status quo* over Central and Eastern Europe. This principle was restated in the Final Act's Decalogue in terms of 'Sovereign equality, respect for the rights inherent in sovereignty', 'inviolability of frontiers', and 'Respect for human rights and fundamental freedoms, including the freedom of thought, conscience, religion or belief'. Looking back, the Soviet Union arguably gained the most from the principle of non-interference, as the Final Act did more than anything else to justify the *status quo*.

Box 5.1   The Helsinki Accords Decalogue

Declaration on Principles Guiding Relations between Participating States

   I. Sovereign equality, respect for the rights inherent in sovereignty
  II. Refraining from the threat or use of force
 III. Inviolability of frontiers
 IV. Territorial integrity of States
  V. Peaceful settlement of disputes
 VI. Non-intervention in internal affairs
VII. Respect for human rights and fundamental freedoms, including the freedom of thought, conscience, religion or belief
VIII. Equal rights and self-determination of peoples
 IX. Co-operation among States
  X. Fulfilment in good faith of obligations under international law
(Conference on Security and Co-operation in Europe, 1975)

Beyond this, the Final Act laid out three security 'baskets'. The first basket was the politico-military dimension of security, which focused on the transparency of military manoeuvres. Foreshadowing the Conventional Force in Europe (CFE) Treaty of 1990, the Final Act even went so far as to suggest how large a group could be moved at any one time without it being made known to the Conference. Such a move towards transparency was to prevent mundane troop movements mistaken as acts of war. Throughout the Cold War, East and West were on tenterhooks as they constantly monitored each other's movements and the 'Iron Curtain' that separated them. Such vigilance even produced its own problems for NATO, like the disagreement between West Germany and the United States over how to respond to Soviet/East German incursions. The USA wanted any incursion to be treated as a threat requiring a robust military response (so-called 'trip-wire' defence), while West Germany, knowledgeable of the fact that it would be the location of a grand land war in such a situation, sought a greater enemy presence before a military response would be required (so-called 'plate-glass' defence). This example, although within the context of NATO, indicates the need for communication and transparency between opposing powers, especially since a lost patrol accidentally crossing the West German frontier had the potential to spark a third world war.

The second basket was the economic and environmental dimension of security. The Final Act set out to make scientific and economic collaboration easier across Europe, the Soviet Union and North America. The economic link to security is not readily apparent, in that the link in contemporary security studies comes from the link between development and conflict. However, the link between economics and security primarily came through discussions around technological innovations. As much as geo-political tensions drove the Cold War, the Cold War drove technology. Greater scientific and technological collaboration fits again into the need for greater transparency, in that the move was to reduce the arms race in the SALT I and SALT II (START) negotiations. Additionally, the Final Act was the first document to set out environmental disasters as a source of regional insecurity. The (largely unfounded) perception of Central and Eastern Europe by the West was of a landscape that had suffered at the hands of socialist modernisation. The fear was that any chemical and nuclear accidents would cross borders into other states or move down rivers (such as the Danube). The Final Act sets out a coordinated framework for responding to disasters, which built in procedures around the international transport of hazardous materials (the IATA protocols).

The final basket was the human dimension of security and was perhaps the most innovative, radical (for its time) and long lasting. As much as the Second World War and the subsequent Cold War had ripped European states apart, they had also ripped European societies apart. The human dimension set out to promote communication between separated families, but also to ascertain the location of relatives who had died in the Second World War on the other side of what became the Iron Curtain. Arguably most important, however, was the focus on the 'freedoms' as set out in the Final Act, for which there was significant debate between the USA and the Soviet Union. The final basket states the freedom of religion, race, ethnicity and language, in terms of promoting these freedoms within the contemporary political realities of Cold War Europe. At the same time, the Final Act does not mention human rights or democracy, but it did provide a framework for so-called 'Helsinki groups' to spring up across Central and Easter Europe that would go on to challenge their governments. As we shall see, the human dimension would have a lasting effect on the CSCE and determined what type of organisation the OSCE would become.

The after-effects of the Helsinki Final Act were mixed in the medium term but important in the short and long term. In the short term, the establishment of a regular meeting between heads of government, foreign and other ministers, as well as politically agreed (although not legal) protocols for increased confidence and security in Europe, was a huge step in the Cold War and undoubtedly made Europe a safer place. However, in the medium term, the Soviet invasion of Afghanistan, the Olympic boycotts and the election of Ronald Reagan as President of the USA ended the era of *Détente* and challenged the continued relevance of the CSCE. By the mid-1980s, questions were being asked about the presence of the CSCE in world affairs (Sizoo and Jurrjens, 1984). Nevertheless, with the rise to power of Mikhail Gorbachev in the Soviet Union in 1985 and the change in Soviet foreign policy in the Eastern Bloc and further afield, the foundations of the CSCE written into the Final Act were once again relevant to European security. This change of fortunes of the CSCE would pave the way for Europe's post Cold War security architecture.

Comprehensive approach to European security

As the geo-politics of the Cold War began to change in Europe (while they continued in other parts of the world), participating states of the CSCE began to meet on challenges to European security. Beginning in 1986, a series of so-called 'Expert Meetings on the Human Dimension' met in various cities to discuss the challenges that would come as the political constraints of the Cold War began to slacken. Chief among these worries was the prospect for ethno-nationalism and the propensity for ethnic conflict. These early meetings set the foundations for many of the underlying features of the OSCE, including a focus on prevention and the use of small-scale political intervention ('quiet diplomacy') to resolve tensions before conflict erupted (see Kemp, 2001). The focus was also on the status of national minorities in Central and Eastern Europe, such as Hungarians in Romania, Czechoslovakia and (Soviet) Ukraine. The agreement among the experts was that the decay in the socialist system would need to be met with democratic reform and the respect for human rights. This initial meeting in 1986 was the first to connect the human dimension of security to democracy and human rights in Europe. This connection would be an underlying theme for the OSCE, EU and NATO throughout the post Cold War era.

By 1990, the Cold War was firmly on its way out. The Soviet Union had held republic level contested elections in 1989, to be followed by union-wide elections to the Supreme Soviet in 1990. Furthermore, 1990 saw the USA and the Soviet Union plan their first ever joint military intervention in the case of Kuwait and Iraq. Also, NATO and Warsaw Pact states came together to establish the CFE Treaty, which would regulate the movement and placement of military units throughout Europe. At the same time, CSCE participating states agreed to the Open Skies Treaty, which allowed for planned aerial surveillance of any signatory state. Both of these treaties are still in effect, although the CFE Treaty has been revised to little effect and the Open Skies Treaty stipulates an outdated photo resolution superceded by today's military and commercial satellites. Nevertheless, 1990 proved to be an important year for the Cold War and it would be also for the CSCE.

The Paris Charter for a New Europe (1990) was the birth of the CSCE as a normal functioning institution that we would ordinarily refer to as an international organisation. Before this point, there were no offices, buildings, CSCE staff, or even planned, regular meetings. The Paris Charter changed this and invested the CSCE in bricks, mortar, and people and set out a new collective (and common) security organisation for post Cold War Europe. The Charter established an institutional body, the Council of Senior Officials (CSO), and that there would be regular meetings between participating state representations. Furthermore, the Paris Charter established a permanent CSCE secretariat in Vienna that would execute the agreed policies of the CSO. Finally, the Paris Charter created the Office for Free Elections in Warsaw that would monitor and advise on democratic elections in the CSCE area, or, in other words, 'East of Vienna'. Overall, the Paris Charter represented a moment in time. NATO and the Warsaw Pact were no longer representative of European security needs, or so it was thought. Without the Soviet threat (and, eventually, the Soviet Union itself) Europe no longer saw itself as a divided continent and needed a regional collective security organisation that would provide it with stability. The Paris Charter suggested that such an organisation would be the newly institutionalised CSCE.

As we see from the previous chapters, European security did not work out like this. The reasons have been discussed but are elaborated upon specifically relating to the OSCE later in this chapter. More importantly, the CSCE continued to grow in terms of institutions and mechanisms to promote security and cooperation in Europe. In 1992, the ministerial councils and summits (of heads of states) in Stockholm and Helsinki established much what we know of the OSCE today. The CSO was changed to the Permanent Council (PC) and the OFE was changed to the Office for Democratic Institutions and Human Rights (ODIHR), the latter with a wider remit. Furthermore, the CSCE established the office of the High Commissioner on National Minorities (HCNM), which to this day remains the only mechanism for promoting good relations between states and their national minorities. The CSCE Conflict Prevention Centre was created within the Secretariat to monitor and respond to growing tensions in the area. At a more diplomatic level, the CSCE established the Forum for Security Co-operation and the Forum for Economic Co-operation, pertaining to the first and second baskets, respectively. Finally, participating states agreed to the precedent of the PC establishing field missions, the first being the CSCE Spillover Mission to Skopje (which remains in place). This presence in the field would be the CSCE/OSCE's most important asset in an otherwise busy European security architecture.

Box 5.2 Current OSCE field operations

- Presence in Albania
- Mission to Bosnia and Herzegovina
- Mission in Kosovo
- Mission to Montenegro
- Mission to Serbia
- Mission to Skopje
- Mission to Moldova
- Project Co-ordinator in Ukraine
- Special Monitoring Mission to Ukraine
- Observer Mission at the Russian Checkpoints Gukovo and Donetsk
- Personal Representative of the Chairperson-in-Office on the conflict dealt with by the OSCE Minsk Conference
- Centre in Ashgabat
- Programme Office in Astana
- Programme Office in Bishkek
- Programme Office in Dushanbe
- Project Co-ordinator in Uzbekistan

(Organization for Security and Co-Operation in Europe website, October 2018)

At this point, the focus on the OSCE is helped by a more in-depth discussion of some of the key features of the organisation. Let us begin with the Permanent Council (PC), as the most important decision-making body within the OSCE. The PC includes representation from every participating state, which at the moment includes 56 diplomats and their representations. Seating around the long oval table is determined by the French alphabet, leaving the Russian Federation to look across the table at the USA and Canada. Decision making at the PC is made unanimously, giving every participating state a veto. Furthermore, EU member states under normal circumstances vote in one block and whoever holds the presidency of the European Council speaks on behalf of the EU at the PC. Given that successful measures require unanimous agreement among participating states, the PC had to come to an agreement as to how it would respond to crises within one state and between states that could obviously block any decision by voting against it. In 1992, the PC agreed that a state could be suspended while it was necessary to act on the crisis in or with the state in question. Furthermore, the PC determined that all warring parties could be suspended. This came to be known as the Moscow Mechanism. As an example of its use, Yugoslavia (and subsequently Serbia and Montenegro) was suspended from the PC in 1992 until Milosevic was ousted from power in 2001. As we shall see in the final section of this chapter, while political cohesion is suited by the use of unanimity, it also allows one state or group of states to block decision making, including budgets, at the PC.

The OSCE Secretariat, first established in the Paris Charter, is the operational side of the OSCE. While the Secretariat provides the OSCE with a bureaucracy, it also provides specific policy initiatives ('thematic units'). As discussed earlier, the Conflict Prevention Centre (CPC) was the first unit to be established in the secretariat. The CPC supports OSCE offices and bodies such as the OSCE Chairman-in-Office (yearly alternating position) and the HCNM. The Action against Terrorism Unit was set up as a monitoring and coordination unit following the attacks on the USA in September 2001. The unit provided a communication platform for discussions between the USA and the Russian Federation, for example. The Combating Trafficking in Human Beings has a far greater reach than any other regional organisation's initiatives with the OSCE's broad range of participating states. The human trafficking unit also illustrates the OSCE's ability to broadcast its conception of security broadly. Other units include that of External Co-operation (with other IOs), the Gender Section, the Borders Team and the Strategic Police Matters Unit. With mechanism building in the OSCE all but stopped by the political impasse, the secretariat initiatives brought on by various Chairmen-in-Office are one of the few ways to make a progressive move in the organisation today.

The Office for Democratic Institutions and Human Rights (ODIHR) evolved out of the OFE established in the Paris Charter. The focus of ODIHR was to be a promotion of democratic reform and human rights. Located in Warsaw, it was (and is) aimed primarily at Central and Eastern Europe and the former Soviet Union. The early focus was on supporting and advising on democratic elections. However, as some states progressed while others regressed, ODIHR became more of a monitoring body. For instance, ODIHR's role in observing elections (along with the OSCE Parliamentary Assembly) was highlighted in 2001 in Serbia and Montenegro with the popular movement to Milosevic and again in 2004 in Ukraine with the deemed faulty elections which produced the 'Orange Revolution'. Up to this time, ODIHR was the primary monitor of elections in the OSCE area. However, as stated elsewhere (Galbreath, 2009), the role of ODIHR in the co-called Coloured Revolutions has led to a greater reluctance for some states to accept ODIHR as election observers, as the Russian Federation did in 2010. Incidentally, ODIHR began to observe elections 'West of Vienna' in 2002 (Canada and the USA).

The OSCE has had an important role to play in the regional governance of national minorities in Europe (Galbreath and McEvoy, 2012). The HCNM embodied many of the recommendations that were born out of the Expert Meetings on the Human Dimension, such as the focus on conflict prevention, 'quiet diplomacy', and political participation. The first High Commissioner was former premier Dutch diplomat and eventual foreign minister Max van der Stoel, who very much embodied what was wanted from the HCNM. Van der Stoel had the support of the Dutch government, as well as a diplomatic passport, that allowed him to build the office of the HCNM into an effective administration for monitoring and intervening in cases of potential conflict over national minorities, as he did in Estonia and Latvia in 1993 and Romania in 1994. While many of the recommendations and guidelines that have come out of the HCNM touch on the remit of ODIHR, such as political partici- pation and education, they also touch on issues of conflict prevention, such as inter-ethnic policing and 'kin-state'-'host-state' relations. Since van der Stoel stepped down in 2001, the HCNM has continued much the same, although arguably less in the public light than the first High Commissioner might have wished.

Intervention of a different order

Even before the breakdown of Yugoslavia and the Soviet Union, ethno-nationalist conflict had begun in these complex multi-ethnic states. There had been low-level violence in Kosovo and Azerbaijan as well as inter-ethnic riots in Tajikistan in the late 1980s and into 1990. With NATO focused on collective defence against a Soviet threat, the Warsaw Pact a deteriorating military alliance itself, and the European community an economic superpower but political lightweight, only the United Nations had the remit to intervene in intra-state conflict. In other words, Europe's security architecture was so directed at preparing for a conflict between the USA and the Soviet Union that there was no mechanism for preventing, resolving, or even monitoring intra-state conflict in Europe. This caused chaos at the top and hundreds of thou- sands of lives at the bottom. By 1992, the former Yugoslavia was in full-blown ethnic conflict in Croatia and Bosnia with the Yugoslav regions of Macedonia and Kosovo nearing open conflict, while in the former Soviet Union the new states of Moldova, Azerbaijan and Georgia saw secessionist violence, just as the Baltic States, Ukraine, and Kazakhstan appeared to be on the brink of exploding into ethnic conflict. Europe was witnessing ethnic conflict on a scale that had not been seen in the region since the Second World War.

The CSCE, shortly to become the OSCE at the Budapest Summit in 1994, had the institu- tions and the security remit given to it by the Helsinki Final Act to intervene in such conflicts.

Despite the overwhelming need to intervene, the participating states of the OSCE chose to build an organisation that would be unable to greatly contribute to any attempt at preventing or resolving conflict. Why was this the case? The USA and many of its NATO allies did not want a direct competitor to the Alliance and stated that the UN had the remit and ability to intervene in the conflicts. Other European states, such as France, did not want to take away from a European approach to regional security, seen in the Western European Union (and eventually the EU's CSDP). Russia and many of its post-Soviet allies, however, sought to make the OSCE transcend NATO and any EU approach to regional security. As president of the Russian Federation (1991–1999), Boris Yeltsin made it clear that the OSCE was to become the regional collective security organisation of the post-Soviet European security architecture. Or, put another way, the OSCE should assume such an architecture. The result was a half-hearted attempt to create a regional collective security organisation that did not directly compete with other trans-Atlantic institutions.

While the OSCE was left to be unable to deal with ethnic conflict and other insecurities on its own, it still played an important role in the resolution of the conflicts in Yugoslavia, although its record in the former Soviet Union is mixed. In the former Yugoslavia, the UN and NATO played the key role in bringing an end to the violence, although not necessarily in tandem, as the USA became increasingly frustrated with the command structures and mandates of the UN mission, as discussed in Chapter 4. The OSCE, however, came into play in the border skirmishes that were occurring in North Macedonia, as the first field mission was sent in 1992 to prevent an escalation between ethnic Albanians and Slavs.

After the Dayton Peace Accords in 1995, the OSCE Mission to Bosnia-Herzegovina was established with the remit of aiding the development of local political and judicial services. The mission to Bosnia would represent a model for future broad agenda missions, such as the missions to Kosovo before and after the 1999 NATO intervention. The focus in Bosnia gave the OSCE a distinct level of operation, as it focused primarily on local elections, police reform, inter-ethnic education and the institutionalisation of progressive policy agendas, such as gender mainstreaming. The OSCE worked within the UN mandate and direction, while it liaised with NATO and Partnership-for-Peace forces that took part in SFOR (the NATO-led Stabilisation Force in Bosnia and Herzegovina, as discussed in the NATO chapter). From the beginning, the OSCE has had to coordinate and cooperate with other international organisations, as the OSCE, UN, NATO and, later, the EU, had to work together to bring a sustainable peace to Bosnia. Whether this has happened appears increasing debatable. Nevertheless, the role of the OSCE was important in that the local, societal levels of a conflict are rarely addressed by third parties, who often seek top-down solutions. The OSCE provided such an approach, even to the point of being referred to as the international organisations' non-governmental organisation (see Krupnick, 1998).

As Bosnia became more stable, the situation in Kosovo continued to worsen. Already, large-scale ethnic violence perpetrated by ethnic Albanians against the Kosovo Serb communities had driven thousands of refugees northwards into Serbia proper, particularly to Vojvodina. As the Kosovo Liberation Army (KLA) escalated the guerrilla war against Yugoslav forces for independence (and possibly eventual inclusion in Albania), Belgrade responded with a full-forced military assault on Albanian communities in Kosovo. As Michael Mann (2005) argues in *Dark Side of Democracy*, Serbs were both the largest set of victims and perpetrators of the violence in the breakdown of Yugoslavia. The result of the military assault was deemed by the UN and human rights NGOs as a gross violation of human rights. As a result, and importantly without a UN resolution mandate, NATO began aerial bombardment of Kosovo and Yugoslavia in March 1999. After a month of bombing Belgrade and Yugoslav positions in Kosovo, Yugoslavia withdrew its forces and the UN ordered a peacekeeping force and peace-building operation in UN Security Council Resolution 1244. The OSCE was included in the UN mandate for Kosovo, responsible for political institutions and local government. The OSCE Mission to Kosovo (2001–) has been one of the largest field missions to be established, retaining over 500 personnel as of 2018. The OSCE's mandate in Kosovo has brought it into close contact with the EU and its EULEX mission (see Chapter 6). The role of the OSCE has had to evolve over time, as the EU has taken on more responsibilities in Kosovo (see Brosig, 2011). Given the centrality of the UN in Kosovo, the OSCE mission to Kosovo has also had to work quite closely with the UN; perhaps even more so than it does with the OSCE Secretariat in Vienna. To date, the role of the OSCE in Kosovo remains sustainable.

The OSCE's role in the former Soviet Union has been far more isolated, at least up to the point of the 2008 Russian–Georgian conflict. As the conflicts in Moldova, Azerbaijan and Georgia began to deteriorate, the OSCE was building up its mechanisms for conflict prevention and resolution. By the end of 1992, cessation of hostilities agreements had been signed in the four breakaway areas of Transdniestra (Moldova), Nagorno-Karabakh (Azerbaijan), Abkhazia and South Ossetia (Georgia). In all four so-called 'frozen conflicts', Russian troops have played the part of peacekeepers and, some would argue, protectors of breakaway regions in Moldova and Georgia. Rather than a mission, the OSCE HCNM began monitoring the 'frozen conflicts' in Transdniestria and South Ossetia in 1994. At the same time, the UN established a monitoring mission in Abkhazia. As a result, the OSCE worked closely with the UN to prevent a resumption of violence. The OSCE also worked with the UN through the OSCE-sponsored Minsk Process, aimed at ending the conflict in Nagorno-Karabakh.

The OSCE role in the former Soviet Union, as the only major international organisation involved in the region, has produced mixed results. With ethnic conflict breaking out in the aforementioned 'frozen conflicts', there was a general fear in Europe that the Russian minorities in Estonia, Latvia, Ukraine and Kazakhstan would be a source of tensions in those countries, whether as perpetrators or victims (see Galbreath, 2005, 2007). The HCNM dispatched to all four states (and others including Lithuania) to meet with state and minority parties. For example, Estonia witnessed the so-called 'Alien's Crisis' where the Riigikogu (Estonian parliament) passed a law restricting the rights of non-citizens, who overwhelmingly represented the Russian-speaking communities in Estonia's capital, Tallinn, and northeast regions of Ida-Virumaa (Laitin, 1998). The city councils of Silimae and Narva declared referenda that questioned the cities' political continuity in the Estonian state (i.e., secession to Russia). In this tense situation, the High Commissioner went to Estonia, meeting separately and together representatives of the Estonian government (foreign minister) and the mayors of the predominantly Russian-speaking cities. The Estonian government agreed to allow the referendum but stated that it would not respect the outcome as it was not a government sanctioned referendum. For their part, the city councils changed the line of questioning that would not directly challenge the territorial integrity of the Estonian state. As a result of moderate minds in Estonia, as well as the role of the OSCE HCNM, ethnic conflict in Estonia was avoided.

While the HCNM has played an important role in Estonia, Latvia, Ukraine (originally over the status of Crimea, now changed) and Kazakhstan, the OSCE's success in the three 'frozen conflicts' in which it was directly involved is mixed. Following the 2004 and 2007 enlargements, the EU became far more engaged in the Transdniestria region, especially the border with Ukraine. Eventually, the EU placed a border-monitoring mission on the Ukraine–Moldova border in 2005. At the same time, the OSCE was never as fully engaged in the Transdniestria conflict as it was with South Ossetia and Nagorno-Karabakh. In the case of South Ossetia, OSCE sponsored initiatives to help build confidence between the breakaway region and Georgia took a step back with the election in 2003 of the nationalist Mikheil Saakashvili, and was firmly blown away by the conflict in 2008 between Russian and Georgia over the region. The failure to bring peace in South Ossetia has led to a situation where Georgia will, more than likely, not see the return of South Ossetia and Abkhazia, which have both declared independence from Georgia (and are recognised by the Russian Federation). However, the Nagorno-Karabakh case raises the most questions about the OSCE's ability to resolve conflicts. At the time of writing, the Azerbaijani government has greatly increased its defence spending while turning up the rhetoric of recapturing the ethnic Armenian-held mountainous region. European leaders and international organisations have made increasing suggestions that Azerbaijan and Armenia are on a collision course towards war without any concerted international effort to prevent the war from re-emerging since its cease-fire in 1994.

With the role of the OSCE declining over time, it was with a great deal of surprise that the OSCE came to the fore in the conflict in Eastern Ukraine in 2014. The OSCE had a prior role in Crimea with the agreement to a *status quo* settlement over the peninsula. With the Russian seizure of Crimea and inclusion into the Russian Federation, pro-Russian forces began assaults in Eastern Ukraine around the cities of Donetsk and Lugansk. The OSCE entered the conflict zone as observers and subsequently as brokers of the Minsk and Minsk II peace deals. As Europe fell into war again, the Ukraine crisis brought European security back from the dead. Nevertheless, the OSCE's role in conflict prevention and peace building *in concert* appears far better than its ability to resolve conflicts in isolation. At the same time, the fact that the OSCE remains the only organisation involved in the region suggests that international interest in the former Soviet Union has not been high.

The OSCE offers several unique contributions to European security (Galbreath, 2007, pp. 130–133). First, the Organization is the only regional institution that includes both the USA (also in NATO) and the Russian Federation (also in the Council of Europe). Furthermore, the breadth of the participation extends all the way to the Central Asian borders of China through Kazakhstan. As an organisation, it covers much of the northern hemisphere, albeit noticeably not the Middle East or North Africa. The fact that the participation sits along Cold War lines perhaps says something about the context and sustainability of the OSCE as events change. No further requests for formal participation have been made since Montenegro became the 56th participating state in 2006. Second, the OSCE 'comprehensive' security approach has given it a nuanced relationship with Europe's security challenges, allowing it to focus on a broader range of underlying sources of conflict and violence. This breadth can be seen in the institutions of the OSCE as well as the units within the Secretariat. At the same time, the EU has begun to incorporate 'comprehensive' security into its own security discourse (Gebhard and Norheim-Martinsen, 2011). Third, the OSCE has unique institutions to deal with national minorities and free media. While the EU and Council of Europe have roles to play in influencing national minorities and the media, this influence is overwhelmingly limited to activities within member states rather than the much broader OSCE area. Fourth, the OSCE has been able to package its conflict prevention approach into a 'quiet diplomacy' method, best personified by the first HCNM, Max van der Stoel, and his successors. Finally, the OSCE has a traditional role in the field, something only recently begun by the EU. Overall, while NATO and the EU have the ability to act robustly in response to Europe's security challenges, the OSCE remains at the coalface of regional stability. To do away with the OSCE would mean either leaving these underlying sources of insecurity to fester – or, more likely, that another organisation chooses to take over these functions, although with severe consequences for the range of confidence and security in Europe.

Unresolved tensions

The future of the OSCE has been in debate since the end of the 1990s, when two presidents who at one time championed the organisation, Bill Clinton and Boris Yeltsin, came out of office. Neither of their successors were interested in the OSCE in the form that it took in the 1990s, while at the same time neither proved able to change it. For this and other reasons, the OSCE remains in doubt in terms of its medium- to long-term sustainability. The first issue is the debate between the USA (and its allies) and Russia (and its allies) as to what form of OSCE they want, harking back to the creation of the CSCE from 1973 to 1975. The institutionalisation and transition of the Conference to the Organization created an actor in the European security architecture which would predominately be concerned with the fallout of failed and contested states in Central and Eastern Europe and the former Soviet Union. As far as Central and Eastern Europe was concerned, other organisations, such as NATO, the EU and Council of Europe, were also interested in the state of contestation and transition in these states, largely for their own purposes of enlargement. However, the same issues in the former Soviet Union were left unresolved. For instance, no movement has occurred in four 'frozen conflicts' in the former Soviet Union, despite the agreement at the 1999 Istanbul Summit (Revised CFE Treaty) that all Russian troops would leave the breakaway regions. The OSCE (and the UN) has been unable to improve the situation, although arguably in some cases it (at times) has helped to prevent the situation from getting worse.

Perhaps more worrying is the established resentment in the former Soviet Union that the OSCE has become an organisation aimed solely at regime transition, citing Georgia in 2003, Ukraine in 2004 and Kyrgyzstan in 2007 as examples. The Russian Federation has stated on numerous occasions, as has Kazakhstan and Uzbekistan, that the OSCE is no longer fit for purpose with its current focus on democratic transition, human rights, and intra-state conflict resolution. Rather, the Russian president Vladimir Putin has encouraged a reform process in the OSCE that would see the organisation return to its inter-state focus on issues such as arms control, economic cooperation and environmental sustainability (see Dunay, 2006). As a result of the decision-making system in the OSCE PC, little resolution has been found. For instance, OSCE institutions like ODIHR are isolated from budget constraints taken at the PC. On the other hand, it is possible for ODIHR to be primarily funded by a certain group of participating states, which maintains the institution but furthers the resentment.

One example of compromise was the Kazakh assumption of the Chairperson-in-Office in 2011, which, for the first time, allowed a government friendly to Moscow into the role. The outcome of the position of Kazakhstan, however, was rather muted. Kazakhstan pushed for a summit at which a new direction of the OSCE would be debated. By the time the USA came around to agreeing to the summit (in the spirit of the 'Reset' policy with Russia), the Russian Federation changed its mind and withdrew its support for the summit. As a result, the OSCE looks much the same as it did before the Kazakh chairmanship, with little prospect for change. Ukraine took up the mantle in 2013, with similar outcomes.

Second, the OSCE faces considerable pressure from other organisations that have come to assume its functions (see Galbreath and Gebhard, 2010). NATO has become the vehicle for arms control discussions with the Russian Federation. The EU has become evident in the field with 37 CSDP field missions throughout the world from 2003. The EU has also become increasingly interested in far Southeast Europe in the cases of the 'frozen conflicts'. There is an EU border mission on the Ukraine–Moldova border. There are EU monitors in Abkhazia and South Ossetia. When push comes to shove in Nagorno-Karabakh, we can assume that the EU will be the primary actor here as well, although they will need to negotiate with the Russian Federation if a lasting peace is to be found. Even the Council of Europe has developed similar functions to the OSCE, with the Secretariat of the Framework Convention for the Protection of National Minorities and Parliamentary Assembly. Overall, there are very few areas on which OSCE has focused left untouched by other international organisations. Contrarily, this may not be a problem for the OSCE or for the other organisations. More specifically, this functional overlap appears to be more burden sharing than competition. For instance, recent work on the European approach to national minorities indicates a strong role played by all of the organisations (see Galbreath and McEvoy, 2012).

Third, and connected to both of the previous issues, is the growing lack of political interest in the OSCE by all sides. Many states do not have full delegations to the OSCE any longer. Any collective good that comes with being a participating state at the OSCE is delivered by other organisations in ways that appear more manageable and dependable, while at the same time being ironically more constraining as legal agreements (as opposed to the political nature of the OSCE). Most problematic is the disinterest in the very areas in which it is the key – if not only – actor. Russia suspended its participation of the Revised CFE Treaty following the USA's insistence on missile defence in Eastern Europe. In parliamentary elections to the State Duma in 2010, the Russian government did not allow the participation of the OSCE ODIHR as election observers. Yet, currently, no major participating state has a desire to do away with OSCE either, for reasons of its uniqueness, as mentioned earlier.

One such example of the OSCE's re-emergence is Ukraine, as one case that had not been able to come to terms with its post-Soviet status. With changes in Ukraine's relationship with the European Union, the Euromaidan movement and eventual Russian annexation of Crimea and subsequent separatist movement in the Donbas, the tension had manifested itself in open warfare, the likes of which had not been seen since the Yugoslav Wars. The OSCE was once again thrust back into the spotlight, as an organisation that had experience in the region, had a degree of trust by both the West and Russia, not to mention Ukraine, and had the specialisation for field missions similar to those in Bosnia-Herzegovina and Kosovo. The OSCE's role has been to monitor compliance around the Minsk II agreement that was accepted by all involved in the conflict. The organisation has many observers across the contact line separating Ukrainian forces and separatist forces. Furthermore, the OSCE has been working with the United Nations on settling internally displaced persons (IDPs) emanating from the conflict affected areas. The OSCE has once again shown its vital role at the heart of European security, often fulfilling a function that no other international organisation or defence alliance could do; something that speaks more to its future than any other single factor.

Conclusion

The OSCE holds a unique place in European security. While NATO remains a collective security alliance and the EU continues to develop a multitude of aims and ambitions in Europe and beyond, the OSCE has a grounded approach to regional security that, while sometimes copied by other organisations, continues to be its hallmark. As the CSCE, the Conference was able to bring East and West together to lay out common security and cooperation goals that would outlast the period of *détente* and into the post Cold War era. Even as the post Cold War era was shaken by the rise of global jihadist terrorism and the wars in Afghanistan and Iraq, the OSCE has maintained a role in fostering security and cooperation in ways and in areas that other organisations cannot, such as parent–teacher associations in Bosnian schools, police training in Kosovo, and observer missions in South Ossetia and now Ukraine. As European security changes in relation to European states, the USA, Russia, and, indeed, the future of the EU itself, the OSCE will continue to have a role to play; one which harks back to the original intent of the Helsinki Final Act to preserve security and encourage cooperation.

Further reading

Ghebali, Victor-Yves, and Warner, Daniel (eds) (2018), *The Operational Role of the OSCE in South-Eastern Europe: Contributing to Regional Stability in the Balkans*. London: Routledge.

Jenichen, Anne, Joachim, Jutta, and Schneiker, Andrea (2018), '"Gendering" European Security: Policy Changes, Reform Coalitions and Opposition in the OSCE', *European Security*, 27 (1), 1–19.

Kropatcheva, Elena (2012), 'Russia and the Role of the OSCE in European Security: A "Forum" for Dialog or a "Battlefield" of Interests?', *European Security*, 21 (3), 370–394.

Organization for Security and Co-operation in Europe Network of Think Tanks and Academic Institutions (2017), *OSCE Confidence Building in the Economic and Environmental Dimension: Current Opportunities and Constraints*. Vienna: CORE Centre for OSCE Research.

Sperling, James, and Kirchner, Emil (1997), *Recasting the European Order: Security Architectures and Economic Cooperation*. Manchester: Manchester University Press.

Weblink

The Organization for Security and Co-operation in Europe: www.osce.org/

References

Brosig, Malte (2011), 'The Interplay of International Institutions in Kosovo between Convergence, Confusion and Niche Capabilities', *European Security*, 20 (2), 185–204.

Conference on Security and Co-Operation in Europe (1975), 'Conference on Security and Co-Operation in Europe Final Act', Helsinki, 1 August. Available at: www.osce.org/helsinki-final-act (accessed: 31 October 2018).

Dunay, Pál (2006), 'The OSCE in Crisis', *Chaillot Paper 88*. Paris: Institute for Security Studies.

Fall, Brian (1977), 'The Helsinki Conference, Belgrade and European Security', *International Security*, 2 (1), 100–105.

Galbreath, David J. (2005), *Nation-Building and Minority Politics in Post-Socialist States: Interests, Influence and Identities in Estonia and Latvia*. Stuttgart: Ibidem.

Galbreath, David J. (2007), *The Organization for Security and Co-operation in Europe*. London: Routledge.

Galbreath, David J. (2009), 'Putting the Colour into Revolutions? The OSCE and Civil Society in the Post-Soviet Region', *Journal of Communist Studies and Transition Politics*, 25 (2), 161–80.

Galbreath, David J., and Gebhard, Carmen (2010), *Cooperation or Conflict? Problematizing Organizational Overlap in Europe*. London: Ashgate.

Galbreath, David J., and McEvoy, Joanne (2012), 'European Organizations and Minority Rights in Europe: On Transforming the Securitization Dynamic', *Security Dialogue*, 43 (3), 265–282.

Gebhard, Carmen, and Norheim-Martinsen, Per Martin (2011), 'Making Sense of EU Comprehensive Security towards Conceptual and Analytical Clarity', *European Security*, 20 (2), 221–241.

Kemp, Walter A. (2001), *Quiet Diplomacy in Action: The OSCE High Commissioner on National Minorities*. The Hague: Kluwer Law International.

Krupnick, Charles (1998), 'Europe's Intergovernmental NGO: The OSCE in Europe's Emerging Security Structure', *European Security*, 7 (2), 30–53.

Laitin, David D. (1998), *Identity in Formation: The Russian-Speaking Populations in the Near Abroad*. Ithaca, NY: Cornell University Press.

Mann, Michael (2005), *The Dark Side of Democracy: Explaining Ethnic Cleansing*. Cambridge: Cambridge University Press.

Sizoo, Jan, and Jurrjens, Rudolph (1984), *CSCE Decision-Making: The Madrid Experience*. The Hague: Kluwer Academic.

European Union **6**

Laura Chappell and David J. Galbreath

Introduction

The basis of the European Union (EU) was a path towards 'ever closer union' (Maastricht Treaty, 1992, p. 7). Yet, the EU's route towards a security and defence institution was not straight or even predictable. The EU (or European Community as it was then) having a defence capability during the Cold War would have been quite unthinkable. This was left to NATO, which would provide the guarantee of defence against any threat to (Western) Europe through the means of nuclear deterrence. However, the Cold War did not remain a constant and NATO as a collective defence organisation was unable to bring Europe together and provide it with a post Cold War defence and security identity. As we shall see in this chapter, the EU has evolved into a security provider, having performed military operations and civilian missions in many parts of the world in addition to creating security strategies and policy initiatives.

The chapter looks at the EU and its role in security, specifically focused on the Common Security and Defence Policy (CSDP). The first section looks at how the EU as a security and defence actor has been conceptualised. This connects to ongoing debates about what type of power the EU utilises in the international system and whether the EU has any form of grand strategy or strategic culture. The second section looks at the rise of security as an EU relevant issue area. Thus, it examines the formulation and initial development of CSDP, paying particular attention to the institutions that have been created within the EU in order to give it strategic direction. The final section looks at CSDP missions, operations and policy initiatives in the context of new challenges.

Analysing the EU as a security and defence actor

In order to understand the EU as a security actor we must have an idea as to what the EU looks like in terms of power projection, which interconnects with the strategy that the EU is able and willing to pursue (Chappell, Mawdsley, and Petrov, 2016). The underlying question for scholars was: what sort of actor is the EU? The question was set against an understanding that it was unlike other traditional powers (e.g., the USA) because its power was not based on military might. Prior to the initiation of CSDP, the EU had no collective military capabilities on which to rely. Thus, if power was going to be separated from military might, where did this leave the EU as an international actor?

The debate about what sort of power the EU is in international relations began in the early 1970s. The first conceptual label used in relation to Europe (although not necessarily the EC as it was then) was that of 'civilian power' (Duchêne, 1972). Duchêne argued that Europe's focus on cooperation and collective action through the rule of law was a force for change in international relations. Bull (1982), on the contrary, argued that without military might to accompany 'civilian power', Europe was not a power at all. This rather delayed debate between Duchêne and Bull set the ground for later discussions and conceptualisations about Europe as a power and security provider and particularly to what degree hard power is related to security. Let us take a broad division between scholars of the EU as a power. The first is the traditional, neorealist, concept of the 'rights of power' (Falk, 2008). That is, there is an assumption that rights are given (and taken away) through the application of hard power; hence, security comes via military power. The alternative view, best encapsulated in Manners' (2002) original conceptualisation of 'Normative Power Europe' (NPE), focuses on the 'power of rights' (Falk, 2008). In other words, by increasing the empowerment of individuals and communities, power is (re-)distributed. Hence, in relation to our discussion, security comes via rights.

In the literature, these two different approaches to power and rights proscribe a different type of EU as a security provider. The 'rights of power' argument underlines the traditional forms of power through 'hard' means (i.e., the military). Although neorealist explanations of international relations traditionally focus on the state rather than on regional organisations, neorealist analysis has been applied to CSDP to argue that the EU is (soft) balancing the USA (Jones, 2007; Posen, 2006). Hence, the EU Member States are using CSDP to ensure the EU is less reliant on the US and to build up its military power (see Posen, 2006). This argument has been criticised by Howorth and Menon (2009), who contend that this misunderstands the rationale behind CSDP (to answer the USA's burden sharing calls) and the actualities of the policy in which the EU has deployed a far greater number of civilian missions than military operations.

More recently, Hyde-Price (2012, p. 34) has applied a neorealist argument to explain the development of CSDP 'as the response of EU member states to the uncertainties of US security policy in the context of global unipolarity' in which it 'establishes an institutional and procedural framework for limited security co-operation in order to collectively shape the Union's external milieu, using military coercion to back up its diplomacy'. This reflects a failure of civilian power, thus concurring with the argument made by Bull in the 1980s as presented above.

The 'rights to power' argument is furthered by a call for grand strategy (Biscop, 2009). Traditionally, strategy, as a concept, implies the connection of military means with political ends (see Chappell et al., 2016, pp. 3–4). Grand strategy broadens this to incorporate the full range of instruments to fulfil policy aims (Chappell et al., 2016, p. 4; Liddell Hart, 1967). In an EU context, a grand strategy will set out the EU's vision of opportunities and risks in the international system and how it will go about trying to respond to them (similar to the US National Security Strategies). Especially in a time of limited resources, one might argue that it is important for the EU (and, thus, its member states) to agree what it takes seriously and what it may focus on as priorities. However, as will be demonstrated below, the EU has yet to create a 'grand' strategy which produces a hierarchy of threats and policy aims, although it has started to develop civilian and military capabilities and operational experience which indicates the potential to create strategy from a bottom up, rather than a top down, perspective (see Chappell et al., 2016, p. 5; Wedin, 2008).

Conversely, the 'power of rights' argument at first sight does not directly address European security as it originally set out, that it is the norms and principles of the EU, rather than its military might, that will have the most impact on the world we live in (see Manners, 2002). A case in point is Manners' (2002) study that provided the initial empirical evidence of the NPE argument, which concentrated on the EU's focus on encouraging the abolition (or suspension) of the death penalty worldwide. While the case study does not offer us much in terms of European security, the argument of norm-driven foreign policy does, especially when we take into account many of the other issues pushed forward by the EU at the international level, such as the trade in small arms (civil wars), land mines (human security), and deliberative democracy (peace-building) (see Chapter 10). Far from being irrelevant to our discussion of the EU and European security, rather it lies at the heart of the EU's post-Westphalian (i.e., post nation state) approach to foreign policy and international relations.

More recently, NPE scholarship has incorporated military instruments (see Diez and Manners, 2007) while also viewing the use of military power as being of decreasing usefulness in international relations (Aggestam, 2008). Indeed, it is the normative underpinning of the EU that guides its use of instruments (whether military or civilian), connecting with key premises such as multilateralism and international law, which are of primary importance. Rather than dismissing military power as being incompatible with NPE, it is feasible to incorporate it as a means of diffusing normative power through symbolic manifestation (Manners, 2006). Hence, military instruments can safeguard EU norms provided they are not used coercively. Therefore, there is not an either/or choice between civilian and military power *per se*, but, rather, that it is the norms underpinning the tools and how these tools are used which is of importance to the 'power of rights' approach.

Circumventing the argument regarding whether a normative or civilian power can use military instruments, strategic culture connects norms to the civilian and military power utilised. Hence, a strategic culture approach seeks to understand why a security community acts as it does in the international environment with a focus on, *inter alia*, cultural beliefs, historical experience, geography and norms, connecting these with the means to carry out its strategic approach (see Chappell et al., 2016; Gray, 1999; Longhurst, 2004; Meyer, 2006). A security community's underpinning beliefs, attitudes and norms should be integrated into strategic documentation and then actioned through crisis management tools – whether these are military or civilian (see Chappell and Petrov, 2014). However, whether the EU has a strategic culture is contested. Those operating from realist perspectives (Heiselberg, 2003; Rynning, 2003) deny the existence of a European strategic culture due to divergences between member states regarding when, where and how force should be applied. Meanwhile, proponents, utilising Gray's (1999) idea of 'culture as context', point to convergences regarding member states' strategic cultures (Chappell, 2012; Meyer, 2006) or to strategic developments at the EU level, including strategies, policy initiatives and military operations (Chappell and Petrov, 2014; Cornish and Edwards, 2005). However, the EU's ability to operationalise elements of strategic thinking based on its underpinning normative basis has been mixed, leading to the conclusion that the EU has no more than an emerging strategic culture (if at all).

This section has outlined two generic approaches to the EU as an actor: the 'rights to power' and the 'power to rights', aligning each with different understandings of strategy (grand strategy and strategic culture). The former connects with neorealist explanations of the use of military power in the international system. Here, unipolarity and European regional multipolarity have combined to create a CSDP which allows member states to address specific second-order security concerns and which is led by the most powerful countries within the EU (Hyde-Price, 2012). Meanwhile, the latter has moved from a classical liberal to social constructivist understanding of the EU's approach to security and defence. Here, the normative underpinning of CSDP enables us to understand the EU's actions in the international security environment. As we shall see, both of these arguments around power and rights represent a side of the EU and how it responds to insecurities in the region and further afield.

The creation and initial development of CSDP

The EU's role in defence and security is a recent 'competence', in the language of the EU treaties. Indeed the failure of the Pleven Plan in 1954, which would have established a European Defence Community, ensured that security and defence was not placed on the EU agenda until the 1990s (see Chapter 2). The EU had begun to take on a more formal political role following the advent of European Political Cooperation in 1970, which had the aim of coordinating member states' foreign policies. This was subsequently institutionalised into the Single Europe Act (1986). However, as will be outlined below, the EU focus on foreign affairs became far more prominent following the end of the Cold War and the subsequent changes in the European security environment. Hence, the Maastricht (1992), Amsterdam (1997), and Nice (2001) Treaties and the Cologne and Helsinki Summits (1999) all pushed forward security and, subsequently, defence within the EU, set against a background of the collapse of the former Yugoslavia and Central and Eastern European enlargement (see Chapter 2).

While the completion of economic and monetary union had been on the EU's agenda in the late 1980s, the end of the Cold War placed constitutional and political elements there, too. In particular, there were fears in the UK and France concerning the reunification of Germany, including whether Germany would acquire a greater military capability and desire to use it.

Hence, the Maastricht Treaty was partly about tying Germany further into the EU. None the less, the lack of agreement concerning whether the EU should have a defence element remained, particularly as this was dealt with through NATO and the WEU (see Chapter 2). Although the Maastricht Treaty included a Common Foreign and Security Policy (CFSP), it also referred to 'the eventual framing of a common defence policy, which might in time lead to a common defence' (Maastricht Treaty, 1992, p. 8). Hence, the question remains, why did the previously contested area of defence suddenly become acceptable at the end of the 1990s?

The answer lies in a number of interconnected external and internal catalysts. First, it was evident that the creation of CFSP did little to help EU member states to formulate an effective response to the collapse of the former Yugoslavia (see Chapter 2). Once again the EU had to rely on the USA to provide for European security. However, the USA had a diminishing interest in playing a defence role in Europe, following the demise of the USSR. This was emphasised by the USA's calls for Europe to take up its share of the burden in defence and was intertwined with the EU's expanding international role following the completion of the single market (Chappell, 2012, p. 69). However, the defining moment was the election of a Labour government, led by Tony Blair, in the UK in 1997. As an Atlanticist country with close ties to the USA, the UK took note of the USA's burden-sharing calls and, thus, moved to increase this as a way of strengthening the alliance, particularly in the wake of Europe's ineptitude in the Balkans. Additionally, with the UK not involved in the EMU, security and defence was an area where the UK could demonstrate leadership. This latter argument was also important for France. Not only was defence an area where France, too, could provide leadership, but it also supported the ability of the EU to have an independent capacity to deploy force.

Hence, at the Franco–British St Malo summit in 1998, both countries proposed the creation of a common security and defence policy. The St Malo declaration stated that 'the Union must have the capacity for autonomous action, backed up by credible military forces, the means to decide to use them, and a readiness to do so, in order to respond to international crises' (Rutten, 2001, p. 8). The European Security and Defence Policy (ESDP), which would subsequently be renamed CSDP in the Lisbon Treaty, was set up to complement, rather than compete with, NATO. This highlighted a compromise for Europeanist France. At the Cologne European Council in 1999, member states agreed that CSDP would be integrated into the EU. For the first time, the world could foresee EU peacekeeping operations, comprising member-states from across the Union (although Denmark has an opt-out from CSDP).

The initial steps involved in creating CSDP incorporated two elements. The first was an institutional structure that was integrated into the Council of the Ministers. This comprised a Political and Security Committee (PSC), which would bring together member state ambassadors, an EU Military Council (EUMC), including member states' chiefs of staff and the EU Military Staff (EUMS), incorporating military experts. Finally, Javier Solana was made High Representative of CFSP. However, adding additional institutions made decision making in EU external affairs more complex, particularly taking into account the role of the Commission in CFSP, which included aid, trade and diplomacy. Arising from a critique by Chris Patten, then European Commissioner for External Relations, Missiroli (2001) examines the substance of CSDP through the prisms of 'consistency' and 'coherence'. The argument surrounding CSDP is that the planning and operations procedures suffered from both inconsistency and incoherence. As Missiroli points out (2001, p. 182), there is a difference between the two concepts legally and practically. Where consistency is ordinarily meant in terms of a lack of contradictions, coherence denotes a level of integration. Practically, this means that a set of policies can either be or not be consistent but they can be varying degrees of coherent. This argument was central to the decision to create the EU External Action Service (EEAS) as part of the Lisbon Treaty, as highlighted below.

The second step was achieved at the Helsinki European Council in December 1999, where the EU agreed 'Headline Goals' set out to establish an autonomous (non-NATO) capacity to engage in conflict prevention and crisis management through military operations. The agreement allowed for the establishment of an EU Rapid Reaction Force of 60,000 troops deployable in 60 days. None the less, troops remained under the responsibility of the EU's member states and could be used for all operations, not just those conducted by the EU. The Treaty of Nice (2001) brought CSDP formally into the EU in addition to integrating the WEU into the policy. The latter included the Petersberg Tasks, the Institute for Security Studies and the Satellite Centre. The EU was now in a position to project power at home and abroad.

Yet, CSDP remained for a long time a set of strategic policies on paper and in the heads of bureaucrats in Brussels. While the EU had institutionalised CSDP within its governance structures prior to the Lisbon Treaty, it suffered from a capabilities perspective, coined in Hill's (1993) capabilities–expectations gap. Hill's conceptualisation encapsulated the idea that there was a gap between what was expected of the EU as a security actor and the capabilities it had available to meet those expectations. While Hill coined the phrase in the early 1990s in the context of the Balkan wars, it became no less relevant with the creation of CSDP. Although CSDP had increased expectations, capabilities, particularly military ones, trailed behind. Hence, the original impetus for creating CSDP, which aligns with the security in power argument presented in the previous section, was missing.

Part of the issue was that the primary defence rationale behind the UK's and France's decision to set up CSDP was not reflected in how other member states viewed security. For the Nordic countries, particularly Finland and Sweden, focus should be placed on the civilian dimension. As Rummel (2011, p. 617) underlines, 'in their analysis, the EU was confronted with intervention cases of a kind that mostly demanded civilian expertise and support, a conclusion which was inspired by the August 2000 Brahimi Report of the UN'. Hence, following its military equivalent, the civilian headline goal was created in 2000, which listed policing, the rule of law, civil protection and civil administration as key priority areas. Even so, the civilian dimension was an afterthought at the outset of CSDP.

Operationalising CSDP pre-Lisbon: strategy and deployments

It is important to see how CSDP went from paper to actual missions and operations. The first of these were the EU Police Mission (EUPM) in Bosnia and Herzegovina and Operation

Concordia in North Macedonia in 2003, although the EU had been playing a post-conflict role in Bosnia and Kosovo prior to this. Operation Concordia was deployed following increased ethnic tension between the Slavic majority and Albanian minority. Furthermore, under the remit of the 'Berlin Plus' agreement, which had been agreed between the EU and NATO in 2002, Operation Concordia used assets belonging to NATO. The EU quickly followed up this operation with Operation Artemis in the Democratic Republic of Congo (DRC). As Knutsen (2009, p. 448) states, Operation Artemis was important because 'it was the first autonomous EU military operation taking place outside Europe and was not based upon common NATO assets and capabilities'. Since then, the EU has conducted 35 military operations and civilian missions, of which only 12 have been military operations. According to Menon (2009, p. 244), 'it is undeniable that the majority of these interventions have had a beneficial – if limited – impact. The sheer number of requests coming in for the deployment of EU missions bears eloquent testimony to this impact'. Menon's central argument is that CSDP has come far in a very short time, although challenges remain. In particular, the majority of the civilian missions are very small, with fewer than 100 personnel, while some of the military operations have suffered from equipment shortfalls and member state caveats which have curtailed where their armed forces are deployed and how long they are deployed for, affecting the length of the operation (e.g., EUFOR RD Congo and EUFOR Tchad/RCA) (see also Chapter 8).

While military operations and civilian missions began to be deployed in 2003, the EU lacked a document which specified what the EU's security position was, including threat perceptions, security objectives and the tools to meet them. This became significant in 2003 with the Iraq War and the division between the then US Defence Secretary Donald Rumsfeld's 'old' Europe and 'new' Europe. Rumsfeld had categorised Europe into these two camps, based on whether or not they supported the USA's intervention in Iraq. The former incorporated largely Europeanist countries, such as France and Germany, who refused to intervene in Iraq, while the latter included Atlanticist countries such as the central and Eastern European candidate countries that supported the USA. The USA had also produced a security strategy in 2002. Hence, there was a need to give the EU strategic direction and highlight where there was agreement between EU member states in security and defence.

The European Security Strategy (ESS) starts with one of the EU's key formative roles; 'successive enlargements are making a reality of the vision of a united and peaceful continent' (European Council, 2003, p. 1). Indeed, the EU as a peace project is the foundation of a European strategic culture (Norheim-Martinsen, 2011, p. 517). However, in the 'Global Challenges' section of the Strategy, the EU lays out its security concerns, all of which point to outside the EU and predominantly outside Europe. For instance, development, resources, health and their link to conflict and Europe's security is at the heart of the challenges. In as much as the EU attempted to distance itself from the USA, the Strategy lists its security concerns much in the same fashion as the US National Security Strategy had done previously. These include terrorism, the proliferation of weapons of mass destruction, regional conflicts, state failure and organised crime. Of these, only organised crime is referenced to Europe itself (European Council, 2003, p. 4).

Beyond this, two themes are highlighted. They are 'effective multilateralism' and Europe's neighbourhood. The first theme concentrated on the inherent nature of Europe towards cooperation and deliberation and away from the USA, seen as a unilateralist actor. More than this though, the statement sets out the EU's consideration for other international and regional organisations, such as the UN and WTO as well as the OSCE, Council of Europe, ASEAN and Mercosur. The second theme accompanied the European Neighbourhood Policy of the same year that attempted to set out a post-enlargement agenda for the 'new outsiders' beyond accession Europe. The focus in the Strategy is specifically the frozen conflicts and geo-politics of the former Soviet Union, as well as the threats of terrorism in the Middle East and the Maghreb. Finally, the strategy stipulates that the EU needs to be 'more active', including preventative engagement, 'more capable' (including both civilian and military capabilities), 'more coherent', focusing on the EU's different foreign policy instruments, and to work with partners (European Council, 2003, pp. 11–12). Overall, the Strategy has been criticised because it is only a partial strategy that does not link the ends of EU strategy with the means to achieve it (Biscop and Coelmont, 2010, p. 3). Rather, it is a declaration that states how Europe sees instability in the world and how the EU sees itself as part of the solution.

A number of initiatives were created to try to meet the call of a more active, capable and coherent EU. The Headline Goal 2010 introduced the EU Battlegroup Concept (see Box 6.1) and the European Defence Agency. The latter was created to 'assist Member States' efforts to improve their military capabilities to sustain CSDP' (European Council, 2004a, p. 12). Meanwhile, the civilian Headline Goal 2008, launched in 2004, specified six priority areas in civilian crisis management (European Council, 2004b). Following this, operations and missions were deployed spanning Europe, sub-Saharan Africa, the Middle East and Asia. However, the report on the implementation of the ESS in 2008 stated that 'for our full potential to be realised we need to be still *more capable, more coherent and more active*' (European Council, 2008, p. 2). The document included cyber security and piracy, reflecting the launch of EUNAVFOR Atalanta, the EU's first naval military operation to deter piracy in the Gulf of Aden. It also articulates the EU's normative underpinnings of human rights, human security and ensuring a combination of military and civilian tools. As Rummel (2011, p. 619) highlights, 'the initial advocacy for a strong civilian ESDP component had moved on from a few pioneer member states . . . to an EU-wide conceptual logic'. Considering the general failure of EU member states to generate additional military capabilities, particularly in the wake of the financial crisis, the question was how the EU was going to develop its CSDP.

Box 6.1   The EU Battlegroup concept

The EU Battlegroup concept was a UK–French idea that was formally launched as a UK, French and German initiative in 2004. A Battlegroup is formed of 1500 armed forces personnel and must be sustainable for 30 days with the possibility to extend this to 120 days. The timeframe for deployment is tight: 'the decision to deploy a Battlegroup should take place five days after the Council's agreement' with the operation commencing ten days after this (Major and Mölling, 2011, p. 11). Battlegroups can be unilateral or multilateral and are rotated every six months. Two Battlegroups are on standby during each six=month period. They have been at full operational capability since 2007; however, they have never been deployed. There are several reasons for this, including the size of a Battlegroup (EU operations have involved a greater number of troops), funding (the majority of military operations are funded through 'costs lie where they fall', that is, on the participating member states) and, most importantly, the lack of political willingness to deploy (see Chappell, 2012). The rotational nature of the Battlegroups means that it depends on whether any potential operation that comes up for discussion has the support of the countries that have Battlegroups on standby. None the less, the Battlegroups have facilitated armed forces reform in certain countries (e.g., Sweden and the Czech Republic) and have enhanced military cooperation and coordination, including training (Jacoby and Jones, 2008; Major and Mölling, 2011). Discussions on making the Battlegroups more usable occurred under the Swedish (2009) and Polish (2011) presidencies and more recently within discussions following the creation of the EU Global Strategy.

A more coherent security and defence actor? The Lisbon Treaty and its impact

The Lisbon Treaty was designed to push CSDP into the next gear, represented by a change in name from ESDP to CSDP, and offered the EU several new or updated features in its security and defence portfolio. First, the Lisbon Treaty introduced a solidarity clause linked to terrorist activities. Second, it created Permanent Structured Cooperation in Defence (PESCO) as outlined in Box 6.2. Third, the Treaty seeks to establish a European defence industry to promote European armaments manufacturing as an economic stimulus and independent strategic capability. The EDA already had a role to promote collaboration across European defence industries, but the Lisbon Treaty was to take this to the next level. Finally, two interconnected innovations were introduced: the High Representative for Foreign Affairs and Security Policy and the EEAS, with the former heading up the latter, in addition to becoming one of the Vice Presidents of the Commission.

CSDP was an attempt to bring defence and security policies under the mandate of the Union and less to each and every state, with the aim of making decision making and planning more efficient and effective. The EEAS was critical in this respect, as it represented the creation of the EU's diplomatic service. The Lisbon Treaty provided no guidelines regarding how the institution should be created or the tasks it would perform. This fell to the first High Representative (HR), Baroness Catherine Ashton. The EEAS was created from the Council Secretariat's Directorate General (DG) External and Politico-Military, the Commission's DG Relex and elements of DG Development, as well as seconded member state personnel. Hence, the idea was to combine all the EU's external relations into one organisation. However, elements remained in the Commission (e.g., trade, aid, the

European Neighbourhood Policy and enlargement) that questioned how far the EU could combine its foreign policy instruments to provide for a coherent and consistent foreign policy founded on a comprehensive approach.

Indeed, criticism of the EEAS's ability is widespread; not least in respect to the EEAS's relations with the Commission. The second issue relates to the idea of the creation of an *esprit de corps* within an institution that has officials coming from three different backgrounds. This has resulted in organisational and cultural clashes (Davis Cross, 2011, p. 454; Vanhoonaker and Pomorska, 2013). Finally, the question remains as to how far the EEAS can become its own autonomous actor (Furness, 2013). Bátora (2013, p. 606) points to the EEAS's role in 'political engagement, development assistance and civil and military crisis management' with mixed results as the EU's delayed response to the Arab Spring highlights. The idea of the EEAS as a civilising force reflected Ashton's perspective on foreign affairs (Vanhoonaker and Pomorska, 2013). This fits into the idea of normative power and goes some way to under-standing Ashton's sidelining of CSDP while HR. Indeed, CSDP stalled in the years following the Lisbon Treaty, despite the promise of a coordinated EU foreign policy.

However, part of the stalling within CSDP did not just relate to the issues highlighted above. While the Treaty eliminated the pillar system, it failed to bring security and defence policy into line with other EU law. Hence, CSDP remained a primarily intergovernmental policy area which effectively left CSDP open to heavy influence by those states that make the most contribution to Europe's combined military forces, namely France, UK, Italy and Germany. The UK's support had declined significantly since 2004. Meanwhile, France's enthusiasm had also waned due to frustration regarding the lack of progress in the area of defence. Additionally, in areas such as counter-terrorism, where more integration is neces-sary, this already happens predominantly outside of CSDP in the area of Justice and Home Affairs. Finally, the EU's ability to establish a defence industry does not begin without healthy collaboration between member-state companies (Mawdsley, 2003, 2008). Multinational col-laboration within the EU has failed to gain much ground and the Lisbon Treaty could be seen more for making a gesture to local economies dependent on armaments manufacturing than laying the grounds for greater collaboration. The Lisbon Treaty did not mark a step change in security and defence policy although it laid the ground work for this to happen should the political will ever exist.

CSDP post-Lisbon: defence matters?

The slow-down in CSDP post-Lisbon, and particularly post the French presidency in 2008, was clear, with very few new operations and missions deployed and the failure of initiatives such as PESCO, to be replaced by the much less ambitious pooling and sharing (see Box 6.2). In respect to the former, the EU's first anti-piracy operation, EUNAVFOR Atalanta, the larg-est civilian mission, EULEX Kosovo, the military operation EUFOR Tchad/RCA, which was deployed to Chad and the Central African Republic, and a small civilian monitoring mission in Georgia were all deployed in 2008 (see also Chapter 8). This demonstrated some of the military and civilian scenarios that the EU could contribute to. However, from 2009 to 2011, there was a notable slowdown with just one new mission – the EU Training Mission (EUTM) Somalia in 2010. Indeed, two military operations were discussed but, in the end, failed to be deployed (one to Eastern Congo at the end of 2008 and one to Libya in 2011). In the case of Libya, there were questions as to whether this marked the end of CSDP, particularly as it was considered to be the type of operation for which CSDP had been designed (Menon, 2011).

However, 2013 saw the beginnings of a reinvigoration of CSDP with the December European Council, which discussed defence for the first time since 2008 and declared that 'defence matters'. The document was separated into three baskets including: 'Increasing the effectiveness, visibility and impact of CSDP', 'Enhancing the development of capabilities' and 'Strengthening Europe's defence industry' (European Council, 2013, pp. 1–8). The first basket outlined the creation of a cyber security strategy and a maritime security strategy as well as making the Battlegroups more flexible and deployable. The second outlined four areas for further capability development (see Box 6.2) while the third focused on the requirement of a strengthened European defence, technological and industrial base, as well as announcing a Preparatory Action on CSDP-related research (European Council, 2013, pp. 8–10). While it may appear that these developments support the rights of power argument, with a concentration on furthering capabilities, these are dual use rather than military. Dual use capabilities relate to equipment that can be used for civilian or military purposes. This, in turn, reflects the idea of the EU's comprehensive approach to security, including the ability to use the full spectrum of tools.

Box 6.2   Developing EU member states' capabilities: PESCO and pooling and sharing

PESCO allowed member states who were able and willing to further integrate in the field of military capabilities. However, the initiative initially failed due to the member states' lack of agreement concerning the political criteria which would need to be fulfilled either prior to participation in PESCO or within a certain period of time after joining. The debate fell down to one of inclusion/exclusion, with some member states concerned about being left behind. Hence, in 2010, Germany and Sweden proposed the idea of pooling and sharing under the Ghent Initiative. This included 'the pooling of military equipment procurement, specialisation and sharing through some integration of force structures, e.g. joint units' (Chappell and Petrov, 2015, p. 195). Member states participate on a project-by-project basis. Eleven projects were initiated under the Polish Presidency in 2011, with a further four announced in 2012. These range from training programmes to air-to-air refuelling and smart munitions. At the 2013 European Council, four priority areas were identified which included air-to-air refuelling, remotely piloted aircraft systems (RPAS), satellite communications and cyber security. None the less, the number and size of the projects are relatively small and primarily attract small and medium member states. More recently, PESCO has come back on to the agenda. In December 2017, PESCO was finally agreed with 25 participating countries (excluding the UK, Denmark and Malta).

While focus had been placed on the creation of capabilities, there was a requirement for a new strategy that underpinned these and reflected the current security environment. This had changed substantially since the 2003 ESS and its update in 2008, not least due to the conflict in Syria and Russian engagement in Ukraine, including the annexation of Crimea. At the December 2013 European Council, the HR had been tasked to produce a report regarding the global environment and the changes therein, including the opportunities and challenges that this created for the EU. This was delivered by Ashton's successor to the HR role – Federica Mogherini – in 2015, who was then tasked with creating the EU Global Strategy (EUGS), which was duly delivered in 2016. Unlike Ashton, Mogherini was more supportive of CSDP and the idea of a strategy that underpinned the EU's external relations (Tocci, 2015).

The EUGS transcends CSDP to include the entirety of the EU's external relations. While the strategy articulates the EU's underpinning values, including their promotion (humanitarianism/human rights, the rule of law and democracy, as well as the idea of the EU as a peace project), connecting with the idea of the power of rights, it moves beyond the idea of a civilian power. As the strategy states, 'the idea that Europe is an exclusive "civilian power" does not do justice to an evolving reality . . . For Europe, soft and hard power go hand in hand' (EEAS, 2016, p. 4). In this way, it embodies a comprehensive approach to security in which the EU uses all its instruments up to and including the use of force along with ensuring the cohesiveness of the different EU institutional efforts. This involves investing in both civil and military instruments. Indeed, the EUGS promotes the idea of 'strategic autonomy' to enable the EU 'to foster peace and safeguard security within and beyond its borders' (EEAS, 2016, p. 19). Effective multilateralism remains key, with this being connected to international law. A diverse array of security threats is mentioned in the EUGS, including 'terrorism, hybrid threats, climate change, economic volatility and energy insecurity', with cyber security also highlighted (EEAS, 2016, pp. 18–21). Geographically, the EUGS focuses, unsurprisingly, on the European continent, while also highlighting that 'it is in the interests of our citizens to invest in the resilience of states and societies to the east stretching into Central Asia and south down to Central Africa' (EEAS, 2016, p. 23). Resilience, along with principled pragmatism, are two new concepts introduced in the EUGS, with the former being defined as, 'the ability of states and societies to reform, thus withstanding and recovering from internal and external crisis' (EEAS, 2016, p. 23), while the latter combines realism and pragmatism. Hence, the question is whether this leaves the EU with a way out of being proactive in its external relations. Overall, the EUGS provides a broader vision of the EU's approach to security and connects the power of rights ideal with the tools to facilitate this through a combination of civil and military tools.

However, the UK voted to the leave the EU (known as Brexit) in the same month that the EUGS was released and after it had been finalised. Rather than acting as a break, Brexit has acted as a catalyst for the realisation of CSDP initiatives. As highlighted, the EU has a number of security crises occurring on its borders. This will require EU cooperation, particularly considering the USA's lessening interest in European security (see Howorth, 2017a; Keohane, 2017, p. 56). Moreover, the election of Donald Trump as US President, who has articulated his support for Brexit, has fed 'into a growing sense of European insecurity' in the context of increasing nationalism in Europe (Keohane, 2017, p. 56). Finally, while the UK has disengaged from CSDP, it is one of the two largest military powers in the EU, along with France, and contributes financially to CSDP through the Athena mechanism, which provides CSDP funding for common costs. Furthermore, the UK and France have similar views on the use of force *vis-à-vis* the majority of other EU member states. However, the EUGS has articulated the idea of 'strategic autonomy', which remains undefined but potentially implies 'the EU's ability to stablise its neighbourhood without being dependent on the US' (Howorth, 2017b, p. 193). Hence, a combination of security crises, the inability of the EU to sufficiently deal with them, as well as the risk to the EU project more generally and EU security specifically, has spurred the EU member states and the EEAS into action with the EUGS providing a foundation for the EU's vision.

This has resulted in a number of policy initiatives and the strengthening of inter-institutional relations in defence, as the declaration on EU–NATO cooperation demonstrated. Following on from the events in June, the EUGS implementation plan on security and defence in November 2016 focused on how to activate the CSDP elements of the strategy. Such ideas as the Coordinated Annual Review on Defence (CARD), whereby member states would voluntarily synchronise their national planning cycles, the initiation of PESCO, making the Battlegroups more usable and reviewing the structures in place for planning CSDP operations and missions were highlighted. These have subsequently been taken up with the initiation of CARD in 2017 and PESCO in December 2017 (see Box 6.2). In terms of the planning and conduct of operations, the Military Planning and Conduct Capability (MPCC) was created in June 2017 and is located within the EUMS. This commands all non-executive military operations (i.e., training operations), which currently number three in total. Thus, the MPCC is the non-executive military equivalent of the Civilian Planning and Conduct Capability (established in 2007), which is the permanent structure within the EEAS for civilian missions. This is a further step towards a full-fledged permanent operational headquarters (OHQ) for military operations, which had been previously vetoed by the UK due to the unnecessary duplication of NATO structures (in the British view).

Finally, the preparatory action on CSDP related research announced in 2013 led to the establishment of a European Defence Fund. This highlights the increasing role of the Commission in CSDP, who proposed the idea and will be central in its implementation. In essence, the capability gaps faced by the EU member states are civil–military in nature, demonstrating the intertwining of these two elements within CSDP. Rather than seeing them as acting against one another, as the military vs. civilian power arguments highlight, rather we should see these as being integral to the EU's view of security and how to activate it, based on a range of normative values which have acted as the foundation of the EU as a project since its inception.

Conclusion

The EU's move into security and defence is a result of changes in the Cold War security architecture and changes in the USA's role in Europe. The result was an EU with the political willingness to play a positive role in ensuring peace and stability in the EU and its neighbourhood. While the EU remained prosperous and stable, the neighbourhood was not and, furthermore, expanded so that eventually the EU found itself in missions from central Asia to the Congo and Indian Ocean. Needless to say, something had changed in the European security architecture, even with the blessing of NATO and the USA. At the turn of the twentieth century, Europe had become a single, even if at times disjointed, provider of security.

The prospect is, what now for the EU? The USA has stated its intention to shift (or 'pivot') away from Europe as a source of insecurity towards other parts of the world, such as Asia. At the same time, the 2007 financial crash and its long legacy have hit national defence budgets hard. Where does this leave the EU, not to mention individual states? The fate of the EU and, of course, NATO may be one in the same: a more European role in European defence. This has become even more critical in light of the ring of fire encircling Europe; from insecurity arising in Libya and Syria to the Russian reawakening in Eastern Europe, as events in Ukraine have attested to. The slowdown of CSDP following 2008 created a situation that placed the policy in doubt, as even France slowly withdrew support, as attested by its unilateral action in Mali in 2013.

However, the EUGS and the UK's announced departure from the EU have had some influence on moving CSDP forward. None the less, care has to be taken not to overemphasise this. The UK's Atlanticist stance and vocal opposition to certain initiatives is supported by other EU member states, who have not always been forthcoming in publicly endorsing some of the UK's positions. Moreover, the UK's active participation in CSDP, including in civilian missions and military operations, has waned since the Blair government.

Finally, it is important to highlight that for all the talk on the creation of structures and capabilities, this does not mean that they will be utilised or that additional civilian or military capabilities will materialise. As the trajectory of CSDP has demonstrated, a number of initiatives have been far from successful and the majority of the military operations and civilian missions deployed have been small and short in duration. None the less, CSDP has come far in a short period of time. Civilian and military structures have been created and operationalised, some capability gaps are being dealt with and the recent raft of policy announcements give some hope that the EU can become an actor without a capabilities–expectations gap. Whatever the outcome, for students of contemporary European security, the future will be interesting, if nothing else.

Further reading

Chappell, Laura, Mawdsley, Jocelyn and Petrov, Petar (eds) (2016), *The EU, Strategy and Security Policy*. Abingdon: Routledge.

Howorth, Jolyon (2014), *Security and Defence Policy in the European Union* (2nd ed). Basingstoke: Palgrave Macmillan.

Irondelle, Bastien, Bickerton, Chris J., and Menon, Anand (eds) (2011), 'Security Cooperation Beyond the Nation State: The EU's Common Security and Defence Policy', *Journal of Common Market Studies*, 49 (1), 1–21.

Missiroli, Antonio (ed) (2015), *Towards an EU Global Strategy – Background, Process, References*. Paris: Institute for Security Studies.

Weblinks

European Defence Agency website for capability development information: www.eda.europa.eu/
EU External Action Service website on CSDP: https://eeas.europa.eu/headquarters/headquarters-homepage_en
EU Institute for Security Studies on CSDP related areas: www.iss.europa.eu/

References

Aggestam, Lisbeth (2008), 'Introduction: Ethical Power Europe?', *International Affairs*, 84 (1), 1–11.
Bátora, Jozef (2013), 'The 'Mitrailleuse Effect': The EEAS as an Interstitial Organization and the Dynamics of Innovation in Diplomacy', *Journal of Common Market Studies*, 51 (4), 598–613.
Biscop, Sven (2009), 'The Value of Power, the Power of Values: A Call for an EU Grand Strategy', *Egmont Paper 33*. Ghent: Academia Press.
Biscop, Sven, and Coelmont, Jo (2010), 'Strategy for CSDP Europe's Ambitions as a Global Security Provider', *Egmont Paper 37*. Ghent: Academia Press.
Bull, Hedley (1982), 'Civilian Power Europe: A Contradiction in Terms?', *Journal of Common Market Studies*, 21 (2), 149–170.
Chappell, Laura (2012), *Germany, Poland and the Common Security and Defence Policy*. Basingstoke: Palgrave Macmillan.
Chappell, Laura, and Petrov, Petar (2014), 'The European Union's Crisis Management Operations: Strategic Culture in Action?', *European Integration Online Papers (EIoP)*, 18 (2). Available at: http://eiop.or.at/eiop/texte/2014–002a.htm (accessed: 18 October 2018), 1–24.
Chappell, Laura, and Petrov, Petar (2015), 'The European Defence Agency and Pooling & Sharing: Moving Out of First Gear?', in Iraklis Oikonomou and Nikolaos Karampekios (eds), *The European Defence Agency – Arming Europe*. Abingdon: Routledge, pp. 191–206.
Chappell, Laura, Mawdsley, Jocelyn, and Petrov, Petar (eds) (2016), *The EU, Strategy and Security Policy*. Abingdon: Routledge.
Cornish, Paul, and Edwards, Geoffrey (2005), 'The Strategic Culture of the European Union: A Progress Report', *International Affairs*, 81 (4), 801–820.
Davis Cross, Mai'a K. (2011), 'Building a European Diplomacy: Recruitment and Training to the EEAS', *European Foreign Affairs Review*, 16 (4), 447–464.
Diez, Thomas, and Manners, Ian (2007), 'Reflecting on Normative Power Europe', in F. Berenskoetter and M. J. Williams (eds), *Power in World Politics*. Abingdon: Routledge, pp. 173–188.
Duchêne, Francois (1972), 'Europe's Role in World Peace', in Richard Mayne (ed), *Europe Tomorrow: Sixteen Europeans Look Ahead*. London: Fontana, pp. 32–47.
European Council (2003), *A Secure Europe in a Better World: European Security Strategy*. Brussels: European Council.
European Council (2004a), *Headline Goal 2010*. Available at: www.europarl.europa.eu/meetdocs/2004_2009/documents/dv/sede110705headlinegoal2010_/sede110705headlinegoal2010_en.pdf (accessed: 18 October 2018).

European Council (2004b), Civilian Headline Goal 2008. Available at: https://eur-lex.europa.eu/legal-content/EN/TXT/HTML/?uri=LEGISSUM:l33239&from=EN (accessed: 2 November 2018).

European Council (2008), *Report on the Implementation of the European Security Strategy: Providing Security in a Changing World*. Brussels: Council of the European Union.

European Council (2013) 'Common Security and Defence Policy'. *European Council Conclusions EUCO 217/13, 19–20 December 2013*. Brussels: European Council.

European External Action Service (EEAS) (2016), *Shared Vision, Common Action: A Stronger Europe. A Global Strategy for the European Union's Foreign and Security Policy*. Luxembourg: Publications Office of the European Union.

Falk, Richard (2008), 'The Power of Rights and the Rights of Power: What Future for Human Rights?', *Ethics & Global Politics*, 1 (1–2), 81–96.

Furness, Mark (2013), 'Who Controls the European External Action Service? Agent Autonomy in EU External Policy', *European Foreign Affairs Review*, 18 (1), 103–126.

Gray, Colin S. (1999), 'Strategic Culture as Context: The First Generation of Theory Strikes Back', *International Affairs*, 7 (1), 49–69.

Heiselberg, Stine (2003), 'Pacifism or Activism: Towards a Common Strategic Culture Within the European Security and Defense Policy?', *ISS Working Paper 2*. Copenhagen: Danish Institute for International Studies, pp. 1–36.

Hill, Christopher (1993), 'The Capability–Expectations Gap, or Conceptualising Europe's International Role', *Journal of Common Market Studies*, 31 (3), 305–328.

Howorth, Jolyon (2017a), 'The EUGS: New Concepts for New Directions in Foreign and Security Policy', *The International Spectator*, 51 (3), 24–26.

Howorth, Jolyon (2017b), 'EU Defence Cooperation after Brexit: What Role for the UK in the Future EU Defence Arrangements?', *European View*, 16 (1), 191–200.

Howorth, Jolyon, and Menon, Anand (2009), 'Still Not Pushing Back: Why the European Union Is Not Balancing the United States', *Journal of Conflict Resolution*, 53 (5), 727–744.

Hyde-Price, Adrian (2012), 'Neorealism: A Structural Approach to CSDP', in Xymena Kurowska and Fabian Breuer Fabian (eds), *Explaining the EU's Common Security and Defence Policy: Theory in Action*. Basingstoke: Palgrave Macmillan, pp. 16–40.

Jacoby, Wade, and Jones, Christopher (2008), 'The EU Battle Groups in Sweden and the Czech Republic: What National Defense Reforms Tell US about European Rapid Reaction Capabilities', *European Security*, 17 (2), 315–338.

Jones, Seth G. (2007), *The Rise of European Security Cooperation*. Cambridge: Cambridge University Press.

Keohane, Daniel (2017), 'Brexit and European Insecurity', in Oliver Thränert and Martin Zapfe (eds), *Strategic Trends 2017: Key Developments in International Affairs*. Zurich: ETH Zurich Center for Security Studies, pp. 55–72.

Knutsen, Bjørn Olav (2009), 'The EU's Security and Defense Policy (ESDP) and the Challenges of Civil–Military Coordination (CMCO): The Case of the Democratic Republic of Congo (DRC)', *European Security*, 18 (4), 441–459.

Liddell Hart, Basil (1967), *Strategy* (2nd ed.). London: Faber.

Longhurst, Kerry (2004), *Germany and the Use of Force*. Manchester: Manchester University Press.

Maastricht Treaty (1992), *Treaty on the European Union*. Available at: http://eur-lex.europa.eu/legal-content/EN/TXT/?uri=LEGISSUM%3Axy0026 (accessed: 18 October 2018).

Major, Claudia, and Mölling, Christian (2011), 'EU Battlegroups: What Contribution to European Defence? Progress and Prospects of European Rapid Response Forces', *SWP Research Paper 8*. Berlin: Stiftung Wissenschaft und Politik.

Manners, Ian (2002), 'Normative Power Europe: A Contradiction in Terms?', *Journal of Common Market Studies*, 40 (2), 235–258

Manners, Ian (2006), 'Normative Power Europe Reconsidered: Beyond the Crossroads', *Journal of European Public Policy*, 13 (2), 182–199.

Mawdsley, Jocelyn (2003), 'On the Way to a Common European Armaments Policy?', in P. Schlotter (ed), *Europa-Macht-Frieden: Zur Politik der 'Zivilmacht Europa*. Baden-Baden: Nomos, pp. 134–158.

Mawdsley, Jocelyn (2008), 'European Union Armaments Policy: Options for Small States?', *European Security*, 17 (2–3), 367–386.

Menon, Anand (2009), 'Empowering Paradise? The ESDP at Ten', *International Affairs*, 85 (2), 227–246.

Menon, Anand (2011), 'European Defence Policy from Lisbon to Libya', *Survival*, 53 (3), 75–90.

Meyer, Christoph O. (2006), *The Quest for a European Strategic Culture: Changing Norms on Security and Defence in the European Union*. New York: Palgrave Macmillan.

Missiroli, Antonio (2001), 'European Security Policy: The Challenges of Coherence', *European Foreign Affairs Review*, 6 (2), 177–196.

Norheim-Martinsen, Per M. (2011), 'EU Strategic Culture: When the Means Becomes the Ends', *Contemporary Security Policy*, 32 (3), 517–534.

Posen, Barry R. (2006), 'European Union Security and Defense Policy: Response to Unipolarity?', *Security Studies*, 15 (2), 149–186.

Rummel, Reinhardt (2011), 'In Search of a Trademark: EU Civilian Operations in Africa', *Contemporary Security Policy*, 32 (3), 604–624.

Rutten, Maartije (2001), 'From St Malo to Nice: European Defence: Core Documents', *Chaillot Paper 47*. Paris: Institute for Security Studies.

Rynning, Sten (2003), 'The European Union: Towards a Strategic Culture?', *Security Dialogue*, 34 (4), 479–496.

Tocci, Nathalie (2015). 'Towards an EU Global Strategy', in Antonio Missiroli (ed), *Towards an EU Global Strategy: Background, Process, References*. Brussels: Institute for Security Studies.

Vanhoonaker, Sophie, and Pomorska, Karolina (2013), 'The European External Action Service and Agenda-Setting in European Foreign Policy', *Journal of European Public Policy*, 20 (9), 1316–1331.

Wedin, Lars (2008), 'The EU as a Military Strategic Actor', in Kjell Engelbrekt and Jan Hallenberg (eds), *The European Union and Strategy: An Emerging Actor*. London: Routledge, pp. 40–55.

Internal security 7

Raphael Bossong and Hendrik Hegemann

Introduction

'European security' most commonly refers to the handling of 'traditional' security threats, such as military conflicts and great power relations in Europe. Without doubt, these problems remain of pivotal importance (see Chapter 10 in this volume). Yet, ever since the end of the Cold War, issues like terrorism, illegal migration and organised crime have clearly risen in prominence on the agenda of bilateral and multilateral security cooperation. In Europe, this wide range of transnational and non-military security threats is typically summarised under the label of 'internal security'.

Three lines of investigation will guide the following critical introduction to the field of European internal security. First, we need to reflect critically on the meaning and political relevance of internal security. The provision of domestic peace and security can be regarded as the foundation of the modern state, but also invites competing interpretations of the boundary between freedom and security. Using the term 'internal security' should, therefore, not be seen as a neutral or purely analytical term, but may contribute to the overall securitisation of European politics (see Chapter 3 in this volume). In addition, it has almost become a cliché to state that the boundary between internal and external security is increasingly blurred and that we should work towards transnational security cooperation in response to transnational threats (Bigo, 2006; Eriksson and Rhinard, 2009). Issues associated with internal security also overlap with alternative framings such as 'homeland security' (Kaunert et al., 2012) or 'societal security' (Wæver et al., 1993), which have further political connotations. Irrespective of the choice of security labels, however, it is clear that the fight against organised crime, terrorism, or illegal migration presents a distinct arena for professional actors from law enforcement and interior ministries. These actors operate increasingly on a transnational scale, alongside other traditional security actors, such as the military or ministries for foreign affairs.

Based on such a critical and heuristic understanding of the notion of internal security, second, we turn to the organisational and legal architecture in Europe that seeks to deal with organised crime, irregular migration and international terrorism. Internal security in this sense is an integral part of the complex multi-level and multi-actor system of European security governance (Bossong and Hegemann, 2015; Ehrhart et al., 2014; Sperling and Webber, 2014). Most notably, the Council of Europe has developed a profile in these areas since the 1950s and remains prominent today. In addition, students should be aware of a very diverse set of bilateral or mini-lateral networks between European police and internal security authorities, which is often most relevant for operational security cooperation. Following a new political emphasis on transnational risks such as human trafficking and cybersecurity, multilateral organisations, for example, the OSCE and NATO, have also integrated some internal security aspects into their more traditional security agendas. However, since the emergence of border-free travel in the Schengen Zone and increasingly since the late 1990s, the European Union (EU) has taken on an increasingly central role. The EU has a common legal space for criminal justice cooperation – the so-called Area of Freedom, Security and Justice – as well as separate EU agencies and infrastructures for internal security cooperation, such as EUROPOL or the Schengen Information System. The 'refugee crisis' and heightened fears of terrorist attacks in Europe since 2015 have deepened this long-term trend and led the EU to establish a so-called 'Security Union' between all (remaining) EU as well as Schengen member states (European Commission, 2015, 2016).

Third, this expansion of European internal security, as well as its relation to salient political issues, has brought into question its traditional focus on informal forums and operational coordination and put it on top of the political agenda. The legitimacy and effectiveness of the existing architecture for internal security, therefore, has increasingly become subject to public debate and contestation. While the existing emphasis on informal forums and operational coordination raised concerns about democratic control and functional efficacy, further integration and constitutionalisation is constrained by the operational prerogative of national security actors and growing political scepticism towards further European integration, partially driven by a general sense of Euroscepticism. Most notably, recent debates about migration, border control and terrorism unveiled fundamental differences among European states and within European societies and spurred a trend towards the politicisation of internal security. This has raised difficult questions about the future development of an increasingly contentious policy field.

Conceptualising internal security

Political philosophy tells us that the provision of domestic security is the core legitimation for the modern state. Thomas Hobbes drew on the experience of civil war and argued for a central 'Leviathan' that protects each individual against a permanent state of violence. Each person gives up the right to exercise force in exchange for protection and general peace inside a state's territory. All threats are dealt with – or crimes are punished – exclusively by the unmatched and undivided power of the Leviathan. In response, however, John Locke argued that this pervasive fear of anarchy and a war of all against all is misguided. It is not other people, but the state (or absolutist monarch) that often poses the greatest risk to the life and liberty of the individual. Hence, legitimate order is based on civil rights and laws, which bind both the individual and the state.

These two stylised opposing positions of the 'maximal state' and 'minimal state' (Buzan, 1991, pp. 57–111) remain relevant for the contemporary debate on the meaning of internal security. Advocates for a maximalist position can point to the serious impact of organised crime and terrorism in many countries (Pinotti, 2015; Vorsina et al., 2017), as well as a growing sense of insecurity and calls for increased protection in European societies, though levels of concerns vary significantly across countries and with regard to different threats (European Commission, 2017a). Crime and disorder have a strong symbolic dimension that challenges the social fabric, community ties, trust and confidence in governments as well as moral views, causing people not only to change their behaviour, but also to demand governments to step in and restore security and order (Farrall et al., 2009). Therefore, there might be good reasons to move beyond traditional military threats, and to see these problems as urgent threats requiring a resolute response.

From the perspective of critical security studies, in contrast, the rise of the notion of internal security reflects a broader process of 'securitisation', which has potentially problematic effects (see Chapter 3 in this volume). In a nutshell, it is argued that securitisation extends the fundamental logic of 'national security', which implies an existential threat and the need for urgent and extraordinary measures, to a growing number of societal and political issues. These securitised issues are then likely to lead to the one-sided executive empowerment of security authorities and illiberal policies (Buzan et al., 1998). This can range from 'zero tolerance' policies against crime and illegal migration to the invocation of a state of exception to combat terrorism. Thus, using the concept of 'internal security' can invite a vision of state–society relations, which limits the space for democratic politics in exchange for maximal protection. This tendency may be aggravated in post-solidaristic, or 'neo-liberal' societies with rising economic inequality and weakening social ties, in which the fear of crime and terrorism can be invoked for political and economic purposes, even if it does not always match official statistics (Furedi, 2005; Garland, 2001). In such a political climate, many issues that could also be associated with welfare or educational policies, such as drugs control and the prevention of 'radicalisation', are dominantly treated as narrow security concerns – which, in turn, may lead to self-reinforcing cycles of state repression and widespread delinquency.

Internal security, therefore, requires a more nuanced understanding than the area of external security, where the pursuit of peace and international order can be conceived of as a more unconditional good. The often-invoked image of a balance between security and liberty is problematic, as infringements upon civil liberties do not necessarily enhance security, while increased security might also be achieved through measures that do not fundamentally constrain citizens' rights (Waldron, 2003). Still, the state and its citizens need to constantly review the necessity and proportionality of internal security measures – which, in turn, lead to difficult debates about which crimes and security risks may need to be accepted as a price for personal and societal freedom. In addition to this classic struggle between liberal and more conservative norms on domestic law and order, in recent decades questions have been raised about the centrality of the state in the provision of internal security as a democratically controlled public good, and which tasks can be left to societal and private actors (Loader and Walker, 2007). For instance, in the fight against terrorism, civil society initiatives for prevention and counter-radicalisation are trying to make an impact, whereas the protection of specific sites or installations, such as airports, is increasingly outsourced to private security companies. This thumbnail sketch of the concept of internal security can only scratch the surface of the ongoing philosophical, political and legal debate. What should be clear, however, is that the notion of 'internal security' is as 'essentially contested' as other central concepts of political life. There never was a historical ideal 'balance' between freedom and security, nor can we expect a future consensus on the degree to which internal security measures have to be strengthened. Hence, this question needs to be determined in public deliberation and debate.

Building on the essentially contested meaning and scope of security, the contemporary condition of globalisation requires us to take a closer look at the distinction between *internal* and *external* security. This terminology derives from a binary distinction between, on the one hand, the partly anarchical realm of international relations occupied by diplomats and militaries and, on the other hand, the supposedly law-governed space under the control of centralised states with their law enforcement agencies exercising the monopoly over the legitimate use of force. While this clear-cut distinction always has been an illusion, structures and patterns of international relations have been substantially transformed since the end of the Cold War, so that many threats to internal security now have clear cross-border dimensions and almost all foreign policy affairs are entangled in transnational regimes and international institutions to some extent. Conversely, the nature of domestic politics has increasingly come to involve more fluid transnational governance systems, including private companies and regulatory networks (Knill and Lehmkuhl, 2002).

At the same time, the end of the Cold War stimulated a reorientation of all security authorities towards alternative threats to European societies. These ranged from organised crime and illegal migration to various other assorted 'unconventional' threats, such as terrorism, critical infrastructure vulnerability and a related new awareness of vulnerabilities related to information and communication technology. These issues along the 'internal–external security nexus' could not be adequately handled through the traditional means of the domestic police, intelligence and justice system and, rather, crossed the traditional boundaries of internal and external security (Eriksson and Rhinard, 2009). This has become manifest, for example, in the growing use of the military for domestic purposes, such as the protection of key public buildings, or the fusion of police and domestic intelligence tasks with regard to precautionary measures in the 'War on Terror' (Amoore and de Goede, 2008; Aradau and van Munster, 2007). The rise of globalisation and international mobility lent further credibility to arguments about the need to forge new international mechanisms for cooperating on these threats. The events of 11 September 2001 amplified or entrenched this narrative about dislocated or ubiquitous risks. Hence, the domestic monopoly on the legitimate use of force has become embedded in an increasingly complex transnational regime (Herschinger et al., 2011). This empirical development is traced further in the second part of this chapter.

Despite this common discourse on a necessary merger of internal and external security, however, one should not jump to the conclusion that the fusion of internal and external security is a natural response to an inevitable trend. Even if police and interior ministries are now increasingly operating on a regional, or even global, scale, they nevertheless remain formally distinct in their outlook, organisation and instruments from external intelligence services, the military, or traditional foreign ministries. From a more sociological understanding, one may instead speak of an increasingly transnational field of internal security, which is constituted by the changing day-to-day actions or practices of law enforcement agencies, domestic intelligence agencies, or interior ministries (Bigo, 2006, 2014). These practices should be understood in a broad sense, ranging from shared discourses, meetings and training, exchanges of information and joint operations, to more competitive aspects, such as bureaucratic struggles over funding and competences. Such practices take place at all levels of governance. However, the transnational field of internal security and its participating actors are usually not concerned with regular policing or administration of justice. Instead, top-level criminal justice and police authorities or internal intelligence agencies' focus on 'high policing' (Brodeur, 2007) that involves more exceptional and politically relevant cases, such as drug trafficking and organised crime, the fight against terrorism and, increasingly, also the containment of illegal migration. The question of border control within and around Europe has gained particular salience over the last decade (see also further below), leading to polarised debates over the alleged human rights violations in the Mediterranean and elsewhere or the perceived necessity to 'take back control' of state borders (Jeandesboz, 2016). In addition, the transnational professional field of internal security has come to include serious cyber-crime and the related concern of critical infrastructure failure. This relates to the inherent vulnerability of modern societies due to unintended side effects of globalisation and high-tech capitalism, which may also be exploited by malignant or criminal actors (Dunn Cavelty and Kristensen, 2008).

This heuristic understanding of a professional and topical field of internal security helps us to go beyond a narrow or outdated understanding of territoriality. In all mentioned issues, areas or security concerns, one can find numerous points of contact with traditional external security actors, such as the military and external intelligence agencies. Yet, for most intents and purposes, this transnational field of internal security issues and practitioners develops on an independent basis. For instance, in the fight against terrorism, one can see intensive cooperation between the US and the European law enforcement community, whereas military coordination and intelligence exchanges are handled in separate channels and institutional frameworks.

We need to recall that this transnational field of internal security can also be described with different labels, which have distinct understandings about the role of the state and the nature of security provision. For example, Wæver et al. (1993) coined the term 'societal security' to denote a growing sensitivity to the need to preserve a sense of collective identity, especially in light of the impact of globalisation, transnational mobility and growing diversity. With a view to recent concerns around migration, terrorism and 'radicalisation', these fears gain salience and public debates frequently address the desire to address issues of integration and

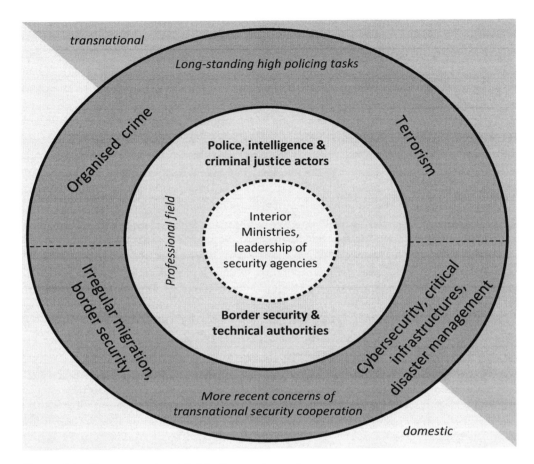

Figure 7.1   The transnational field of internal security

'social cohesion', beyond a functionalist concern with border or crime control. The concept of 'homeland security', which emerged after '9/11' as part of the US-led 'War on Terror' also carries the notion of protecting a mystified homeland and helped to legitimate the massive expansion of executive power across different economic and societal sectors, well beyond a conventional understanding of police and criminal justice (Mueller and Stewart, 2011). And, despite its supposed inward-looking and defensive nature, the concept of homeland security also had transnational ramifications. While most European states did not endorse the overall framing of 'homeland security' and the proclaimed 'War on Terror', the USA pressured European states to adopt a range of coercive security measures, such as the inclusion of biometric data in passports and the transfer of passenger name records (Argomaniz, 2009).

In short, the notion of internal security cannot be considered as a clear-cut sub-field of the overarching security role of the modern state. On the one hand, the notion of internal security is potentially connected with shifting legitimating rationales that move away from a strictly constitutional, liberal understanding to a more executive and hierarchical under-standing of political rule. While there may be growing asymmetric threats, such as terrorism and organised crime, that may require new security measures, the classic debate about the appropriate balance between freedom and security, or the potentially problematic effects of securitisation, are absolutely central to this issue. On the other hand, the territorial dis-tinction between internal and external security cannot be taken at face value. The rise of globalisation has challenged such clear-cut understandings, while threats of organised crime and terrorism have long been a transnational concern. However, this is not to say that the distinction between internal and external security has become meaningless. The main actors of internal security, that is, high-level police and criminal justice authorities and interior ministries, remain formally distinct from military and foreign policy actors, even if they are increasingly operating alongside on an international level. This empirical development can be conceived of as a transnational field of internal security – while not forgetting about other political framings, such as 'societal' or 'homeland' security. The following section builds on this reflective understanding of the possible meaning of internal security, and outlines the main European governance patterns in this field.

The evolution of internal security governance in Europe

To understand the substance and dynamic of European internal security governance, it is not sufficient to start with a conventional narrative of the impact of 9/11 or the latest secu-rity crises. International cooperation against various forms of crime has a long tradition and includes a wide array of issues and institutions, though it has often received limited public attention (Andreas and Nadelmann, 2006; Deflem, 2002; Jakobi, 2013). INTERPOL – the only worldwide platform for police cooperation – was founded in 1923 in Vienna as a response to the then pressing problem of transnational anarchist terrorism, which had contributed to the outbreak of the First World War. And as soon as the horrors of two World Wars and the rise of totalitarianism had somewhat subsided, political extremist and nationalist–separatist terrorism raged in many areas of the world. Moreover, the global problem of drug consump-tion has been present since the 1960s, with the USA driving a first truly global campaign under the aggressive label of the 'War on Drugs'. Ever since then, questions of international legal harmonisation and cross-border law cooperation have steadily risen on the political agenda. This trend also is reflected in the work of international organisations, as exemplified by the creation of the Single Convention on Narcotic Drugs in 1961 and the United Nations Interregional Crime and Justice Research Institute (UNICRI) in 1968.

However, European states could be seen as pioneers of cross-border legal and criminal justice cooperation. After the Second World War, the Council of Europe, which served as the first political, rather than economic, venue for European integration, developed a number of conventions, mechanisms and forums for criminal justice cooperation as well for the defence of the liberal constitution of its member states. Thus, the Council of Europe pioneered a con-vention for extradition (1957) and mutual legal assistance for criminal proceedings (1959). In the 1970s, a first convention against international terrorism (1977) was agreed. These political developments were flanked by a number of informal working groups among West European states, such as the Pompidou or Dublin Group dealing with drug trafficking. Other flexible professional networks for various aspects of counterterrorism, drugs and related financial crime developed beyond the remit of the Council of Europe, such as the Club of Berne connecting national intelligence officials or the Police Working Group on Terrorism between West European states. To the present day, this trajectory shapes the field of European internal security governance, which continues to heavily rely on a multitude of long-standing as well as newly founded informal networks (Bures, 2012; den Boer et al., 2008). Yet, perhaps equally importantly, the Council of Europe was founded on the basis of the European Convention on Human Rights – defended by the European Court of Human Rights in Strasbourg – which was meant to safeguard European states against totalitarianism after the end of the Second World War. Consequently, the Convention and the jurisdiction of the European Court of Human Rights developed as a counterweight to overly security-orientated conceptions of the role of the modern state, and repeatedly ruled against European member states in their approach against terrorism and migration or with regard to additional aspects of the criminal justice systems, such as penitentiary conditions. This also applied to key Western European states, such as the UK and its confrontation with Irish terrorism in the 1970s and 1980s.

Building on these dual tracks of transnational security cooperation and protection of human rights, further European security institutions have started to look into these issues since the 1990s. The OSCE built on its established role as a 'soft' security infrastructure (see Chapter 5) through new programmes on issues such as 'violent extremism' and human trafficking, while also seeking to promote the Rule of Law and criminal justice reform in parallel. Meanwhile, the Council of Europe expanded its membership to the former Soviet bloc and sought to raise respective standards for the protection of human rights. These activities took an added importance as organised crime took on a new quality in Europe. Rather than as a regionally focused phenomenon, such as the original Italian Mafia, or thematically focused phenomenon, such as the global drugs trade since the late 1960s, organised crime emerged as a structural feature of the rapid economic, social and political transitions in Eastern Europe and the former Soviet Union. Soon the groups and networks of criminal entrepreneurs and former state security professionals, which had comparatively easy access to weapons, moved across borders and became a security concern in Western Europe. Last, but not least, the protracted wars in former Yugoslavia added to rising structural immigration pressures to Northwestern Europe. Over the course of the 1990s, asylum seekers and irregular migration were not only regularly seen as possible sources of crime, but were increasingly seen as a serious threat to European identities and social welfare systems (Huysmans, 2006). This rising concern with migration led to further international dialogues and European platforms to control this phenomenon, such as, for instance, the so-called Budapest Process.

Against this background, the EU started to take on a more central security role. The transformation of the European Economic Communities into the European Union in 1992 laid the foundation to move beyond economic integration under the so-called 'First Pillar' and to include the work of police and criminal justice authorities under the so-called 'Third Pillar' – while European foreign policy coordination occupied the middle 'Second Pillar'. The formation of the Third Pillar built on some older mini-lateral initiatives in the fight against

Table 7.1   Legacies and overlapping forums for internal security governance
(non-exhaustive)

Institution/Network	Current member states	Foundation	Issue area(s) of internal security
INTERPOL	192	1946	Drugs, terrorism, organised crime, cybercrime
Council of Europe (CoE)	47	1949	Human rights, criminal justice, terrorism, migration
OSCE	57	1975	Terrorism, human rights
Club of Berne	31	1971	Terrorism (and espionage)
Police Working Group on Terrorism	31	1979	International terrorism
Pompidou Group	39	1971	Drugs trafficking and abuse
Schengen Convention	26	1985	Border security, police cooperation, irregular migration
Budapest Process	50	1993	Migration
Lyon/Roma Group	7 (G7)	1997	Drugs, organised crime, terrorism

international terrorism in the 1970s – the so-called TREVI Group – but was mainly triggered by the 1985 Schengen Agreement for the abolition of border controls between France, Germany, and the Benelux countries. This groundbreaking commitment set a long-lasting integration dynamic into motion which is to compensate for the abolition of national border controls by increased transnational cooperation between police and border control authorities (Monar, 2001). This momentum for increased transboundary security cooperation matured by the mid-1990s into a first shared European data network for internal security purposes, the Schengen Information System (SIS) and a detailed set of rules on police cooperation, the Schengen Codex. By the late 1990s, the Third Pillar and the Schengen Codex were integrated and gave rise to formal integration objectives of the EU, which was to create the so-called 'Area of Freedom, Security and Justice', which should allow a seamless, trustworthy and efficient cross-border cooperation between police and criminal (as well as civil) justice authorities in the EU. 1999 also saw the formal creation of the first common European police institution, EUROPOL, which took inspiration from the global organisation, INTERPOL. In this sense, the rise of internal security in the EU could mainly be seen as a political 'spill-over' from Schengen and the Common Market, even though external developments and broader processes of securitisation, such as the rise of organised crime and irregular migration, also played a role (Huysmans, 2004).

Hence, the attacks of 11 September 2001, when a group of terrorists associated with al Qaida killed close to 3,000 people in New York, Pennsylvania and Arlington, Virginia, marked a decisive date, but not the crucial foundation for European internal security governance.

Just as after the end of the Cold War, existing European security institutions and platforms sought to adapt and expand their work to the evolving political priorities. The OSCE increased its emphasis on reforming the justice and law enforcement sector in former Communist countries and added 'countering violent extremism', including the role of religion, as a key dimension to its previous work on minorities and ethnic discrimination (Wuchte and Knani, 2013). The Council of Europe expanded its existing legal convention on terrorism in the direction of prevention and increased criminalisation of support for terrorist organisations. NATO used its existing expertise to address the possible use of chemical, biological and radiological weapons and materials by terrorists (de Nevers, 2007). Overall, the USA exerted considerable pressure on partners and international organisations to shift their priorities and policies, ranging from increased biometric and financial data collection over intensified collaboration in the (occasionally illegal) detention and prosecution of terrorist suspects to contributions to flexible military coalitions. It, thereby, managed to install the now so-called 'War on Terror' as a global meta-narrative (Buzan, 2006).

At the time, the EU could contribute little to this harder approach to global counterterrorism. However, the EU boosted its profile across all areas of internal security (Argomaniz, 2011; Bossong, 2013). In particular, the implementation of the planned Area of Freedom, Security and Justice was accelerated, exemplified by the adoption of the Single European Arrest Warrant in 2001. Instead of a traditional intergovernmental coordination process between justice and interior ministries, this new instrument was based on the assumption of 'mutual trust' between European member states and should allow any national police and criminal justice authorities to issue an arrest warrant that could be directly enforced across borders. Similarly, in 2002, EUROJUST was founded as a dedicated EU-agency for supporting criminal justice authorities across borders. The subsequent serious terror attacks in Madrid 2004 and London 2005 underlined the momentum for increased security cooperation, ranging from new preventive efforts against radicalisation into terrorism over regulation for aviation security standards to financial sanctions against terrorist suspects. Over the following years, the range of European internal security issues continued to expand, especially in the fields of critical infrastructure protection, cybersecurity and disaster management. This could be illustrated by a large-scale blackout across Northwestern Europe in 2006 (van der Vleuten and Lagendijk, 2009) or the European financial support to the serious earthquakes in Italy in 2009 (European Commission, 2009). Elsewhere, we have argued that this created a new field of European 'civil security governance', where traditional concerns over natural disasters, such as floods, and new fears of technological risks and vulnerabilities increasingly came to overlap with the internal security field as outlined above (Bossong and Hegemann, 2015).

The Eastern enlargement of the EU in 2004 provided a further impetus to enact more stringent border controls for the Schengen Zone and led to the formation of FRONTEX as a new European agency for border control and internal security. Yet, just as EUROPOL was founded not as an operational police agency, but one focused on information exchange and analysis, FRONTEX was primarily conceived as an institution for risk assessment and as a coordination forum for national border guards (Neal, 2009). In parallel, European member states set up further platforms for migration control with view to the Mediterranean and

EU member states fully participating the in the Schengen Area

Non-EU states which have fully implemented the Schengen Agreement

EU member states which have not implemented the Schengen Agreement

EU member states which have only implemented parts of the Schengen Agreement

Figure 7.2   The Schengen Area

Source: Wikimedia Commons (2017), 'Schengen Zone Map', Available at: https://commons.wikimedia.org/wiki/File:Schengenzone.svg (accessed: 22 October 2018).

Africa, such as the Rabat or Khartoum Processes. But the 2000s were also a period when EU laws on irregular migration and border control, but also on asylum and international protection, became increasingly binding on EU member states (Thym, 2016).

The next major stepping stone for the development of European internal security governance was the adoption of the EU Lisbon Treaty.[1] In the comparatively quiet period in the fight against terrorism and illegal migration between 2007 and 2012, the EU member states agreed to transfer the remaining aspects of the so-called Third Pillar for police and criminal justice cooperation to the regular EU decision-making and legal system.[2] While previously internal security cooperation remained almost fully under the control of interior ministries, the Lisbon Treaty led to a growing involvement of the European Parliament, the European Commission and the Court of Justice of the European Union. The Lisbon Treaty also made the so-called Charter of Fundamental Rights a legal foundation for all European policies and actions, including in internal security. In other words, the Lisbon Treaty could be seen as a critical milestone in a long process of moving from professionally driven networks to a full-blown institutional and political system for internal security governance at the EU level. This strategic shift was also flanked by a first explicit Internal Security Strategy of the EU (European Commission, 2010), which touched upon all possible threats emerging from organised crime, terrorism, irregular migration and, increasingly, also cybersecurity. Yet, the Treaty of Lisbon also underlined the ambiguities and historical legacies of European internal security cooperation. It highlighted that the operational provision of internal security – or the executive work of police, border and criminal justice authorities – would remain with the member states.[3] Hence, the EU level remained focused on analysis, best practice and information exchange, which is the forte of EU agencies such as EUROPOL or FRONTEX, or on broad legal harmonisation. The EU remains far from a truly unified European criminal and internal security law.

This complex and ambiguous state of European internal security governance intersected with the last and – in the eyes of many observers most serious – crisis of European internal security that has developed since 2014. Around that time, the rise of the 'Islamic State' (IS) led to a new surge of international terrorism and a large flow of so-called 'foreign fighters' from Western European nations to conflicts in Syria, Iraq and beyond. Inside Europe, a string of attacks by lone attackers and organised cells put terrorism at the top of the security agenda. Meanwhile, the aftermaths of the Arab Spring in 2011 and the later escalation of the war in Syria created a dramatic spike in refugee movements to Europe. While dramas and deaths on the Mediterranean have occurred on a regular basis since the late 1990s, the accumulation of drownings between 2013 and 2016 and the march of hundreds of thousands of refugees from Greece through South Eastern Europe to Germany and Northwestern Europe caused a new sense of crisis. The unilateral decision of Germany to accept a large number of refugees and asylum-seekers relieved some of the immediate pressures on other European countries, but also invited the charge of a loss of control over European borders. The numbers of arrivals in South and Southeastern Europe during the peak period between summer 2015 and spring 2016 was such that many people could not be registered properly, let alone decently housed or properly managed through the regular asylum process. Finally, the fact that some of the terrorist attackers and IS supporters were (deliberately) channelled through the large-scale flow of refugees, or were subsequently recruited among disillusioned asylum seekers, added to a sense of overwhelming insecurity and failure of European internal security.

Unsurprisingly, this led to growing public demands for action from European security institutions. A Eurobarometer survey from November 2017, for example, found that the public considered immigration and terrorism the two most important issues facing the EU (European Commission, 2017b, p. 4). Internal security, thereby, moved from merely operational fora and professional communities to the political centre stage. In response, the EU entered a new period of deepening and extending its cooperation. This included, for instance, upgrading EUROPOL's counter-terrorism capacities, boosting the European border agency FRONTEX, outsourcing border controls to the European neighborhood, and the integration of EU databases for migration control and police cooperation. At the time of writing, many projects and legislative proposals were still to be implemented or were under negotiation.

The most explicit formulation of the long-standing trend of treating European internal security issues as increasingly integrated, from both a thematic and geographic perspective, could be seen in the European Commission's call for the formation of a so-called 'Security Union' as an overarching ideal (European Commission, 2015, 2016). In this official reasoning, organised crime, terrorism and irregular migration, thus came to be seen as one single 'insecurity continuum' (Bigo, 2006), while the borderless travel in the Schengen Zone was supposed to necessitate a truly unified European approach. In contrast to this narrative, a rising chorus of critical voices pointed to the increasingly illiberal or repressive nature of European internal security policies. This showed especially in the debates over the control of irregular migration, where the cooperation with neighboring countries such as Turkey and Libya raised harsh dilemmas (Carrera and Guild, 2016). While policy makers claimed that they wanted to save migrants from the dangerous and often deadly passage over the Mediterranean Sea, civil society organisations argued that the projection of internal security interests to third countries led to massive abuses of human rights and the exclusion of vulnerable persons beyond the eyes of the European public. The increasing rhetorical linkages between irregular migration and organised crime – and occasionally even terrorism – accentuated the danger that basic normative standards were being ignored and that illiberal populist forces could gain further ground.

Limits and challenges to European internal security cooperation

So far, we have argued that the notion of internal security remains contested and may legitimate overly forceful responses to regular police and criminal justice issues. At the same time, the distinction between internal and external security may be less one of functional substance and territorial scope, as there is an entrenched discourse on the need to fight asymmetric threats across borders and in a comprehensive manner. Instead, it may be more useful to look at the different actor-sets that relate to these security discourses in their own way. Thus, one may discern a transnational field of police and criminal justice authorities as well as interior ministries, which engage with each other on a transnational level, and mostly work in parallel to, rather than directly with, traditional external security actors. Building on this perspective, we illustrated that this transnational field has a long history, reaching all the way to the beginning of the twentieth century. European institutional arrangements shadowed these growing professional networks and practices for 'high policing' issues. After the Second World War, the Council of Europe served as the first focal point, providing a legal framework for international police and criminal justice cooperation as well as a regime for the protection of human rights. The end of the Cold War, increased personal mobility and a more fragmented regional environment in Europe boosted the importance and salience of this transnational internal security cooperation. The European Union, in particular, took on an increasingly central role since the mid- to late 1990s, as it forged a link between the abolition of internal border controls in the Schengen Zone and the creation of a common 'Area of Freedom, Security and Justice'. This overarching political development was spurred on by repeated terrorist attacks and political debates over irregular migration between 2000 and the late 2010s.

The resulting rich tapestry of networks and institutional frameworks for internal security cooperation does not necessarily translate into positive policy outcomes. First, the revelations by Edward Snowden showed how security agencies can evade established formal institutional limitations and accountability structures. Long-standing links between security agencies and security professionals, often relying heavily on new technologies for data gathering and surveillance, have evolved into a non-transparent transnational web of exchanges (Bauman et al., 2014). Security services may, thus, exchange data sets on citizens between each other that each single service could not legally collect by itself. Executive and administrative actors can also resort to the international level in order to evade domestic scrutiny or present national decision-making structures with pre-set policy choices. During the 1990s and 2000s, many European interior ministries sought to advance harsher migration controls through transnational forums, which fell beyond the view and control of national parliaments and courts (Guiraudon, 2000). As outlined above, the growing constitutionalisation of EU internal security policy has partially rectified this procedural imbalance, but has not necessarily led to more liberal policy outcomes (Trauner and Ripoll Servent, 2016). The increasing involvement of non-European countries in the provision of internal security and border control for the EU adds a further layer of complexity and controversy. In any case, the persistence of multiple informal and non-transparent forums for operational internal security cooperation remains a serious challenge to central norms of democratic legitimacy and accountability (den Boer et al., 2008). This especially applies to harder aspects of internal security provision and the cooperation of intelligence services. Here, the European level has not (yet) been able to develop full-fledged oversight and control processes that could be compared to the domestic institutional checks and balances of European liberal democracies.

Second, it is not clear that the proliferation of international cooperation venues is effective and efficient. For sensitive security cooperation and intelligence sharing, it might help to have multiple professional networks and forums that may be tailored to specific needs. For instance, the European states that were most affected by the threat from IS have good reasons to focus on mutual cooperation without involving all other EU member states, who may lack the respective intelligence capacities or simply have little direct need to track large numbers of suspects. Yet, if one seeks a reliable level of protection and information sharing against transnationally mobile threats and suspects, it may be necessary to create more centralised and formalised frameworks for cooperation (Bures, 2012). In other words, one 'weak link' may be enough to critically undermine the cooperation chain between security authorities, be they at national or transnational level. It is for this reason that the EU has been building up shared databases for border control and agencies such as EUROPOL that should allow for a common threat perception and joint action.

Yet, the further centralisation and institutionalisation of internal security at a supranational level cannot be the only answer, either. The preservation of national sovereignty in internal security affairs is not just a legacy of the past, but also reflects the deeper differences between democratic publics that are also concerned with symbolic or subjective aspects of internal security. Most notably, since 2014, the migration crisis has illustrated how the mobilisation of national identities and diverging threat perceptions overstretched all European mechanisms of negotiation and crisis management. Transnational policy forums, or 'integration by stealth', thus reach their limits when faced with open contention in national democratic publics (Börzel and Risse, 2018; Hegemann and Kahl, 2018). Further obstacles arise when supposed threats to internal security are also looked at from the perspective of social or welfare policies. This not only relates to legitimate differences in problem-framing, say of the causes of crime or violent radicalisation, but also to the use of financial resources, which largely remain tied to the nation-state. Substantial investments in community cohesion, crime prevention and social integration – which many observers continue to see as the most effective and important contribution to long-term internal security (Savage et al., 2008) – can only be made through taxation. This power of taxation and corresponding democratic accountability have yet to be successfully transferred to international organisations.

On an abstract level, one could argue that we are in an interim historical period and that a further politicisation of internal security at the European level will provide a way out of these dilemmas, leading to an integrated polity or, at least, a transnational internal security community. Further politicisation and debate might bring more transparency and enable public deliberation on the question of which security tasks should reasonably and legitimately be transferred to the European level. Yet, a growing politicisation might also provide incentives to pursue excessive security measures that target minorities and undermine civil liberties, or deepen and entrench political conflicts between different European countries and, thereby, make further cooperation more difficult. This was exemplified in the debates over the distribution of refugees across European countries or the lead-up to the Brexit referendum. In sum, we should be wary of adding ever more threat conceptions to the political debate and underlining the importance of European internal security cooperation. But instead of retreating to professional (and largely hidden) venues, the political management of identity conflicts and possible de-securitisation of societal threat perceptions could offer a more constructive way forward, which would also provide room to uphold shared European fundamental rights.

Notes

1 Treaty on the European Union (TEU) as well as the Treaty on the Functioning of the European Union (TFEU).
2 Chapter V TFEU, Art. 67–89.
3 Art. 4 (2) TEU.

Further reading

Andreas, Peter, and Nadelman, Ethan (2006), *Policing the Globe: Criminalization and Crime Control in International Relations*. Oxford: Oxford University Press.
Bigo, Didier, Guild, Elsbeth, Carrera, Sergio, and Walker, Rob M. (eds) (2010), *Europe's 21st Century Challenge: Delivering Liberty*. Farnham: Ashgate.
Bossong, Raphael, and Rhinard, Mark (eds) (2016), *Theorizing Internal Security in the European Union*. Oxford: Oxford University Press.
Kaunert, Christian, Léonard, Sara, and Pawlak, Patryk (eds) (2012), *European Homeland Security: A European Strategy in the Making?* London: Routledge.

Weblinks

Centre for European Policies Studies, Rights and Security Section: www.ceps.eu/research-areas/rights
Council of Europe: www.coe.int/en/web/portal
European Parliament, Committee for Civil Liberties, Justice and Home Affairs: www.europarl.europa.eu/committees/en/libe/home.html
Statewatch: www.statewatch.org

References

Amoore, Louise, and de Goede, Marieke (eds) (2008), *Risk and the War on Terror*. London: Routledge.
Andreas, Peter, and Nadelmann, Ethan (2006), *Policing the Globe: Criminalization and Crime Control in International Relations*. Oxford: Oxford University Press.
Aradau, Claudia, and van Munster, Rens (2007), 'Governing Terrorism Through Risk: Taking Precautions, (Un)Knowing the Future', *European Journal of International Relations*, 13 (1), 89–115.
Argomaniz, Javier (2011), *The EU and Counter-Terrorism: Politics, Polity and Policies after 9/11*. London: Routledge.
Argomaniz, Javier (2009), 'When the EU Is the "Norm-Taker": The Passenger Name Records Agreement and the EU's Internalization of US Border Security Norms', *Journal of European Integration*, 31 (1), 119–136.
Bauman, Zygmunt, Bigo, Didier, Esteves, Paulo, Guild, Elspeth, Jabri, Vivienne, Lyon, David, and Walker, R. B. J. (2014), 'After Snowden: Rethinking the Impact of Surveillance', *International Political Sociology*, 8 (2), 121–144.
Bigo, Didier (2006), 'Internal and External Aspects of Security', *European Security*, 15 (4), 385–404.
Bigo, Didier (2014), 'The (In-)Securitization Practices of Three Universes of EU Border Control: Military/Navy – Border Guards/Police – Database Analysts', *Security Dialogue*, 45 (3), 209–225.

Börzel, Tanja, and Risse, Thomas (2018), 'From the Euro to the Schengen Crisis: European Integration Theories, Politicization, and Identity Politics', *Journal of European Public Policy*, 25 (1), 83–108.

Bossong, Raphael (2013), *The Evolution of EU Counter-terrorism: European Security Policy after 9/11*. London: Routledge.

Bossong, Raphael, and Hegemann, Hendrik (2015), 'Introduction: European Civil Security Governance – Towards a New Comprehensive Policy Space?', in Raphael Bossong and Hendrik Hegemann (eds), *European Civil Security Governance: Cooperation and Diversity in Crisis and Disaster Management*. Basingstoke: Palgrave Macmillan, pp. 1–23.

Brodeur, Jean-Paul (2007), 'High and Low-Policing in Post-9/11 Times', *Policing*, 1 (1), 25–37.

Bures, Oldrich (2012), 'Informal Counterterrorism Arrangements in Europe: Beauty by Variety or Duplicity by Abundance?', *Cooperation and Conflict*, 74 (4), 495–518.

Buzan, Barry (1991), *People, States and Fear: An Agenda for International Security Studies in the Post-Cold War Era*. Boulder, CO: Lynne Rienner.

Buzan, Barry (2006), 'Will the "Global War on Terrorism" Be the New Cold War?', *International Affairs*, 82 (6), 1101–1118.

Buzan, Barry, Wæver, Ole, and Wilde, Jaap de (1998), *Security: A New Framework for Analysis*. Boulder, CO: Lynne Rienner.

Carrera, Sergio, and Guild, Elspeth (2016), 'EU–Turkey Plan for Handling Refugees Is Fraught with Legal and Procedural Challenges', *CEPS Commentary*. Available at: www.ceps.eu/publications/eu-turkey-plan-handling-refugees-fraught-legal-and-procedural-challenges (accessed: 22 October 2018).

Deflem, Mathieu (2002), *Policing World Society: Historical Foundations of International Police Cooperation*. Oxford: Oxford University Press.

Den Boer, Monika, Hillenbrand, Claudia, and Nölke, Andreas (2008), 'Legitimacy Under Pressure: The European Web of Counter-Terrorism Networks', *Journal of Common Market Studies*, 46 (1), 101–124.

De Nevers, Renée (2007), 'NATO's International Security Role in the Terrorist Era', *International Security*, 31 (4), 34–66.

Dunn Cavelty, Myriam, and Kristensen, Kristian Søby (eds) (2008), *Securing the 'Homeland': Critical Infrastructure, Risk and (In)Security*. London: Routledge.

Ehrhart, Hans-Georg, Hegemann, Hendrik, and Kahl, Martin (2014) 'Towards Security Governance as a Critical Tool: A Conceptual Outline', *European Security*, 23 (2), 145–162.

Eriksson, Johan, and Rhinard, Mark (2009), 'The Internal–External Security Nexus: Notes on an Emerging Research Agenda', *Cooperation and Conflict*, 44 (3), 243–267.

European Commission (2009), 'The Commission Proposes Granting 494 Million Euros to Italy to Help Cope with the Aftermath of the Abruzzo Earthquake', Press Release IP/09/1185, 23 July 2009, European Commission, Brussels. Available at: http://europa.eu/rapid/press-release_IP-09–1185_en.htm?locale=en (accessed: 10 April 2018).

European Commission (2010). 'The EU Internal Security Strategy in Action. Five Steps towards a More Secure Europe', Memo COM/2010/673 final, 22 November 2010, European Commission, Brussels. Available at: https://eur-lex.europa.eu/legal-content/EN/TXT/PDF/?uri=CELEX:52010DC0673&from=en (accessed: 22 October 2018).

European Commission (2015) 'European Agenda on Security', Communication COM/2015/185 final, 28 April 2015, European Commission, Strasbourg. Available at: www.cepol.europa.eu/sites/default/files/european-agenda-security.pdf (accessed: 22 October 2018).

European Commission (2016) 'Delivering on the European Agenda on Security to Fight against Terrorism and Pave the Way Towards an Effective and Genuine Security Union', Communication COM/2016/230 final, 20 April 2016, European Commission, Brussels. Available at: https://ec.

europa.eu/home-affairs/sites/homeaffairs/files/what-we-do/policies/european-agenda-security/legislative-documents/docs/20160420/communication_eas_progress_since_april_2015_en.pdf (accessed: 22 October 2018).

European Commission (2017a). *Special Eurobarometer 464b: Europeans' Attitudes towards Security*. Brussels: European Commission.

European Commission (2017b) *Standard Eurobarometer 88: Autumn 2017: Public Opinion in the European Union*. Brussels: European Commission.

Farrall, Stephen D., Jackson, Jonathan, and Gray, Emily (2009), *Social Order and the Fear of Crime in Contemporary Times*. Cambridge: Cambridge University Press.

Furedi, Frank (2005), *Culture of Fear: Risk-Taking and the Morality of Low Expectation*. London: Continuum.

Garland, David (2001), *Culture of Control: Crime and Social Order in Contemporary Society*. Oxford: Oxford University Press.

Guiraudon, Virginie (2000), 'European Integration and Migration Policy: Vertical Policy-Making as Venue Shopping', *Journal of Common Market Studies*, 38 (2), 251–271.

Hegemann, Hendrik, and Kahl, Martin (2018), 'Security Governance and the Limits of Depoliticisation: EU Policies to Protect Critical Infrastructures and Prevent Radicalization', *Journal of International Relations and Development*, 21 (3), 552–579.

Herschinger, Eva, Jachtenfuchs, Markus, and Kraft-Kasack, Christiane (2011), 'Scratching the Heart of the Artichoke? How International Institutions and the European Union Constrain the Monopoly of Force', *European Political Science Review*, 3 (3), 445–468.

Huysmans, Jef (2004), 'A Foucaultian View on Spill-Over: Freedom and Security in the EU', *Journal of International Relations and Development*, 7 (3), 284–318.

Huysmans, Jef (2006), *The Politics of Insecurity: Fear, Migration and Asylum in the EU*. London: Routledge.

Jakobi, Anja (2013), *Common Goods & Evils: The Formation of Global Crime Governance*. Oxford: Oxford University Press.

Jeandesboz, Julien (2016), 'Justifying Control: EU Border Security and the Shifting Boundaries of Political Arrangement', in Raphael Bossong and Helena Carrapico (eds), *EU Borders and Shifting Internal Security: Technology, Externalization and Accountability*. Cham: Springer, pp. 221–238.

Kaunert, Christian, Léonard, Sarah, and Pawlak, Patryk (eds) (2012), *European Homeland Security: A European Strategy in the Making?* Abingdon: Routledge.

Knill, Christoph, and Lehmkuhl, Dirk (2002), 'Private Actors and the State: Internationalization and Changing Patterns of Governance', *Governance*, 15 (1), 41–63.

Loader, Ian, and Walker, Neil (2007), *Civilizing Security*. Cambridge: Cambridge University Press.

Monar, Jörg (2001), 'The Dynamics of Justice and Home Affairs: Laboratories, Driving Forces and Costs', *Journal of Common Market Studies*, 39 (4), 747–764.

Mueller, John, and Stewart, Mark G. (2011), *Terror, Security and Money: Balancing the Risks, Benefits and Costs of Homeland Security*. Oxford: Oxford University Press.

Neal, Andrew (2009), 'Securitization and Risk at the EU Border: The Origins of Frontex', *Journal of Common Market Studies*, 47 (2), 333–356.

Pinotti, Paolo (2015), 'The Causes and Consequences of Organised Crime: Preliminary Evidence across Countries', *The Economic Journal*, 125 (586), 158–174.

Savage, Joanne, Bennett, Richard R., and Danner, Mona (2008), 'Economic Assistance and Crime: A Cross-National Investigation', *European Journal of Criminology*, 5 (2), 217–238.

Sperling, James, and Webber, Mark (2014), 'Security Governance in Europe: A Return to System', *European Security*, 23 (2), 126–144.

Thym, Daniel (2016), '"Citizens" and "Foreigners" in EU Law: Migration Law and Its Cosmopolitan Outlook', *European Law Journal*, 22 (3), 296–316.

Trauner, Florian, and Ripoll Servent, Ariadna (2016), 'The Communitarization of the Area of Freedom, Security and Justice: Why Institutional Change Does Not Translate into Policy Change', *Journal of Common Market Studies*, 54 (6), 1417–1432.

Van der Vleuten, Erik, and Lagendijk, Vincent (2009), 'Europe's Electrical Vulnerability Geography: Historical Interpretations of the 2006 "European Blackout"', *Tensions of Europe/Inventing Europe Working Paper*. Eindhoven: Technische Universiteit Eindhoven.

Vorsina, Margarita, Manning, Matthew, Fleming, Christopher, Ambrey, Cristopher, and Smith, Cristine (2017), 'The Welfare Cost of Terrorism', *Terrorism and Political Violence*, 29 (6), 1066–1086.

Wæver, Ole, Buzan, Barry, Kelstrup, Morten, and Lemaitre, Pierre (1993), *Identity, Migration and the New Security Agenda in Europe*. London: Pinter.

Waldron, Jeremy (2003), 'Security and Liberty: The Image of Balance', *The Journal of Political Philosophy*, 11 (2), 191–210.

Wuchte, Thomas, and Knani, Mehdi (2013), 'Countering Violent Extremism and Radicalization that Lead to Terrorism: The OSCE's Unique Regional Blueprint', *Journal EXIT-Deutschland*, 2, 76–86.

Europe and the human security agenda

8

Jocelyn Mawdsley

Introduction

The end of the Cold War opened up new possibilities in both academic thinking about international relations and their practice. The Cold War security agenda had been driven by the assumption that security was about the territorial integrity of the nation-state, and that its protection was best served by immense investment in militaries and armaments, which had led to an arms race between East and West. For Cold War analysts, the balance of power, bipolarity, containment and deterrence were the core security concepts. This concentration on hard security for the nation-state, and the resources needed to supply it, meant that most academics and practitioners were distracted from thinking more broadly or idealistically about global security. As immediate military security threats largely disappeared for the permanent members of the United Nations Security Council (UNSC), broader security concerns, such as the environment, health and poverty emerged as topics for discussion. The then UN Secretary-General Boutros Boutros-Ghali's 1992 Agenda for Peace can be seen as the most significant early iteration of these wider concerns. They were, however, quickly and widely adopted as mainstream issues. The 1990s saw a broad acceptance among academics and policy makers that international security was about more than just military security, and that forms of collective action would be needed to combat threats such as climate change and the spread of HIV / AIDS (Buzan et al., 1998).

At the same time, the development policy agenda had been driven throughout the 1980s by a neoliberal model of development that stressed the role of markets in delivering economic growth, rather than directly targeting poverty alleviation. The end of the arms race promised a peace dividend, and the United Nations (UN) and, specifically, the UN Development Programme (UNDP) saw an opportunity to refocus development efforts (in terms of both finance and personnel) on human development indicators rather than just economic ones. As Thomas (2001) argued, these developments saw a convergence of the international security and development agendas. The concept of human security is at the heart of this convergence.

Boutros Boutros-Ghali's Agenda for Peace also made the suggestion that security should be understood not just in terms of state security, but should extend to the people within states. This is often referred to as the deepening of the security agenda to consider threats to the individual. In other words, the referent object of security is the individual, not the state. As the 1993 Human Development Report pointed out, 'The concept of security must change – from an exclusive stress on national security to a much greater stress on people's security, from security through armaments to security through human development, from territorial security to food, employment and environmental security' (United Nations Development Programme, 1993, p. 2).

While this proposal fitted the early 1990s' Zeitgeist, its necessity became tragically apparent. The 1994 Rwandan genocide drew horrified international attention to the human suffering that could occur when a state did not protect its citizens from violence, or was complicit in that violence (Suhrke, 1999). The 1990s and early 2000s saw not just the development of the concept of human security but also an ambitious international policy agenda to implement it. It was an agenda that was initially very popular in Europe but has subsequently faltered.

This chapter will start by exploring the concept of human security. It will consider differing definitions, the link between human security and the 'responsibility to protect' (R2P) agenda and how human security was adopted by the UN. It will then go on to examine why the debates around human security had particular resonance for many European states and how the European Union (EU) responded. The chapter focuses on the EU, as, of the three institutions in this book, it has engaged the most intensively with the concept. The OSCE lacks the resources to really implement a human security approach, and while there have been recent calls for NATO to adopt the concept, such debates are still under-developed – rather, NATO's involvement has centred around questions about how legitimate their claims to be implementing the principle of R2P in its operations in Kosovo, Afghanistan and Libya are. The final substantive section will ask why both European states and the EU became disillusioned with human security and, thus, it has not come to occupy as central a role as had been expected.

Human security: definitions and development

As Duffield and Waddell (2006) point out, human security rapidly acquired substantial institutional support following its emergence in the early–mid 1990s. They suggest that while Boutros Boutros-Ghali's 1992 Agenda for Peace shaped the security dimension of human security, the UNDP Human Development Reports played a similar role in shaping the development side. In particular, the UNDP contributed by developing the idea that human security should be characterised by 'freedom from want' and 'freedom from fear'. As a concept, it was rapidly adopted by UN agencies, NGOs and civil society.

Despite this rapid adoption, critics have pointed out that human security remained conceptually vague and that there is little agreement on its definition, meaning that implementation in terms of policy or research is near impossible (Paris, 2001). Kerr (2007) points to tensions between what she dubs the narrow and broad schools of human security (see Box 8.1). The narrow school, which is particularly attached to Andrew Mack and his Human Security Centre at the Canadian University of British Columbia, emphasises the freedom from fear dimension of human security. Mack (2004) argues that for human security to have conceptual clarity and analytical rigour, it should concentrate on freeing individuals from the threat or use of political violence. He argues that while there are other threats to the individual, these are often correlated with violence.

The broad school of human security moves beyond the freedom from fear agenda, and tackles the second element of the UNDP definition, namely, freedom from want. This approach became particularly associated with Ramesh Thakur and his institution, the United Nations University in Tokyo. Thakur and Newman (2004), for instance, argue that human security should be concerned with all critical life-threatening dangers to people, not just those caused by political violence (see Box 8.1), although they do limit this to those situations that have become crises. Some, like Alkire (2004, p. 360) called for an even more expansive definition, suggesting that human security was 'to protect the vital core of all human lives in ways that advance human freedoms and human fulfilment'.

Box 8.1   Key definitions

UNDP definition

Human security means '. . . first, safety from such chronic threats as hunger, disease and repression. And second, it means protection from sudden and hurtful disruptions in the patterns of daily life – whether in homes, in jobs or in communities' (United Nations Development Programme, 1994, p. 23).

Narrow definition

Human security is 'the protection of individuals and communities from war and other violence' (Human Security Centre, 2005).

Broad definition

Human security is 'concerned with the protection of people from life-threatening dangers, regardless of whether the threats are rooted in anthropogenic activities of natural events, whether they lie within or outside states, and whether they are direct or structural. Human security is "human centred" in that its principle focus is on people both as individuals and as communal groups. It is "security-orientated" in that the focus is on freedom from fear, danger and threat' (Thakur and Newman, 2004, p. 4).

Kerr (2007) points out that disagreements on definitions were and are joined by disagreements on how the concept might be implemented in practice. She highlights questions of what means are required, what the role of the state should be and, most controversially, when the case for international humanitarian intervention should override the principle of state sovereignty.

An important element of the UN's institutional involvement in shaping the concept of human development was a concern for what this might mean for its own practices. One element of key concern was its peacekeeping role. The UN had published two reports in 1999 that highlighted the UN failure to prevent genocide in Rwanda in 1994 and to protect the inhabitants of Srebrenica (Bosnia and Herzegovina) in 1995. In response, the then Secretary-General, Kofi Annan, appointed the Panel on UN Peace Operations. The panel was tasked with assessing the shortcomings of the existing peace operations system and to make recommendations for change. The Brahimi Report (Lakhdar Brahimi was the Chair of the Panel) called for renewed political commitment on the part of Member States, significant institutional change, and increased financial support. They also argued that if UN peacekeeping operations were to be effective, then they must be properly resourced and equipped, and operate under clear, credible and achievable mandates.

The early 2000s saw the publication of two further major reports, both of which were intended to give substance to the question of what human security might mean in practice. In 2003, the Commission on Human Security presented its report 'Human Security Now' to the then UN Secretary-General, Kofi Annan, and, in 2001, the International Commission on Intervention and State Sovereignty (ICISS) presented its report 'Responsibility to Protect' (see Box 8.3). The former report is associated with the broad school of human security and with development concerns and the latter with the narrow school and security questions. As Duffield and Waddell (2006, p. 8) point out, 'These two reports reflect, in a practical sense, how, until recently, the governance networks of human security were being constructed in two complementary but different ways'.

Finally, in 2012, after multiple further reports, the UN General Assembly agreed a resolution on human security that seemed to gain widespread consent, and which was closer to the broad school's definition.

Box 8.2   UN General Assembly Resolution 66/290, point 3

3. Agrees that human security is an approach to assist Member States in identifying and addressing widespread and cross-cutting challenges to the survival, livelihood and dignity of their people. Based on this, a common understanding on the notion of human security includes the following:

(a)   The right of people to live in freedom and dignity, free from poverty and despair. All individuals, in particular vulnerable people, are entitled to freedom from fear and freedom from want, with an equal opportunity to enjoy all their rights and fully develop their human potential

(b)   Human security calls for people-centred, comprehensive, context-specific and prevention-oriented responses that strengthen the protection and empowerment of all people and all communities

(c)   Human security recognizes the interlinkages between peace, development and human rights, and equally considers civil, political, economic, social and cultural rights

(d)   The notion of human security is distinct from the responsibility to protect and its implementation

(e)   Human security does not entail the threat or the use of force or coercive measures. Human security does not replace State security

(f)   Human security is based on national ownership. Since the political, economic, social and cultural conditions for human security vary significantly across and within countries, and at different points in time, human security strengthens national solutions which are compatible with local realities

(g)   Governments retain the primary role and responsibility for ensuring the survival, livelihood and dignity of their citizens. The role of the international community is to complement and provide the necessary support to Governments, upon their request, so as to strengthen their capacity to respond to current and emerging threats. Human security requires greater collaboration and partnership among Governments, international and regional organizations and civil society

(h)   Human security must be implemented with full respect for the purposes and principles enshrined in the Charter of the United Nations, including full respect for the sovereignty of States, territorial integrity and non-interference in matters that are essentially within the domestic jurisdiction of States. Human security does not entail additional legal obligations on the part of States.

(United Nations General Assembly, 2012)

However, as the text shows, it continues to attract considerable tensions over the extent to which the concepts of human security and respect for state sovereignty are compatible. As the ICISS report predicted, many of the controversies that have emerged have been around questions of when, by whom and under what circumstances international humanitarian intervention in a sovereign state using military force is acceptable. When does the international community have a responsibility to protect?

Box 8.3   International Commission on Intervention and State Sovereignty (ICISS)

What was ICISS? In September 2000, the Canadian Government, together with a group of major foundations, announced at the UN General Assembly the establishment of the International Commission on Intervention and State Sovereignty (ICISS). In December 2001, ICISS produced a report that aimed to establish global consensus on the conditions that permitted humanitarian intervention.

Why was it set up? To answer the question posed by Kofi Annan (then UN Secretary-General) '. . . if humanitarian intervention is, indeed, an unacceptable assault on sovereignty, how should we respond to a Rwanda, to a Srebrenica – to gross and systematic violations of human rights that affect every precept of our common humanity?'

Who was involved? Founders: Gareth Evans (Australia) and Mohamed Sahnoun (Algeria). Members: Gisèle Côté-Harper (Canada), Lee Hamilton (United States), Michael Ignatieff (Canada), Vladimir Lukin (Russia), Klaus Naumann (Germany), Cyril Ramaphosa (South Africa), Fidel V. Ramos (Philippines), Cornelio Sommaruga (Switzerland), Eduardo Stein Barillas (Guatemala) and Ramesh Thakur (India).

What did they recommend? That sovereignty entailed rights and responsibilities, including a responsibility to protect (R2P) citizens from major human rights violations, and that if a state is 'unable or unwilling' to do this the responsibility to protect passes to the international community and that this R2P overrode the principle of non-intervention. Any military intervention should be 'an exceptional and extraordinary measure', and must meet certain criteria, e.g.,

- Just cause: there must be 'serious and irreparable harm occurring to human beings, or imminently likely to occur'.
- Right intention: the main intention of the military action is to prevent human suffering.
- Last resort: every other measure besides military intervention has to have already been considered and only military intervention is thought likely to succeed.
- Proportionality: the military force must not exceed what is necessary to 'secure the defined human protection objective'.
- Reasonable prospects: the chance of success must be reasonably high, and unlikely that the consequences of the military intervention would be worse that the consequences of non-intervention.
- Right authority: the military action has to have been authorised by the UN Security Council.

See International Commission on Intervention and State Sovereignty (2001).

While the ICISS criteria seem at first glance to be robust, in crisis situations it remains very difficult to judge whether they can be, or have been, met, and political motivations have often seemed paramount in UN Security Council debates over whether or not an intervention should be permitted. In fact, political will is crucial in determining whether or not an intervention will take place. This factor was also crucial in evoking early European enthusiasm for human security and provoking some subsequent disillusionment. The reasons why the concept was so popular in European political circles will be explained in the next section.

In short, human security was very much a product of an optimistic 1990s, when it was hoped that a new, more peaceful era was beginning, although it owes its roots to the much older philosophy of liberalism (Kerr, 2007; see Chapter 3). Its underlying principles did meet with much acceptance, and international initiatives such as the establishment of the International Criminal Court or the Ottawa Treaty banning the use of landmines owe much to the concept. Nevertheless, tensions between state sovereignty and human security remain, and even though the idea of human security is now embedded in UN institutions, its implementation has been patchy at best. The war in Syria stands testament to this.

Human security and Europe: initial positive reactions

Although Canada, Norway and Japan are probably the states that have been most associated with the development of human security, as Fukuda-Parr and Messineo (2012) point out, it also became the spur for much of the debate with the EU as it tried to develop and define the Common Security and Defence Policy (CSDP). Indeed, Martin and Owen (2010) made the claim that, as the debate on definitions floundered in the UN, it was the EU that drove human security forward. This section looks at why human security was a good fit for EU security deliberations, reflecting on how the continent's 1990s' experiences with peacekeeping and enforcement made the questions raised by human security pertinent. It will also consider why particular political figures endorsed the human security agenda, the involvement of civil society, and why the human security agenda enabled progress on certain key European international concerns.

Individual European states, the EU itself, and NATO gained considerable experience, often bruising, in peacekeeping and peace enforcement throughout the 1990s and early 2000s. In his Millennium Report of 2000, the then UN Secretary-General, Kofi Annan, asked how the international community should respond to gross violations of human rights, such as those in Rwanda or Srebrenica, if intervention was such an affront to state sovereignty. This was a question that had become a matter of major concern to European states. Not only had the massacre at Srebrenica happened on European soil, a continent where the 'never again' lesson of the Holocaust was deeply embedded, but European UN peacekeepers were heavily involved in both Rwanda and Srebrenica and bore a share of responsibility for the failures. It was not just a question for the continent's politicians, but also one of wider public concern.

In Rwanda between early April and mid-July 1994, the army, government-backed militias and Hutu civilians massacred ethnic Tutsi people. Approximately 800,000 people were killed in what is widely recognised as an act of genocide. The UN and the international community in general are accused of being slow to act, ineffective and lacking the political will to halt the genocide (Eriksson et al., 1996). The role of both Belgium, and, more particularly, France in what happened was also strongly criticised. Both states were accused of intelligence failures despite having good intelligence gathering abilities in Rwanda and for evacuating their own citizens but not the threatened Tutsi people. France was accused of continuing to sell arms to, and support, a regime known to have committed serious human rights violations. Although, in June, France launched a unilateral intervention, Operation Turquoise, which saved some lives, it was viewed as problematic as it did not disarm or apprehend genocide perpetrators. Belgium was criticised for succumbing to political pressure following Belgian fatalities (ten peacekeepers were brutally murdered) to withdraw from the existing UN peacekeeping operation UNAMIR, thus weakening it even as the killings were under way (Eriksson et al., 1996). While Belgium formally apologised in 2000 to Rwanda for its mistakes, the extent of French complicity in the genocide remains fiercely disputed (Louw-Vaudran, 2014).

In general, Europeans judge the EU and its member states harshly for failures in dealing with the violent break-up of the former Yugoslavia, and particularly over the war in Bosnia. Srebrenica is seen as one of the worst examples. In 1995, a Dutch battalion, known as

Dutchbat, was part of the UN Bosnian peacekeeping mission UNPROFOR, and was tasked with safeguarding the Muslim enclave and UN designated safe zone of Srebrenica. In July 1995, Bosnian Serb forces overran the area. Dutchbat was poorly equipped and was operating under a UN mandate that forbade them from actively defending the enclave unless they were directly attacked. Their requests for NATO air support were ignored. Bosnian Serb forces forcibly deported the Bosnian Muslims in a policy of ethnic cleansing, and approximately 8,000 men and boys were separated from their families and then systematically killed. A 2002 report blamed the Dutch authorities and the UN for sending ill-equipped troops without a strong enough mandate to prevent the massacre, and led to the resignation of the then prime minister, Wim Kok, and his cabinet. Following a series of court judgements and appeals, in 2013 the Dutch Supreme Court found the Netherlands liable for the deaths, and, in 2014, a Dutch civil court ordered the Netherlands to compensate the families of the men Dutchbat handed over to Bosnian Serb forces and who were later killed. Dutchbat and Srebrenica remains a widely debated and controversial topic in the Netherlands (van de Bildt, 2015).

The experience of failing to prevent mass killing began to colour European opinions about military interventions. In complete contrast to what happened during the Bosnian War, when Serbia began to ethnically cleanse Kosovar Albanians from the province of Kosovo between March and June 1999, following the collapse of peace talks, NATO launched air strikes against Serbia. It is estimated that approximately 500 civilians and a similar number of Serbian military were killed in the NATO air strikes. The NATO intervention was controversial, as it was not sanctioned by the UN Security Council, but the Independent International Commission on Kosovo (2000) deemed it illegal but justified. A military intervention in Sierra Leone by the UK in 2000 was also widely seen as being the decisive step that brought a decade-long civil war to an end with a peace settlement that has lasted (Williams, 2001). Initially deployed to evacuate foreign citizens, the British military forces began to assist struggling UN peacekeepers and to train the Sierra Leonean army. Their expanded mandate, coupled with economic pressure on the rebels, seems to have made a decisive difference in ending the civil war.

What did shift European opinions away from the norm of non-intervention that had flourished globally until the late 1980s? In part, experiences of particular missions, as outlined above, were responsible. Kaldor (2007) argues that a major growth in civil society activism on human rights is also an important factor. Throughout the 1990s, a vibrant civil society drew attention to human rights abuses during what Kaldor dubs 'new wars', campaigned against the use of certain types of weapons, seen as being particularly inhumane and, in short, actively promoted humanitarianism and, with it, human security. The Bosnian war in particular evoked high levels of concern, particularly during the siege of Sarajevo – Yugoslavia pre-war had been a popular summer holiday destination and the destruction of familiar sites perhaps gave a sense of greater involvement for Europeans. Kaldor (2007) also points to the role played by individuals such as Bernard Kouchner, the co-founder of Médecins Sans Frontières, in advocating humanitarian intervention. Similarly, popular left-leaning politicians of the late 1990s–early 2000s, such as Germany's Joschka Fischer, Britain's Tony Blair and Sweden's Anna Lindh became strong advocates of humanitarian intervention. Blair's

New Labour government, for example, actively espoused this as part of their ethical foreign policy. As Glasius and Kaldor (2005) point out, the interventions of the late 1990s–early 2000s also enjoyed high levels of public support.

In the late 1990s–early 2000s, many of the issues on the human security agenda, such as the establishment of an International Criminal Court (ICC), the Ottawa process that led to the convention banning the use of anti-personnel landmines, UN action on small arms and light weapons, or the Kyoto Protocol on climate change, were a good fit for both the foreign policies of European states and the concerns of their citizens. In particular, as Glasius and Kaldor (2005) argued, activism on these topics was a popular way of differentiating European foreign and security policies from the aggressive unilateralism of the USA's security policy following the 9/11 terrorist attacks. But, for the European Union in particular, the human security agenda had another potential purpose; it offered the opportunity to give sense and purpose to its fledgling security agenda. The next section charts the EU's engagement with human security.

Human security and the EU: institutional adoption?

At first sight, the EU could be viewed as an enthusiastic adopter of the human security agenda (Martin and Owen, 2010). The language of human security is certainly used across the EU's external relations' portfolios, but its use in the 2016 EU Global Strategy was decidedly limited, when compared to other key EU concepts (four mentions of human security compared to 34 for resilience), which suggests that it has not been thoroughly internalised. More importantly, human security has not come to act as a strategic narrative, which, in the 2000s, human security advocates hoped would be the outcome of their engagement. This section first looks at why there was a policy gap that human security might have filled, then it considers the role of EU human security advocates and the degree to which they were successful.

In 1999, the EU decided to develop what was initially the European Security and Defence Policy (ESDP) and subsequently became the CSDP. Sparked by the Franco–British Saint Malo Agreement, which called for this development, for the UK and France it was obvious that European states, either within NATO (UK preference) or the EU (French preference), needed to invest more in defence and improve their military capabilities (see Chapter 6). Although other EU states were less interested in possessing military power for its own sake, the need for the USA to intervene first in Bosnia and then in Kosovo, as the EU proved unable, had been humiliating, and the ESDP plans were popular. Initially, they were designed around what would have been useful in the former Yugoslavia, and indeed the first missions were predominantly Balkan-based peacekeeping and security sector reform missions. But it soon became clear that there needed to be more of a narrative about the purpose of the CSDP, not least to quell fears that France was using the CSDP to mask its neo-imperialist interventions in Africa. To quote Eric Remacle (2008, p. 17),

> after having used and abused all possible post-modern discourses about 'civilian power Europe' and its 'sui generis nature' to justify why there was no military dimension to the EU for decades, there was now a need to justify why the EU needed one.

Finding a coherent narrative for the CSDP was quite challenging. The member states disagreed on when and where the EU might use military force, and had highly divergent levels of both military capabilities and experience of the use of force. Unlike national defence policies, the CSDP concentrated on crisis management capabilities – tacitly at least, there was an acceptance that the defence element would be left to NATO. This crisis management focus, along with the EU's claim that its added value as a security actor was its ability to draw on not just military but development, economic and civilian crisis management resources, meant that the EU could have adopted human security as an overarching security narrative. There were signs throughout the 2000s that this was indeed a possibility. As Haine (2011) pointed out, human security's emphasis on the civilian component of crisis management was attractive to EU figures for three reasons. First, it would clearly differentiate between the EU and US as security actors at a time when the Iraq invasion was turning into a disaster. Second, it offered a role for small EU states, who lacked meaningful military capabilities. Third, it offered a risk-averse EU a way of framing missions that was unlikely to result in casualties.

Human security entered the EU discourse on security largely because of the advocacy of some key individuals. Both Christou (2014) and Remacle (2008) point to the roles played by Javier Solana and Benita Ferrero-Waldner. Solana had served as NATO Secretary-General before taking up the role of EU High Representative for the Common Foreign and Security Policy, and had long advocated the human security approach. Ferrero-Waldner, who was then the Commissioner for External Relations and the European Neighbourhood policy, was from Austria, which, along with Greece, Ireland, the Netherlands, and Slovenia, had become a member of the Human Security Network in the late 1990s. Ferrero-Waldner was Austrian foreign minister between 1999 and 2004 and had moved the country's foreign policy quite considerably from its traditional neutrality to a more assertive and interventionist stance on international affairs. Solana and Ferrero-Waldner played an important role in making human security visible on the EU scene, however there is some doubt about how successful this has really been.

Solana was active in his efforts to find a purpose for the CSDP by beginning a dialogue with human security advocates from NGOs and academia. After all, the EU's policies, as displayed in Solana's 2003 European Security Strategy, were not dissimilar to the policies espoused by Canada, Norway or Japan, all of which overtly used the concept of human security. In 2003, he commissioned a report from a group of scholars led by Mary Kaldor (London School of Economics) called the Study Group on Europe's Security Capabilities on human security and the EU (Glasius and Kaldor, 2005). As Christou (2014) points out, the report and its follow-up, the Madrid report, did lay out a vision for how human security could act as a strategic narrative for EU security policy in practice. They argued that there are moral, legal and enlightened self-interest cases for the EU to adopt a doctrine of human security, which they suggested should rest on the following seven principles:

1. The primacy of human rights
2. Clear political authority
3. Multilateralism

4. Bottom-up approach
5. Regional Focus
6. Use of legal instruments
7. Appropriate use of force.

(Glasius and Kaldor, 2005, pp. 72–78)

Morally, they point to the need to accept human rights as a universal not just a European norm, that the EU is legally bound to promote human rights worldwide, and that fixing failed states is in the EU's long-term security interests. Their interest was in making the concept workable, so while endorsing the broad definition of human security the Barcelona Report focused more narrowly on responding to the depth of threat and the needs of people in severe insecurity (Christou, 2014). While warmly received in some quarters, the report was criticised for both being a cloak for EU neo-imperialism and for promoting a concept that was both soft and highly ambitious.

The follow-up report in 2007, the Madrid Report offered a chance to respond to these criticisms and to lay out what added value human security had and what a mission would look like on the ground. Arguably the Barcelona Report (A Human Security Doctrine for Europe) from 2004 and its follow up, the 2007 Madrid Report (A European Way of Security) and the ongoing work of the Human Security Study Group have served to embed human security in EU security thinking (Martin and Owen, 2010). Practical proposals, however, like the formation of a 15,000 strong human security response force – 5,000 of which would be on permanent stand-by – did not win the necessary institutional support for adoption.

Partly, this was because the two main internal advocates, Ferrero-Waldner and Solana, did not really share the same vision of human security. Ferrero-Waldner's advocacy role was largely about consistently using the language of human security but she espoused a broad definition. As the EU's external interests and involvement expanded during her tenure, she used her role to reinforce the connections between security, development, environmental concerns, counter-terrorism and individual human rights (Remacle, 2008). However, while there was no doubt of her personal commitment, after she left office, there is little evidence that human security was used consistently by the EU external policy-making mainstream (Christou, 2014). Rather, it was one concept among many, and the EU has a preference for using those that it has internally developed.

Moreover, within the CSDP, the need to find a way for states uncomfortable with the military dimension to contribute had already led to a strong emphasis on developing civilian crisis management capabilities (Remacle, 2008). The language of holistic security, which evolved into the twin tracks of effective multilateralism and the comprehensive approach, acted as a catch-all solution, which while not particularly strategic, already served to differentiate the EU's security policy from the unilateralism and aggressive approach to security shown by the US post 9/11 and keep the EU states with very different traditions and interests involved in the CSDP (see Chapter 6). They are not that dissimilar to what was proposed in the Barcelona and Madrid reports. One critic of the reports' call, Janne Haaland Matlary (2008) asked the pertinent question of whether the adoption of a human security doctrine would change anything fundamentally about the CSDP. She suggested that much of what is proposed can already be found in existing EU documents and practices and that simply calling it human security would change nothing.

Solana meanwhile had a narrower definition of human security and so was a tentative advocate of the Barcelona and Madrid Reports. He is known to have been uncomfortable by some of the recommendations such as the insistence on civilian leadership of all external engagements (Christou, 2014). There were also substantial concerns from member states about how useful human security could be as a strategic narrative for the CSDP. Critics like Matlary (2008), for instance, considered the assertion in the Madrid report that military force could be used in an entirely new and harmless way to be unrealistic. Pointing out that military interventions are unlikely to be carried out solely for human security purposes, she argued that there were dangers of being unable to live up to the human security rhetoric. While Solana was supportive of a human security agenda, it seems in practice he came to think that narrower concepts like R2P were of greater utility (Christou, 2014).

It is undeniable that throughout the 2000s there was considerable EU interest in human security, which peaked in the mid-2000s. Ultimately though, it did not come to be a guiding strategic narrative for the CSDP. The differing views of its main internal advocates and the similarity of its key ideas to internally developed ideas played a role in this but it was probably the growing operational experience of the EU and the worsening security situation globally and in the EU's neighbourhood that stymied EU interest in human security as a strategic narrative. The following section will address these points.

Disillusionment sets in: human security in a less secure Europe

The initial hope that the EU might be able to use human security as a strategic narrative informing its engagement as a security actor was short-lived. The War on Terror led to a changing agenda on development and security. As Duffield (2006) argued, whereas in the initial formulations of human security, development and security were seen as different but equal, the War on Terror both deepened the interconnections for policy makers between security and development, but also focused attention on particular regions and states considered to pose a threat to homeland security. While at first this shift was most noticeable in US policy, European states and the EU were not immune. This shift also came at a time when the utility of military interventions was being questioned by the general public and it is this issue that the section will address first.

During the 1990s, a substantive peace-building agenda had emerged underpinned by liberal internationalist values such as democracy, the free market and the liberal state. Post-conflict societies were expected to accept these externally designed models and evolve into liberal democracies. These practices became closely associated with the practical implementation of human security and particularly R2P doctrine. As Newman (2011) points out, these agendas often failed to pay sufficient attention to everyday, basic human needs and were criticised both by scholars and local stakeholders. While these practices were criticised in both

Bosnia and Kosovo for example, their very public failure following the two major Western military interventions of the 2000s, Iraq and Afghanistan, has been harshly judged by public opinion. In both cases the motives for intervention were mixed and questionable, and have served to discredit both military intervention and the belief that failed states can be rescued.

For some, the liberal internationalist paradigm of intervention has been overridden by the preventive human security practices of resilience. The EU Human Security Study Group's 2016 Berlin Report, for example, speaks of a second generation of human security, while Chandler (2012) argues that the reason human security is less often used as a concept is because it is so widely accepted. He sees resilience as being differentiated from liberal internationalism thus:

> The resilience paradigm clearly puts the agency of those most in need of assistance at the centre, stressing a programme of empowerment and capacity-building, whereas the liberal internationalist paradigm puts the emphasis upon the agency of external interveners, acting post hoc to protect or secure the victims of state-led or state-condoned abuses.
> (Chandler, 2012, p. 216)

He argues that the NATO-led coalition's bombing of Libya was clearly different to that of the Kosovan campaign, in that rather than being about the responsibility to protect, it was about giving the Libyan rebels agency to secure themselves (Chandler, 2012, pp. 220–221). Although, given that post-Ghadafi Libya is neither secure nor peaceful, this approach appears to have failed as badly. Given the multiple references to resilience in the 2016 EU Global Strategy, might this mean that the EU is more committed to human security than it seemed?

The picture is in fact very mixed, at least as far as the CSDP domain is concerned. First, it is necessary to admit that the recent CSDP record has not been successful. Haine (2011) argues that the 2008 EUFOR Chad mission was really the last idealistic human security type of military operation. He judges it was ineffective, made unnecessarily risky by the insistence on neutrality and forced the main contributor, France, to act against its own national interests. He compares EUFOR Chad unfavourably with the anti-piracy Atalanta mission that was interests-driven and both better supported and more successful. Haine (2011) echoes Matlary's (2008) judgement that the use of military force on purely idealistic grounds can go very wrong. Indeed, the lesson the major European military powers appear to have taken is not to carry out military peace enforcement operations through the EU. Recent European major crisis interventions have been unilateral (France), through coalitions of the willing (Syria) or through NATO (Libya).

Second, the costs and difficulties of a human security approach to CSDP have become very evident in the EU's own neighbourhood. How can you justify choosing to intervene in some conflicts but not others? The EU's inability to find consensus over how best to intervene in Libya has now been outdone by the international community's collective failings in Syria. Previous red lines like the use of chemical weapons against civilians have been crossed. But there is also a genuine dilemma – in conflicts spreading across multiple states with many different armed groupings, how even if couched in Chandler's (2012) language of resilience, do you choose which group to give agency to secure themselves through the provision of military assistance?

Third, the EU's own security situation has markedly worsened in the last five years on two different fronts, both of which work against the mainstreaming of a human security approach to its external action. On the one hand, there is a large-scale refugee crisis stemming from the conflicts in the Middle East and North Africa, to which despite the efforts of the EU institutions, there has yet to be a unified humanitarian response from the member states (with some praiseworthy exceptions). Major terrorist attacks in France and Belgium have further raised tensions amid fears that terrorists are among the refugees (although almost all the terror attacks in Europe carried out in the name of Islamic State have thus far been by home-grown extremists). This has pushed the EU into trying to agree deals with third states to prevent the refugees reaching Europe. This is hardly a human security approach. On the other hand, the conflict in Ukraine and Russia's annexation of Crimea have reignited the Cold War security agenda. Once more the language is about inter-state conflict, deterrence and territorial defence. Again, while NATO rather than the EU might be the main actor, the member states, especially those forced to implement austerity measures, have other calls on their defence spending, and so are less likely to be able to contribute to human security type interventions. In short, even if the EU wanted to use human security, however defined, as its strategic narrative, the current situation is likely to work against a practical implementation.

Conclusion

This chapter has charted the development of the human security concept and its reception both by European states and by the EU. In many ways, the end of the Cold War opened up the possibilities of broadening and deepening both academic and practitioner understandings of security. Human security is one such concept. In its initial iterations, as Duffield (2006) put it, development and security were treated as equal but different. It seems at present that the narrower security-focused definition may have passed its period of popularity, damaged by both ill-judged military interventions and by the intractability of some conflicts. The so-called second generation using the broader definition and reworking the concept as resilience may have greater success.

The extent to which human security has been internalised as an EU norm is contested. This is not an unusual finding when trying to assess the extent to which an external concept has had purchase. It is indisputable that the Human Security Study Group's reports have enjoyed unusual degrees of institutional interest, but after Solana and Ferrero-Waldner left their roles, similar powerful internal advocates have not emerged. As Pace states when discussing the EU's levels of internalisation of a similar Normative Power Europe, 'the extent to which NPEU constructions come from EU agents or from academics operating independently outside the EU – which then could possibly influence the way EU agents see themselves – is not crystal clear' (Pace, 2007, p. 1050). Nor it is a given that the use of a term in official documentation means that the authors understand it in the same way as academics. What is clear though is that human security is not currently acting as a strategic narrative for the CSDP, and given the rising insecurity in and around the EU, it is unlikely to do so in the near future.

Further reading

International Commission on Intervention and State Sovereignty (2001), *The Responsibility to Protect: Report of the International Commission on Intervention and State Sovereignty*. Ottawa: International Development Research Centre.

Kaldor, Mary, Martin, Mary, and Selchow, Sabine (2007), 'Human Security: A New Strategic Narrative for Europe', *International Affairs*, 83 (2), 273–288.

Martin, Mary, and Owen, Taylor (eds) (2013), *Routledge Handbook of Human Security*. London: Routledge.

Paris, Roland (2001), 'Human Security - Paradigm Shift or Hot Air?', *International Security*, 26 (2), 87–102.

Weblinks

International Coalition For The Responsibility To Protect: http://responsibilitytoprotect.org/
United Nations Development Programme Human Development Reports: http://hdr.undp.org/
United Nations Trust Fund for Human Security: www.un.org/humansecurity/

References

Alkire, Sabina (2004), 'A Vital Core that Must be Treated with the Same Gravitas as Traditional Security Threats', *Security Dialogue*, 35 (3), 359–360.

Buzan, Barry, Waever, Ole, and de Wilde, Jaap (1998), *Security: A New Framework for Analysis*. Boulder, CO: Lynne Rienner.

Chandler, David (2012), 'Resilience and Human Security: The Post-Interventionist Paradigm', *Security Dialogue*, 43 (3), 213–229.

Christou, George (2014), 'The European Union's Human Security Discourse: Where Are We Now?', *European Security*, 23 (3), 364–381.

Duffield, Mark (2006), 'Human Security: Linking Development and Security in an Age of Terror', in Stephan Klingebiel (ed), *New Interfaces Between Security and Development*. Bonn: German Development Institute, pp. 11–38.

Duffield, Mark, and Waddell, Nicholas (2006), 'Securing Humans in a Dangerous World', *International Politics*, 43 (1), 1–23.

Eriksson, John, with Adelman, Howard, Borton, John, Christensen, Hanne, Kumar, Krishna, Suhrke, Astri, Tardif–Douglin, David, Villumstad, Stein, and Wohlgemuth, Lennart (1996), *The International Response to Conflict and Genocide: Lessons from the Rwanda Experience, Synthesis Report*. Copenhagen: Steering Committee for the Joint Evaluation of Emergency assistance to Rwanda. Available at: www.oecd.org/derec/norway/50189495.pdf (accessed: 23 October 2018).

Fukuda-Parr, Sakiko, and Messineo, Carol (2012), 'Human Security', in Graham Brown and Arnim Langer (eds), *Elgar Handbook of Civil War and Fragile States*. Cheltenham: Edward Elgar, pp. 21–38.

Glasius, Marlies, and Kaldor, Mary (2005), 'Individuals First: A Human Security Strategy for the European Union', *Internationale Politik und Gesellschaft*, 2005 (1), 62–84.

Haine, Jean Yves (2011), 'The Failure of a European Strategic Culture – EUFOR CHAD: The Last of Its Kind?', *Contemporary Security Policy*, 32 (3), 582–603.

Human Security Centre, University of British Columbia (2005), *Human Security Report 2005: War and Peace in the 21st Century*. Oxford: Oxford University Press.

Independent International Commission on Kosovo (2000), *The Kosovo Report: Conflict, International Response, Lessons Learned*. Oxford: Oxford University Press.

International Commission on Intervention and State Sovereignty (2001), *The Responsibility to Protect: Report of the International Commission on Intervention and State Sovereignty*. Ottawa: International Development Research Centre.

Kaldor, Mary (2007), *Human Security*. Cambridge: Polity Press.

Kerr, Pauline (2007), 'Human Security', in Alan Collins (ed), *Contemporary Security Studies*. Oxford: Oxford University Press, pp. 91–108.

Louw-Vaudran, Liesl (2014), 'Rwanda and France: The Blame-Game Continues', *ISS Today*, 11 April. Available at: www.issafrica.org/iss-today/rwanda-and-france-the-blame-game-continues (accessed: 23 October 2018).

Mack, Andrew (2004), 'A Signifier of Shared Values', *Security Dialogue*, 35 (3), 366–367.

Martin, Mary, and Owen, Taylor (2010), 'The Second Generation of Human Security: Lessons from the UN and EU Experience', *International Affairs*, 86 (1), 211–224.

Matlary, Janne Haaland (2008), 'Much Ado About Little: The EU and Human Security', *International Affairs*, 84 (1), 131–143.

Newman, Edward (2011), 'A Human Security Peace-Building Agenda', *Third World Quarterly*, 32 (10), 1737–1756.

Pace, Michelle (2007), 'The Construction of EU Normative Power', *Journal of Common Market Studies*, 45 (5), 1041–1064.

Paris, Roland (2001), 'Human Security: Paradigm Shift or Hot Air?', *International Security*, 26 (2), 87–102.

Remacle, Eric (2008), 'Approaches to Human Security: Japan, Canada and Europe in Comparative Perspective', *Journal of Social Science*, 66, 5–34.

Suhrke, Astri (1999), 'Human Security and the Interests of States', *Security Dialogue*, 30 (3), 265–276.

Thakur, Ramesh, and Newman, Edward (2004), 'Introduction: Non-Traditional Security in Asia', in Ramesh Thakur and Edward Newman (eds), *Broadening Asia's Security Discourse and Agenda: Political, Social and Environmental Perspectives*. Tokyo: United Nations University Press, pp. 1–16.

Thomas, Caroline (2001), 'Global Governance, Development and Human Security: Exploring the Links', *Third World Quarterly*, 22 (2), 159–175.

United Nations Development Programme (1993), *Human Development Report 1993: People's Participation*. Oxford: Oxford University Press.

United Nations Development Programme (1994), *Human Development Report 1994*. Oxford: Oxford University Press.

United Nations General Assembly (2012), 'Resolution Adopted by the General Assembly on 10 September 2012', A/RES/66/290: Follow-up to Paragraph 143 on Human Security of the 2005 World Summit Outcome. Available at: www.un.org/en/ga/search/view_doc.asp?symbol=%20A/RES/66/290 (accessed: 23 October 2018).

Van de Bildt, Joyce (2015), 'Srebrenica: A Dutch National Trauma', *Peace, Conflict & Development*, 21, 115–145.

Williams, Paul (2001), 'Fighting for Freetown: British Military Intervention in Sierra Leone', *Contemporary Security Policy*, 22 (3), 140–168.

Gendering European security

9

Katharine A. M. Wright

Introduction

Feminist scholars have proved that gender is of central importance to European security both in terms of its conceptualisation and practice. This chapter sheds light on the gendered structures and practices of European security. The first question to ask is why is a feminist perspective necessary and what does it add to our understanding of European security? To do so, the chapter introduces students to feminist conceptions of European security through the lens of Feminist Security Studies. This means situating Feminist Security Studies in wider debates on the shape and scope of Security Studies as a project and drawing attention both to the continued silences inherent within wider disciplinary conceptions of security and the value of feminist approaches in exposing the way in which gendered hierarchies are upheld and reified. In so doing, it is possible to expose why gender remains marginal to mainstream accounts of European security.

In addition to considering the place of gender in theorising European security, it is also necessary to consider its role in practice, in terms of how European security institutions are gendered, but also in respect to contemporary developments in gender and security and the place of a key global gender norm and Europe's role in shaping it. Here we discuss the Women, Peace and Security (WPS) agenda embodied in UN Security Council Resolution 1325 and its seven follow-up resolutions. This Resolution was intended to challenge the marginalisation of gender (specifically women) from international security. In particular, the chapter focuses on the passage of WPS through the Security Council to help explain some of the contradictions inherent within the agenda. This analysis also highlights the role of key actors, both UN member states and civil society groups, who continue to shape its implementation at a global, national, local and European level. Only with this understanding is it possible to establish the ways in which it has shaped the value placed on the agenda by European actors, but also how Europe has become a key site for ascribing meaning to WPS.

Finally, the case studies of the EU and NATO as regional security actors provide a point for comparison on the gendered composition of two key European security institutions. This highlights the ways in which gender underpins European security structures and practice as far more than just a peripheral concern. Specifically, in so doing the chapter explores the role of both structures and practices in gendering European security. These institutions also provide useful sites for analysing the integration of WPS into European level security. Europe has been at the forefront of engagement with the WPS agenda, but as this Chapter demonstrates WPS has been used to support instrumental gains rather than to transform the gendered structures and practices of European security. Examining how the EU and NATO are gendered as security actors, helps explain why WPS has been understood this way, rather than as a means to 're-gender' European security institutions to ensure better gender representation in terms of both personnel and within policy.

A Feminist Security Studies perspective

Feminist scholars have made important contributions to our understanding of security. This has, more recently, mirrored wider developments in the practice of security which has also begun to take gender seriously since the adoption of UN Security Council Resolution (UNSCR) 1325 on WPS in 2000. Yet, critical feminist insights continue to remain on the margins of Security Studies. Both mainstream/traditional and critical scholarship on security remains, on the whole, gender blind, with the decades of feminist theorising of issues of security largely ignored (Wibben, 2010, p. 7). Yet, somewhat paradoxically, while mainstream/traditional scholars are resistant to feminist approaches, they are rarely well informed about them (Peterson, 2004, p. 43). In part, and as a result, approaches to European security that specifically take gender seriously as a point of analysis (rather than just a variable) have been few and far between. In order to understand why this might be and the implications of this marginalisation, it is necessary to consider the nature of the feminist challenge to the study and practice of security.

Feminist approaches to security are nothing new. For example, the feminist challenge to the study of war has been ongoing for decades and has its roots in peace research in the 1960s. Here, feminists began to incorporate an explicit focus on power into their analysis (Wibben, 2010, p. 4). In the late 1980s and early 1990s, feminists began to frame their analysis in terms of 'security' and specifically as a challenge to the mainstream/traditional state-centred conception of security (Wibben, 2010, p. 4). This provided a critique of military force as the primary means of securing the core values of the state: sovereignty and territory. In doing so, feminist scholars contend that security defined purely in militarist terms presents a false image of reality (Hudson, 2005, p. 164). Feminist security scholars seek not only to challenge the state centric focus of security, but to reclaim it from its co-option within a militarist framework (Basu, 2013, p. 456). This critique also leads to the claim that the focus of many Security Studies' scholars on the state as the primary actor in global politics creates the state as such, reifying a particular form of knowledge. This has led feminist scholars to study the margins of international politics, looking to the spaces and people absent from mainstream analysis. In identifying these silences, they are concerned not just with exposing how international politics functions, but in challenging the existing system, ultimately with the aim of provoking transformative change to both the study and practice of international politics. One of the central contributions of critical Feminist Security Studies has been to demonstrate that the personal is not only political but international (Enloe, 1989, p. 195). This notion underpins feminist approaches to international relations and builds on the second wave feminist assertion that the personal is political.[1] This has meant shedding light on 'the complex interrelationship of local, national and global scales implicated in the study of security concerns' (Shepherd, 2013, p. 17). It also includes widening the definition of security to include individual and group security, while arguing that security is about all forms of violence, including structural violence, for example, whereby those on the margins of the international system have a shorter life expectancy because capitalism creates an uneven distribution of resources (Tickner, 1992, p. 22).

Much feminist work on security draws across disciplines, including, but not limited to, history, sociology and peace studies, with the multidisciplinary nature of feminist work one of its core strengths. Feminist Security Studies' scholars may take different approaches to their analysis (for example, post-structural, constructivist, normative) but are united in viewing international relations through 'gender lenses' and seek not only to explain, but to transform and disrupt. They view the study and practice of security as co-constitutive. For example, feminist scholars have critiqued the authoritative discourse of mainstream/traditional approaches to security as 'cool, objective, scientific, and overwhelmingly male', drawing attention to how this has allowed scholars (and policy makers) to separate themselves from the reality of what their discussions concern (Elshtain, 1987, p. 245). Carol Cohn's (1987, p. 688) seminal work has also exposed how language and social practice among defence intellectuals is gendered, serving to separate those making life and death decisions from the real lives impacted by them. These findings underpin the necessity for feminist scholars to ask questions about 'how and why masculinist institutions at the heart of this exercise of power function' (Cohn, 2011, p. 585). This includes those operating within European security.

Feminist Security Studies' scholars have made important inroads in both exposing and challenging the silences within mainstream approaches' explanations of international security. As a result, feminist insights make a valuable contribution to the study and our understanding of security. Yet, within European security scholarship specifically, gender approaches have remained marginalised. This poses the question, what is special about the study of European security? In part, the answer lies in broader silences within feminist approaches to security that have sought to challenge the mainstream preoccupation with states and international organisations. It also speaks to what we consider European security. In this chapter, the focus is on European security institutions, but feminist scholarship has been concerned with European security more broadly defined at the individual and group level, and beyond the EU and NATO (see, for example, Kronsell and Svedberg, 2012). We also need to consider the place of feminist scholarship within the wider context of European Studies and in particular on the EU. Feminist accounts are by no means absent from the study of the EU.

In fact, they have provided important insights into the gendered nature of EU policies and critiqued dominant theories of integration. Yet, little feminist work has achieved substantial traction within EU Studies. In part, this can be attributed to the limited systematic engagement by feminist scholars (with the notable exception of Abels and MacRae, 2016; Kronsell, 2016) with the gendered nature of the EU integration project itself (Guerrina et al., 2018b). The result is that, until recently, there was little feminist scholarship concerning 'high politics' issues within the EU, including security and defence. Feminist scholars are, therefore, playing catch-up in theorising European security institutions.

Women, Peace and Security in Europe: opportunities and pitfalls

European security does not operate in a bubble. Global gender norms shape security and defence policy at both national and regional levels. A case in point here is the WPS agenda. This has provided a key lobbying tool for civil society actors across Europe to hold governments (and the EU, NATO and OSCE) to account for their record on integrating gender concerns into external relations. It is this agenda, and European engagement with it, which this chapter turns to examine.

On All Hallows Eve 2000, the UN Security Council passed Resolution 1325 (United Nations Security Council, 2000). This Resolution encapsulated the WPS agenda. The date led some to question whether this Resolution was a 'trick' or a 'treat' (Tryggestad, 2009). The Resolution acknowledges both the disproportionate impact of conflict on women, and their crucial role in resolving it. The intention was to transform international security through challenging its gendered construction. Yet, in so doing, it painted women as both victims and agents of change, roles that appear difficult for any individual to reconcile (Shepherd, 2011, p. 510). Ultimately, the Resolution was the result of the necessary compromises resulting from its passage through the Security Council. Indeed, it was the first time the UN Security Council had formally discussed gender.

The Resolution was also groundbreaking because of the role of feminist civil society in realising its adoption. They worked through the NGO Working Group on Women, Peace and Security, an umbrella grouping bringing together a number of NGOs interested in WPS, to lobby for, draft and redraft the final Resolution (Hill, Aboitiz, and Poehlman-Doumbouya, 2009, pp. 1258–1260). Their intention was not to 'make war safe for women'. Rather, it was to gain an acknowledgement that war has a different and disproportionate impact on women and also that women have an important role in conflict prevention and resolution (Cook, 2009, p. 126). The efforts of women positioned in civil society at the local and international level, within member states, as academics and at the UN were critical to the realisation of the Resolution and were unprecedented at the Security Council. This led to the Resolution being claimed as a 'feminist achievement' (Cockburn, 2011).

The adoption of the Resolution was far from a foregone conclusion in 2000. The role of 'a lucky coincidence' of supportive permanent and non-permanent Security Council members was also key (Otto, 2010, p. 100). These included Namibia, Bangladesh, Jamaica, Canada, the Netherlands, and the UK. In addition to lobbying for the Resolution, these states led a series of initiatives that culminated in UNSCR 1325. Namibia initiated the open debate on WPS preceding the Resolution, building on the findings of a workshop it had hosted on gender mainstreaming in peace operations, and Bangladesh laid some of the groundwork during its presidency of the Security Council by releasing the first ever statement to mark International Women's Day (Tryggestad, 2009, p. 547). Canada also provided support, in particular through launching the 'Friends of 1325' initiative, bringing together like-minded states to support and monitor the implementation of WPS going forward and working closely with the NGO Working Group on WPS (Hill, 2005, p. 4; Tryggestad, 2009, p. 547). The UK, as a permanent member, became the 'penholder' for WPS and has taken the lead in drafting Security Council decisions on this theme going forward (Green, 2016, p. 8).

The actors involved in championing the Resolution had to ensure its adoption by the Security Council and compromises were necessary. Among the NGO Working Group, the majority of whose members did not define themselves as 'feminist' or 'anti-war', there was also a lack of consensus on the extent to which the Resolution should challenge existing practices (Cohn, 2011, p. 134). As a result, some of the groups making up the NGO Working Group viewed discussion of the arms trade or militarism as off limits because they found the subject 'too political' (Cohn, 2011, p. 134). This contributes to explaining the noticeable absence from UNSCR 1325 of the Security Council's own responsibilities under the UN Charter to establish arms regulations systems (Otto, 2004, p. 12). A key member, the Women's International League for Peace and Freedom (WILPF), regretted the absence of any mention of ending war itself, one of the founding principles of the UN and the Security Council's brief (Cockburn, 2007, p. 147). Certainly, there continues to be a contradiction between the Security Council, with an implicit support for a militarised interstate system, and a normative Resolution on women and armed conflict, precisely because of the challenges to women's security resulting from the current setup of the international arena (Basu, 2010, p. 289).

The passage of UNSCR 1325 through the Security Council also removed some of the political and radical feminist understandings of gender and reproduced them in a non-challenging way, palatable for a conservative institution. One prime example of this is the language within the Resolution that consistently associates 'gender' with 'women', making 34 references to women and none to men. The Resolution's calls for gender mainstreaming are, therefore, read as only applicable to the concerns of women. This leaves gender transformed into a 'safe idea' for policy makers, leaving behind its radical potential to produce change (Puechguirbal, 2010, p. 184). The language of the Resolution is also relatively weak compared to other Security Council Resolutions, for example, the inclusion of 'urges', 'encourages' and 'calls', rather than stronger language demanding action from states (Tryggestad, 2009, p. 544).

Another key area of contention is the framing of women as both victims and agents of change within UNSCR 1325. On the one hand, the Resolution presents women as victims of conflict, identifying the 'particular' and 'special needs' of women in conflict situations, making reference to the protection of women five times. In contrast, it also frames women as agents, 'stressing the importance of their equal participation and full involvement in all efforts for the maintenance and promotion of peace and security' (United Nations Security

Council, 2000). For some, including Cohn et al. (2004, p. 139), there is no contradiction here and it is possible to acknowledge both the disproportionate impact of war on women while still 'making women's agency vibrantly visible'. For others, the language of the Resolution has created a victim–agent dichotomy, in particular missing an opportunity to challenge myths that sustain beliefs about women's helplessness in the face of sexual violence by also acknowledging their capacity to be agents of change (Otto, 2010, p. 117).

Realising the Women, Peace and Security agenda beyond UNSCR 1325

After an initially slow engagement with the agenda by the international community and the Security Council, the UN Secretary General called for states to produce National Action Plans (NAPs) for its implementation. The intention was to provide a means to hold states to account in their efforts to implement WPS. European states, specifically Denmark and the UK, were at the forefront of producing NAPs and Europe remains at the vanguard of formal engagement with the agenda. Indeed, Europe, and the Global North more broadly, is often assumed to lead engagement with WPS as the 'conceptual, material and (not least) institutional home of the resolutions' (Basu, 2016, p. 362). Engagement by IOs and states in Europe has been criticised for being outward facing and resembling an 'imperialist' project (Pratt, 2013, p. 774). However, while these claims have validity, they do not exclude the agency of the Global South in contributing to, and shaping, the WPS agenda more broadly – as has been evidenced above with their role in the adoption of UNSCR 1325. We should, therefore, understand the Global South as far from *just* a passive recipient of WPS interventions from the Global North but, rather, constitutive of the WPS agenda at both the local and intergovernmental levels (Basu, 2016, p. 362). So, while our focus in this chapter is on European engagement with WPS, it is important that WPS should not be understood as *solely* a European project.

A few years after states began to produce NAPs, work began in the Security Council to broaden and widen the WPS agenda. While UNSCR 1325 focused primarily on women's participation (WP) and protection, a focus began to emerge on sexual and gender based violence (SGBV) in conflict. The seven resulting WPS resolutions (see Table 9.1) at once serve to provide a more nuanced understanding of WPS, while also widening the agenda.

Table 9.1   UN Security Council Resolutions on Women, Peace and Security

Resolution	1325	1820	1888	1880	1960	2106	2122	2242
Year	2000	2008	2009	2009	2010	2013	2013	2015
Focus	WP	SGBV	WP	SGBV	SGBV	SGBV	WP	WP & CVE
Proposer	Namibia	USA	USA	Vietnam	USA	UK	Azerbaijan	Spain
Month	Oct.	June	Sept.	Oct.	Dec.	June	Oct.	Oct.

As Table 9.1 also demonstrates, European states have not been at the forefront of proposing new WPS Resolutions. However, the two Resolutions supported by the UK and Spain, UNSCRs 2106 and 2242, are worth examining in further detail here given what they can tell us about European perspectives on WPS. The first, UNSCR 2106 on SGBV in conflict, was proposed as part of a series of initiatives forming part of the UK's high profile foreign policy deliverable on preventing sexual violence in conflict (PSVI). Critiques of this high-profile engagement with PSVI have underscored the initiative's value as political capital for then UK Foreign Secretary, William Hague. They also draw attention to the disparity between the rhetoric on this agenda, and the reality that at the same time the UK government was championing PSVI, it was cutting funding for women's refugees in the UK (Meger, 2016, p. 154). UNSCR 2242, proposed by Spain in autumn 2015, brought together the WPS agenda and countering violent extremism (CVE) for the first time. The widening of the agenda has proved problematic in some instances. For example, the pairing of the WPS and CVE agendas sit uncomfortably together and pose a risk that WPS will be hijacked and commodified as an agenda, rather than viewed as an agenda of value in its own right (Aoláin, 2016, p. 277). That is, WPS will become only of value to advancing CVE, rather than as an agenda in its own right.

The focus here has been on the WPS Resolutions. And while it has been important to outline these and their passage through the Security Council in order to understand the politics and wider context underpinning WPS, it is not the whole story. Rather, the WPS agenda should be understood as more than the sum of the Security Council Resolutions. The role of civil society remains crucial for holding the Security Council, governments and international organisations to account for their implementation of the agenda. They serve a crucial role in helping to mitigate some of the weaknesses inherent in the Resolutions. Civil society actors are not the only actors who provide meaning to the WPS beyond a strict reading of the Resolutions. WPS is also interpreted by states and regional institutions seeking to implement it. These interpretations can provide new meaning to WPS beyond that envisaged at the Security Council. Within Europe at the regional level, the EU has been somewhat of a laggard on engagement with WPS. Rather, it has been NATO that has become the leading forum for state engagement on the issue, while the OSCE also engaged early on with the agenda (Tryggestad, 2009, p. 549). It is European regional level engagement with WPS that the chapter now turns to examine.

Gendered structures and practices of European security: the case of the EU

Gender equality is a foundational myth of the EU (MacRae, 2010). Article 119 of the Treaty of Rome (1957) introduces the principle that 'men and women should receive equal pay for equal work'. It is important to note here that the inclusion of this statement was not as a result of feminist demands, but to ensure equal competition in the market and mollify the French government, which had just introduced equal pay legislation (Hoskyns, 1996, p. 56).

Nevertheless, repeated rhetorical statements by the EU and EU officials seek to reinforce the notion that gender is part of the 'European Union's "DNA"' (European Commission, 2014). In reality, the evidence to support such a claim is much more mixed, and calls for its reconsideration. Despite the EU's engagement with WPS, as well as the creation of the position of Principle Gender Adviser within the European External Action Service (EEAS), addressing gender inequalities remains marginal to the institution.

The EU is underpinned by neoliberal values and it is an economic focus that has underpinned the institution's engagement with the issue of gender equality. This has acted as a constraint on internal policy making in this domain and has also led to a liberal understanding of equality devoid of the ability to conceptualise difference (Woodward and van der Vleuten, 2014, p. 69). For example, the European Neighbourhood Policy, the instrument through which the EU engages with its southern and eastern neighbours to promote stabilisation and security, focuses predominately on improving women's access to employment, reinforcing the argument that the EU's rationale for pursuing gender equality is an economic one (David and Guerrina, 2013, p. 60). A cross-cutting feature is that gender is understood in a particular manner which draws heavily on gender stereotypes and binaries. Women are understood within a neoliberal framework as subjects responsible for their own emancipation but also as a resource for military action in relation to the Common Security and Defence Policy (CSDP) (Muehlenhoff, 2017, p. 156). CSDP, as an intergovernmental area reliant on member states to fill positions, has reproduced 'dominant norms and forms' in the shape of masculine bodies (Kronsell, 2015, p. 7). Further, the women mentioned in CSDP texts are women located outside of the EU and this reinforces the notion of a 'vulnerable other feminity' in places of conflict and the EU's role as a masculinist protector (Kronsell, 2016, p. 112).

The creation of the EEAS with the Treaty of Lisbon presented an opportunity to address gender inequalities within EU external relations, and security and defence specifically. The EEAS was formerly launched in 2011. As a new institution, it lacked institutional memory and, initially, an *esprit de corps*, the latter opening the possibility for the introduction of new agendas, such as WPS (Guerrina et al., 2018a, p. 1043). The creation of the EEAS was a result of time-consuming negotiations about composition, budget, organisation and accountability (Juncos and Pomorska, 2013). It involved the transfer of staff from the Commission and Secretariat General, as well as newly seconded staff from member states (see Chapter 6). The newly created Staff Regulations put an emphasis on meritocracy, but there was also a concern that adequate geographical and gender balance be ensured (Juncos and Pomorska, 2013, p. 1335). In reality, this has yet to be realised, with the notable exception of the position of High Representative/Vice-President, a position which has been held by two women, Baroness Catherine Ashton and the current incumbent, Federica Mogherini. There remain significant institutional barriers to the representation of women within the EEAS. For example, while Mogherini appointed women to positions surrounding the High Representative (intentionally or not), reinforcing the visibility of women in the EEAS, EU member states did not reciprocate (Novotná, 2017, p. 179). Indeed, the institutional structure of the EEAS, specifically Mogherini's over-reliance on EU member states to fill key positions, has led to a missed opportunity to create an institution fulfilling the EU's stated commitment to gender equality.

Another opportunity missed to push for the mainstreaming of gender within the EEAS came with the creation of the position of Principle Gender Adviser. On the one hand, the creation of such a position should be welcomed as a starting point for overseeing the integration of gender and WPS concerns into the EEAS, a key part of the position's mandate. Yet, the institutional location of the position means the incumbent, Ambassador Mara Marinaki, despite being an outspoken advocate of gender issues (Bindi, 2015, p. 98), lacks the seniority to push for change (Guerrina and Wright, 2016, p. 312). Marinaki does not report directly to the High Representative and is positioned as a support service for the Secretary General, Helga Schmidt. This falls short of the recommendation of a UN Women report on the implementation of WPS that regional organisations appoint a high-level special representative on WPS to replicate the best practice identified at NATO and the African Union (Coomaraswamy, 2015; Guerrina et al., 2018a, p. 1046).

The EU's Engagement with WPS

Given the EU's stated commitment to gender equality, we could expect that the EU would have been at the forefront of engagement with WPS. Yet, it was not. The EU's engagement with WPS has also assigned specific values to the agenda. If WPS is to be understood as more than the sum of the Security Council Resolutions but shaped by the actors engaging with it, then we need to examine the EU as a site for assigning meaning to WPS. In seeking to implement WPS, the EU interprets the agenda in line with its own foundational values. This both provides both new meaning for WPS and serves to reproduce the EU's own gender order (Guerrina and Wright, 2016, p. 294). The key policies concerned specifically with WPS are the *Comprehensive approach to the EU implementation of the United Nations Security Council Resolutions 1325 and 1820 on Women, Peace and Security* and the *Implementation of UNSCR 1325 as reinforced by UNSCR 1820 in the context of ESDP*, both adopted in 2008. Neither of these policies is referred to in the EU's Gender Action Plan adopted in 2015, which makes only two references to WPS more broadly (European Commission, 2015). This indicates that WPS is not the only means through which the EU engages with gender issues, but given the applicability of WPS to external relations also represents a significant silence on a salient global gender norm.

In order to understand the particular values placed on WPS by the EU, it is necessary to consider how the EU's interaction and engagement externally has shaped this at an institutional level. The notion that the EU primarily exports gender norms is flawed. Rather, gender equality norms are also imported through engagement and interactions with a range of international actors (Woodward and van der Vleuten, 2014, p. 86). WPS is a case in point here. The EU's engagement with WPS has provided an integral role for third parties in both promoting and implementing the WPS agenda. However, rather than providing a platform for deepening existing strategic partnerships, and, thus, demonstrating a commitment to further developing the WPS agenda, the EU has used WPS instrumentally as a means to forge new and specific strategic partnerships with other regional and international organisations (Haastrup, 2017, p. 208). There are some noticeable contradictions in the EU's approach to mainstreaming WPS which belie its commitment to supporting gender equality in peace and security more broadly. On the one hand the EU has prioritised co-operation with both international and regional organisations in order to keep WPS high on the international agenda as evidenced by the EU's relations with the Africa Union which have prominently featured WPS (Haastrup, 2017, p. 208). Yet, in its strategic partnerships with third states, gender is barely visible. For example, the EU strategic partnership with South Africa makes just one reference to gender (Haastrup, 2017, p. 208). Thus, we see that, through interaction with selected third parties, the EU comes to value WPS specifically as of instrumental value.

The instrumentalisation of WPS in EU partnerships speaks to the colonial logics underpinning European security. A case in point here is the European Security Strategy, in which the EU is represented through a gendered and colonial lens as a 'benevolent (masculine), robust, ethical, civilising/normative power' in contrast to those states beyond Europe and its partners (Stern, 2011, p. 36). This could contribute to explaining why it is that the EU has focused on WPS as an issue relevant to new partnerships, rather than as a central concern for existing partnerships. In this light, WPS can be seen as part of the EU's civilising mission and WPS a tool to promote the benefits of European values. Deiana and McDonagh's (2018, p. 44) interviews with gender advisers within the EEAS confirm these findings. They found WPS was valued either as something connected to another institution, primarily the UN, or as something they can pick and choose when to apply, rather than mainstreaming throughout their work. This aids an understanding of the specific way in which the EU has understood the WPS agenda within a neoliberal framework (Guerrina and Wright, 2016; Muehlenhoff, 2017).

Gender stereotypes also underpin the EU's engagement with WPS, with gender framed as an individual social attribute and something groups negotiate (Muehlenhoff, 2017, p. 3). In so doing, EU engagement with WPS lacks consideration of how gender power hierarchies privilege masculinities over femininities and the ways in which these structures serve to both produce and entrench gendered inequalities (Deiana and McDonagh, 2018, p. 38). This has been perpetuated by the way in which WPS has been incorporated into CSDP, which has led to the narrowing of its scope to issues concerning gender balance in peacekeeping and sexual and gender based violence in conflict (Deiana and McDonagh, 2018, p. 37). The specific and limited mandate of CSDP has also led to the incorporation of WPS as a 'security tool', rather than a wider, all-encompassing, approach, seeking broader transformation (Deiana and McDonagh, 2018, p. 42). Specifically, engagement with WPS has focused instrumentally on increasing operational effectiveness (Guerrina et al., 2018a). The focus on gender, and women, as a tool for military action instrumentalises women's bodies. It rests on a premise that women embody something 'different' from men. This expectation, in turn, further genders CSDP, normalising the existing majority (men) and constructing them as a 'homogenous and naturally associated' part of the institution (Kronsell, 2012).

Gendered structures and practices of European security: the case of NATO

NATO has an important place in terms of European security architecture. Its constituents may span the North Atlantic, but the alliance's heart is in Europe. Gender has always mattered to NATO. For example, the NATO Committee on Gender Perspectives has its origins in the 1960s (Wright, 2016, p. 354). Unsurprisingly then, NATO has also been the most visible among the European security institutions (EU CSDP, OSCE) in its engagement with the WPS agenda. The chapter now turns to examine NATO as an institution of hegemonic masculinity, before contextualising this against the alliance's engagement with WPS.

The 'family photos' taken of Heads of State at NATO Summits (see Figure 9.1) demonstrate the continued underrepresentation of women at the decision-making table. They show how small and fluctuating gains in women's broader political representation across Europe have been. NATO Summits provide a space for 'vital diplomatic and political activity' and provide 'additional shape, purpose and impetus' to the alliance (Park, 1996, p. 89). In other words, they matter. The near absence of women is, therefore, cause for concern, if not unsurprising in a military institution based on masculine bodies and practices (Kronsell, 2015). It also reflects a lack of gender balance more broadly within the alliance.

NATO has been elusive in publishing data on gender balance within its organisational structure. A case in point is the fact that the last publicly available report was published six years ago (NATO, 2012). This means it is difficult to ascertain the overall representation of women within NATO. The most recent data on gender balance among NATO civilian staff

Figure 9.1 Family portrait of NATO Heads of State and Government at the NATO Brussels Summit, 2018

Source: NATO (2018) 'Family Portrait', NATO Summit Brussels 2018: Official Portrait and Opening Ceremony, 11 July 2018. Available at: www.nato.int/nato_static_fl2014/assets/pictures/2018_07_180711g-summit-portrait-ceremony/20180711_180711g-025.jpg (accessed: 24 October 2018).

come instead from the global study on the implementation of UNSCR 1325 commissioned by UN Women. This finds that just six of the 38 (16%) executive leadership positions at NATO headquarters are held by women. In the regional offices, this figure is slightly higher, with two of the seven (28%) held by women. In 2015, this meant that just 19% of all civilian leadership roles within NATO were held by women (Coomaraswamy, 2015, p. 258). Today, this figure has increased slightly with the appointment of Rose Gottemoeller as NATO Deputy Secretary General, the first woman to hold such a senior post within the alliance. While this is welcome, it belies the fact that masculine bodies are significantly over-represented in decision-making roles in the alliance. The lack of up-to-date figures on gender balance within NATO makes it difficult to hold NATO to account and indicates that gender balance is a sensitive issue among allies. The lack of transparency is particularly concerning given the alliance's commitment to implement the WPS agenda.

NATO's engagement with Women, Peace and Security

On the surface, the most up-to-date NATO Action Plan on Women, Peace and Security[2] seems to support the increased representation of women in NATO. One of the core outcomes is the 'improved gender balance at all levels at NATO Allies and partners' defence and security institutions'. Yet, if we dig a little deeper into this statement, we find it omits mention of the representation of women within the International Staff or International Military Staff (NATO, 2016). So, while increasing the representation of women in allies' own forces or in national delegations, if realised, is likely to have some trickle down impact on gender balance within delegations to NATO and seconded staff, it will not address the gender imbalance among those employed directly by the alliance.

The gender imbalance within NATO should be a pressing issue for the alliance given its stated commitment to the WPS agenda. That it is not indicates this is an issue with considerable political sensitivities among the allies and one considered separate from WPS. In 2007, NATO formally engaged with the WPS agenda. For many, NATO's adoption of a policy on WPS was the first time the alliance's concern with gender issues became visible to them and took them by surprise (Cockburn, 2011). However, this overlooks the decades of consideration given to 'manpower' issues and, relatedly, the status and role of women in the armed forces by the alliance. It upholds the notion that international security is above concern with gender relations, rather than constituted through them. In order to challenge this view, it is necessary to start from the conception of NATO as a gendered institution. This exposes how gender is not a 'new' issue for the alliance, but, rather, one that is at the core of how it functions day-to-day. NATO has been concerned with gender issues under the guise of 'manpower' for decades. The alliance formally recognised the Committee on Women in NATO Forces within the military structure in 1976 (Wright, 2016, p. 353). This committee would become the institutional locus for NATO's initial engagement with WPS when it was renamed the NATO Committee on Gender Perspectives in 2009. Later, the creation in 2014 of the high-level position of the NATO Secretary General's High-Level Special Representative on WPS would shift the focus to NATO's civilian structure. UN Women pointed to the creation of such a position, reporting directly to the Secretary General on NATO's engagement with WPS, as one of best practice in a 2015 report (Coomaraswamy, 2015). The position has had three incumbents, all of whom have been women, pointing to a broader issue within NATO that it is women who have tended to staff roles with responsibility for gender issues, despite their broader underrepresentation within the alliance (Hurley, 2018, p. 74).

Like the EU, NATO's engagement with WPS has continued to provide a central role for partner states. The NATO policy on WPS was adopted in 2007 in conjunction with the Euro–Atlantic Partnership Council. Indeed, it was NATO partner states, primarily Austria and Sweden, which proved pivotal to realising this (Wright, 2016, p. 356). NATO has also relied on partner states to staff key positions on gender within NATO HQ, including within the Office of the Special Representative on Women, Peace and Security (Ministry of Foreign Affairs, 2014). This indicates that WPS serves an instrumental purpose for both NATO and partners. For partners, it provides a non-contentious issue on which to engage NATO (Wright, 2016, p. 351). Japan, for example, had no formal ties to NATO prior to seconding a member of its foreign service to take up a support role within the office of the NATO Special Representative on WPS. For NATO, it has provided a shared starting point and means to foster a sense of community with partners, in particular those that were engaged in the NATO-led International Security Assistance Force in Afghanistan (Wagnsson, 2011, p. 598).

In respect to operations, NATO has also underscored the instrumental value of WPS as a means to increase operational effectiveness. WPS has been tied to NATO's pre-existing concern with the status of women in NATO militaries and has been used to reinforce the essentialist notion that better gender representation will lead to more effective outcomes. In framing women soldiers as adding something 'different' to NATO militaries, the gendered underpinning of NATO as a militarised institution is not challenged. Rather, the existing masculine practices are normalised and constructed as naturally associated with the institution (Kronsell, 2012, p. 67).

Conclusion

Drawing on a Feminist Security Studies' approach shows that security is a deeply gendered issue. It also challenges the preoccupation of Security Studies' scholars with 'high politics', demonstrating how the personal is not only political, but also international (and, in this case, regional). While the focus of this chapter has been on two key European security institutions, the EU's CSDP and NATO, their engagement with the WPS agenda has the potential to challenge traditional understandings of security and to provide for wider consideration of what security means, and for whom. The politics underpinning WPS, its origins in civil society and the journey the agenda has been on since its adoption by the Security Council have not stripped the agenda of its efficacy. The WPS agenda provides a catalyst for states and other international actors to consider how their own institutional structures support deeply gendered outcomes. For example, the marginalisation of women from decision-making roles creates institutions premised upon masculine bodies and practices. Even with their engagement with WPS, this gender imbalance has proved difficult to challenge given that both the

EEAS/CSDP and NATO are reliant on member states to improve gender balance within them. This has created a significant barrier to increasing gender representation, despite both institutions adoption of policies on WPS. As a result, European engagement with WPS has drawn attention to the ways in which the agenda has been used instrumentally, to support neo-liberal logics or as a tool to increase operational effectiveness, rather than as a means to challenge gendered structures. This speaks to some of the weakness of the WPS agenda. Nevertheless, their public-facing engagement with WPS provides a tool for civil society actors to hold NATO and the EU to account for their lack of measures to effectively address gender imbalances within their institutions.

Notes

1 For further explanation on how the personal is both political and international, this short clip of an interview with Cynthia Enloe is helpful: www.youtube.com/watch?v=COkWGNpV_Wk
2 Adopted in conjunction with the Euro–Atlantic Partnership Council (NATO, 2016).

Further reading

Kronsell, Annica, and Svedberg, Erika (eds) (2012), *Making Gender, Making War: Violence, Military and Peacekeeping Practices*. London: Routledge.
Whitworth, Sandra (2018), 'Feminisms', in P. Williams and M. McDonald (eds), *Security Studies: An Introduction*. London: Routledge, pp. 74–85.
Wibben, Annick T. R. (2010), *Feminist Security Studies: A Narrative Approach*. Abingdon: Routledge.
Wright, K. A. M., Hurley, M., and Gil Ruiz, J. (2019), *NATO, Gender and the Military: Women Organising from Within*. London: Routledge.

Weblinks

Collated documents pertaining to the EU's engagement with WPS at the European Peace Liaison Office: http://eplo.org/activities/policywork/gender-peace-security-2/gender-mainstreaming-eu/
NATO WPS action plans and NATO activities pertaining to the agenda: www.nato.int/cps/en/natohq/topics_91091.htm
NATO International Military Staff Office of the Gender Advisor: www.nato.int/cps/en/natohq/topics_101372.htm
PeaceWomen, the WPS programme of the Women's International League for Peace and Freedom (WILPF) monitoring the global implementation of the WPS agenda: www.peacewomen.org

References

Abels, Gabriele, and MacRae, Heather (eds) (2016), *Gendering European Integration Theory: Engaging New Dialogues*. Columbia: Columbia University Press.

Aoláin, Fionnuala N. (2016), 'The "War on Terror" and Extremism: Assessing the Relevance of the Women, Peace and Security Agenda', *International Affairs*, 92 (2), 275–291.

Basu, Soumita (2010), 'Security Council Resolution 1325: Toward Gender Equality' in Peace and Security Policy Making', in B. A. Reardon and A. Hans (eds), *The Gender Imperative: Human Security vs State Security*. Abingdon: Routledge, pp. 287–316.

Basu, Soumita (2013), 'Emancipatory Potential in Feminist Security Studies', *International Studies Perspectives*, 14 (4), 455–458.

Basu, Soumita (2016), 'The Global South Writes 1325 (Too)', *International Political Science Review*, 37 (3), 362–374.

Bindi, Federiga (2015), 'Cracks in the IR Glass: The Evolving Relationship between International Relations and Gender', *Seton Hall Journal of Diplomacy and International Relations*, 17 (1–2), 89–107.

Cockburn, Cynthia (2007), *From Where We Stand: War, Women's Activism and Feminist Analysis*. London: Zed Books.

Cockburn, Cynthia (2011), 'Snagged on the Contradiction: NATO, UNSC Resolution 1325, and Feminist Responses', *No to War – No to NATO: International Network to Delegitimize NATO Annual Meeting*. Dublin, 15–17 April. Available at: https://no-to-nato.org/wp-content/uploads/2013/03/NATO13251.pdf (accessed: 25 October 2018).

Cohn, Carol (1987), 'Sex and Death in the Rational World of Defense Intellectuals', *Signs*, 12 (1), 687–718.

Cohn, Carol (2011), '"Feminist Security Studies": Toward a Reflexive Practice', *Politics & Gender*, 7 (4), 581–585.

Cohn, Carol, Kinsella, Helen, and Gibbings, Sheri (2004), 'Women, Peace and Security Resolution 1325', *International Feminist Journal of Politics*, 6 (1), 130–140.

Cook, Sam (2009), 'Security Council Resolution 1820: On Militarism, Flashlights, Raincoats, and Rooms with Doors – A Political Perspective on Where It Came from and What It Adds', *Emory International Law Review*, 23 (1), 125–140.

Coomaraswamy, Radhika (2015), *Preventing Conflict, Transforming Justice, Securing the Peace: A Global Study on the Implementation of United Nations Security Resolution 1325*. New York: UN Entity for Gender Equality and the Empowerment of Women (UN WOMEN).

David, M., and Guerrina, R. (2013), 'European External Relations: Dominant Discourses and Unintended Consequences of Gender Mainstreaming', *Women's Studies International Forum*, 39, 53–62.

Deiana, Maria-Adriana, and McDonagh, Kenneth (2018), '"It is Important, But . . .": Translating the Women Peace and Security (WPS) Agenda into the Planning of EU Peacekeeping Missions', *Peacebuilding*, 6 (1), 34–48.

Elshtain, Jean B. (1987), *Women and War*. Brighton: Harvester.

Enloe, Cynthia (1989), *Bananas, Beaches and Bases: Making Feminist Sense of International Politics*. London: Pandora.

European Commission (2014), 'Gender Equality: EU Action Triggers Steady Progress', Press Release IP/14/423, 14 April, European Commission, Brussels. Available at: http://europa.eu/rapid/press-release_IP-14–423_en.htm (accessed: 27 February 2017).

European Commission (2015), 'New Framework for Gender Equality and Women's Empowerment: Transforming the Lives of Girls and Women through EU External Relations (2016–2020) Adopted', Press Release IP/15/5690, 22 September, European Commission, Brussels. Available at: http://europa.eu/rapid/press-release_IP-15–5690_en.htm (accessed: 22 October 2015).

Green, Caroline (2016), 'Assessing UK Government Action on Women, Peace and Security in 2015', Gender Action for Peace and Security (GAPS) Report. Available at: http://gaps-uk.org/wp-content/

uploads/2016/01/GAPS-Shadow-Report-Assessing-UK-Government-Action-on-WPS-in-2015.pdf (accessed: 25 October 2018).

Guerrina, Roberta, and Wright, Katharine A. M. (2016), 'Gendering Normative Power Europe: Lessons of the Women, Peace and Security Agenda', *International Affairs*, 92 (2), 293–312.

Guerrina, Roberta, Chappell, Laura, and Wright, Katharine A. M. (2018a), 'Transforming CSDP? Feminist Triangles and Gender Regimes', *Journal of Common Market Studies*, 56 (5) 1036–1052.

Guerrina, Roberta, Haastrup, Toni, Wright, Katharine A. M., Masselot, Annick, MacRae, Heather, and Cavaghan, Rosalind (2018b), 'Does European Union Studies Have a Gender Problem? Experiences from Researching Brexit', *International Feminist Journal of Politics*, 20 (2), 252–257.

Haastrup, Toni (2017), 'The Undoing of a Unique Relationship? Peace and Security in the EU–South Africa Strategic Partnership', *South African Journal of International Affairs*, 24 (2), 197–213.

Hill, Felicity (2005), 'How and When Has Security Council Resolution 1325 (2000) on Women, Peace and Security Impacted Negotiations Outside the Security Council'. Masters Thesis. *Uppsala University*. Available at: www.peacewomen.org/sites/default/files/1325_1325scnegotiations_hill_2005_0.pdf (accessed: 25 October 2018).

Hill, Felicity, Aboitiz, Mikele, and Poehlman-Doumbouya, Sara (2009), 'Nongovernmental Organizations' Role in the Buildup and Implementation of Security Council Resolution 1325', *Signs: Journal of Women in Culture and Society*, 28 (4), 1255–1269.

Hoskyns, Catherine (1996), *Integrating Gender: Women, Law and Politics in the European Union*. London: Verso.

Hudson, Heidi (2005), '"Doing" Security As Though Humans Matter: A Feminist Perspective on Gender and the Politics of Human Security', *Security Dialogue*, 36 (2), 155–174.

Hurley, Matthew (2018), 'The "Genderman": (Re)Negotiating Militarised Masculinities When "Doing Gender" at NATO', *Critical Military Studies*, 4 (1), 72–91.

Juncos, Ana E., and Pomorska, Karolina (2013), '"In the Face of Adversity": Explaining the Attitudes of EEAS Officials Vis-à-Vis the New Service', *Journal of European Public Policy*, 20 (9), 1332–1349.

Kronsell, Annica (2012), *Gender, Sex and the Postnational Defense: Militarism and Peacekeeping*. New York: Oxford University Press.

Kronsell, Annica (2015), 'Sexed Bodies and Military Masculinities: Gender Path Dependence in EU's Common Security and Defense Policy', *Men and Masculinities*, 19 (3), 1–26.

Kronsell, Annica (2016), 'The Power of EU Masculinities: A Feminist Contribution to European Integration Theory', *Journal of Common Market Studies*, 54 (1), 104–120.

Kronsell, Annica, and Svedberg, Erika (eds) (2012), *Making Gender, Making War: Violence, Military and Peacekeeping Practices*. Abingdon: Routledge.

MacRae, Heather (2010), 'The EU as a Gender Equality Polity: Myths and Realities', *Journal of Common Market Studies*, 48 (1), 153–172.

Meger, Sara (2016), 'The Fetishization of Sexual Violence in International Security', *International Studies Quarterly*, 60 (1), 149–159.

Ministry of Foreign Affairs (2014), 'Dispatch of a Female Self-Defense Force Personnel to NATO Headquarters', Press Release, 4 November, Ministry of Foreign Affairs: Tokyo. Available at: www.mofa.go.jp/press/release/press4e_000488.html (accessed: 25 August 2015).

Muehlenhoff, Hanna L. (2017), 'Victims, Soldiers, Peacemakers and Caretakers: The Neoliberal Constitution of Women in the EU's Security Policy', *International Feminist Journal of Politics*, 19 (2), 153–167.

NATO (2012), 'Gender Balance in NATO HQ International Staff – 2012', NATO document. Available at: www.nato.int/nato_static_fl2014/assets/pdf/pdf_topics/20120301_gender_and_diversity-gender_2012.pdf (accessed: 25 October 2018).

NATO (2016), 'NATO/EAPC Action Plan for the Implementation of the NATO/EAPC Policy on Women Peace and Security', NATO policy document. Available at: www.nato.int/nato_static_fl2014/assets/pdf/pdft_2016_07/160718-wps-action-plan.pdf (accessed: 25 October 2018).

Novotná, Tereza (2017), 'The EU as a Global Actor: United We Stand, Divided We Fall', *Journal of Common Market Studies*, 55 (S1), 177–191.

Otto, Diana (2004), 'Securing the "Gender Legitimacy" of the UN Security Council: Prising Gender from Its Historical Moorings', in Hilary Charlesworth and Jean-Marc Coicaud (eds), *Faultlines of International Legitimacy*. New York: United Nations University Press, pp. 1–32. Available at: https://papers.ssrn.com/sol3/papers.cfm?abstract_id=585923 (accessed: 25 October 2018).

Otto, Diana (2010), 'Power and Danger: Feminist Engagement with International Law Through the UN Security Council', *Australian Feminist Law Journal*, 32 (1), 97–121.

Park, Bill (1996), 'NATO Summits', in David H. Dunn (ed), *Diplomacy at the Highest Level – The Evolution of International Summitry*. Basingstoke: Palgrave Macmillan

Peterson, V. Spike (2004), 'Feminist Theories Within, Invisible to, and Beyond IR', *Brown Journal of World Affairs*, 10 (2), 35–46.

Pratt, Nicola (2013), 'Reconceptualizing Gender, Reinscribing Racial–Sexual Boundaries in International Security: The Case of UN Security Council Resolution 1325 on "Women, Peace and Security"', *International Studies Quarterly*, 57 (4), 772–783.

Puechguirbal, Nadine (2010), 'Discourses on Gender, Patriarchy and Resolution 1325: A Textual Analysis of UN Documents', *International Peacekeeping*, 17 (2), 172–187.

Shepherd, Laura J. (2011), 'Sex, Security and Superhero(in)es: From 1325 to 1820 and Beyond', *International Feminist Journal of Politics*, 13 (4), 504–521.

Shepherd, Laura J. (ed) (2013), *Critical Approaches to Security: An Introduction to Theories and Methods*. New York: Routledge.

Stern, Maria (2011), 'Gender and Race in the European Security Strategy: Europe as a "Force for Good"?', *Journal of International Relations and Development*, 14 (1), 28–59.

Tickner, J. Ann (1992), *Gender in International Relations: Feminist Perspectives on Achieving Global Security*. New York: Columbia University Press.

Tryggestad, Torunn L. (2009), 'Trick or Treat? The UN and Implementation of Security Council Resolution 1325 on Women, Peace, and Security', *Global Governance*, 15 (4), 539–557.

United Nations Security Council (2000), 'Resolution 1325', S/RES/1325, 31 October, New York, United Nations Security Council. Available at: https://daccess-ods.un.org/TMP/7169836.75956726.html (accessed: 25 October 2018).

Wagnsson, Charlotte (2011), 'A Security Community in the Making? Sweden and NATO Post-Libya', *European Security*, 20 (4), 585–603.

Wibben, Annick T. R. (2010), *Feminist Security Studies: A Narrative Approach*. Abingdon: Routledge.

Woodward, Alison E., and van der Vleuten, Anna (2014), 'EU and the Export of Gender Equality Norms: Myth and Facts', in Anna van der Vleuten, Anouka van Eerdewijk, and Conny Roggeband (eds), *Gender Equality Norms in Regional Governance: Transnational Dynamics in Europe, South America and Southern Africa*. Basingstoke: Palgrave Macmillan, pp. 67–92.

Wright, Katharine A. M. (2016), 'NATO's Adoption of UNSCR 1325 on Women, Peace and Security: Making the Agenda a Reality', *International Political Science Review*, 37 (3), 350–361.

New threats to European security   **10**

Peter Viggo Jakobsen

Introduction

The destabilisation of the Middle East and North Africa (MENA) in the wake of the Arab Spring in 2011 and the Russian resort to force in Ukraine marked the end of the post Cold War era in Europe – the era characterised by the absence of direct threats to the national security of the European states. The bloody break-up of Yugoslavia in the 1990s (see Chapter 2) had not posed direct military threats to its state neighbours, and Russia and NATO's member states had ceased viewing each other as adversaries and threats.

From the perspective of liberal international relations (IR) theory, the 1990s were a dream come true. The Paris Charter, signed by all members of the Commission on Security and Cooperation in Europe (CSCE) in 1990 had liberalism written all over it:

> The era of confrontation and division of Europe has ended . . . Europe is liberating itself from the legacy of the past . . . Ours is a time for fulfilling the hopes and expectations our peoples have cherished for decades: steadfast commitment to democracy based on human rights and fundamental freedoms; prosperity through economic liberty and social justice; and equal security for all our countries.
>
> (Organization for Security and Co-operation in Europe, 1990)

Realist scholars were much less optimistic about Europe's future. Mearsheimer (1990) published a much-cited article with the provocative title, 'Why we will soon miss the Cold War'. He argued that the transition from bipolarity to multipolarity would result in increased great power rivalry, and that the best way to maintain stability would be to arm Germany with nuclear weapons. Mearsheimer and other realists were wrong to predict that NATO would wither away and pave the way for increased rivalry between Europe's old great powers: Germany, France, Russia and the UK. But they were right in predicting that the liberal recipes for peace and prosperity – disarmament, democratisation, institutionalisation, integration and free trade – would be insufficient to create the undivided and peaceful Europe that many were hoping for, and that liberal and constructivist scholars believed was within reach. The liberal recipes failed *vis-à-vis* Russia and the MENA region , and their failure contributed to the rise of new threats to the East and in the South. The direct threats to national and European security that disappeared with the end of the Cold War have made a comeback.

The purpose of this chapter is to trace the resurgence of direct threats to European security. It does so by tracing the gradual breakdown of relations between Russia and Western states, and particularly Europe's two key security organisations: the EU and NATO. These organisations completely marginalised the OSCE, which played a key role in ending the Cold War and laying out the liberal visions for a new and undivided Europe (see Chapter 5).

The chapter has five parts. The first part shows how the liberal-inspired peace policies, which brought prosperity and security to the states joining the EU and NATO, helped bring about a renewed rivalry between Russia and the West. The second part analyses the different Russian and Western perceptions driving the confrontation, the rise of hybrid threats, and considers the likelihood of a direct military confrontation between the two sides. The third section turns south, showing how failed EU and NATO attempts to democratise and stabilise the MENA region helped create the cocktail of terrorism, state collapse, migration and refugees that now pose a direct threat to European security. The fourth examines how the EU and NATO have perceived and tackled the new direct threats from the South. The fifth and final part sums up the main findings and discusses their implications for the future of the EU, NATO and European security.

From partnership to rivalry: the deteriorating Russian–Western relationship

In 1998, George Kennan, the American diplomat who conceived the containment strategy that the USA employed against the Soviet Union during the Cold War, deplored the decision to expand NATO eastwards:

> I think it is the beginning of a new cold war . . . I think the Russians will gradually react quite adversely and it will affect their policies. I think it is a tragic mistake. There was no reason for this whatsoever. No one was threatening anybody else . . . It shows so little understanding of Russian history and Soviet history. Of course there is going to be a bad reaction from Russia, and then [the NATO expanders] will say that we always told you that is how the Russians are – but this is just wrong.
>
> (cited in Friedman, 1998)

Unlike realist scholars, Kennan did not consider a return to Cold War-style rivalry inevitable, because of the anarchic structure of the international system or human nature. Kennan took a more constructivist view of the Russo–Western relationship. He believed that a positive relationship with Russia was possible if the West understood Russian concerns, considered them and treated Russia with respect.

Liberal scholars and practitioners shared the view that a positive relationship with Russia was possible, but only if Russia adopted the liberal ideals and ways of the West unconditionally. Russia could only become a true partner of the West if Russia met the criteria for EU and NATO membership (see Box 10.1). In the Western perspective, partnership was about westernising Russia. The EU partnership and cooperation agreement was based on the 'respect for democratic principles and human rights as an essential element of the partnership' and the objective is to 'support Russian efforts to consolidate its democracy, develop its economy and complete the transition into a market economy' (European Union, 1994). NATO also based its cooperation agreement with Russia on the premise that Russia would continue its process of transition towards democracy and market economy, and 'that democracy, political pluralism, the rule of law, and respect for human rights and civil liberties and the development of free market economies' was key to the development of a successful partnership (North Atlantic Treaty Organization, 1997).

Box 10.1   EU and NATO membership criteria

'[EU] Membership requires that candidate country has achieved stability of institutions guaranteeing democracy, the rule of law, human rights, respect for and protection of minorities, the existence of a functioning market economy as well as the capacity to cope with competitive pressure and market forces within the Union. Membership presupposes the candidate's ability to take on the obligations of membership including adherence to the aims of political, economic and monetary union.'
(European Council, 1993, Section 7.A.iii)

'NATO membership is potentially open to all of Europe's emerging democracies that share the alliance's values and are ready to meet the obligations of membership. We have made clear that, at a minimum, candidates for membership must meet the following six requirements:

- New members must uphold democracy, including tolerating diversity.
- New members must be making progress toward a market economy.
- Their military forces must be under firm civilian control.
- They must be good neighbours and respect sovereignty outside their borders.
- They must be working toward compatibility with NATO forces.
- New members must be invited by a consensus of current members.'
(U.S. State Department, 1997)

This constructivist-style socialisation approach worked well in stabilising and democratising the central and Eastern European countries, who were willing to do virtually anything to join the two organisations. It did not work with Russia, however. The Western understanding of partnership made its realisation contingent upon a successful Russian transformation to a liberal Western democracy with an open market economy compatible with EU standards.

This was a tall order, and it made a deterioration of the relationship with Russia inevitable, when its democratisation process went into reverse after Putin's accession to power in 1999.

The Russian understanding of partnership was very different. Russia wanted the West to respect it as a great power with privileged interests in its "near abroad". In the Russian perspective, the partnership never became real because the Western powers consistently refused to respect its great power interests. They dismissed repeated Russian proposals for a new pan-European security organisation based on the OSCE, and ignored Russian protests against NATO's bombing of the Bosnian Serbs (1995), NATO's air war over Kosovo (1999), the Western recognition of Kosovo's independence (2008) and NATO's air war against Libya (2011). Yet, the principal cause of disagreement was NATO expansion. When President Yeltsin pleaded with the USA's President Clinton not to expand the alliance, Clinton told him not to worry; Russia's security would benefit from it. Then he added, 'No country will be allowed to veto expansion' (cited in Marshall, 1994). NATO expansion was a *fait accompli* that Russia had to learn to live with.

President Putin begged to differ. He made clear at NATO's Bucharest Summit in 2008 that he regarded Georgian and Ukrainian membership as a 'direct threat to Russian security' and that 'the efficiency of our co-operation will depend on whether NATO members take Russia's interests into account' (cited in Blomfield and Kirkup, 2008). He was serious. Later that year, Russia intervened militarily in Georgia in support of Abkhazian and South Ossetia's separatists, subsequently recognising the two regions as independent states.

Russia's reaction was equally hostile when the EU launched its Eastern Partnership, offering Armenia, Azerbaijan, Belarus, Georgia, Moldova and Ukraine closer economic and political links. Moscow perceived this as an attempt 'to extend the EU's sphere of influence' (Pop, 2009). It responded by launching a competing plan for a Eurasian Customs Union (ECU) and lobbied hard to persuade these countries to join the ECU instead of signing Association Agreements with the EU. The EU fuelled the rivalry, insisting that ECU membership was incompatible with its Association Agreements, and the EU unwillingness to engage in dialogue with Russia over Ukraine reinforced Russian perceptions that the objective was to reduce Russian influence (Marocchi, 2017, pp. 4–5). It was the Ukrainian government's decision to yield to Russian pressure that triggered the violent protests that brought down Ukrainian President Yanukovych in 2014. When the new Ukrainian government declared its intention to sign the Association Agreement and speed up integration with the West, Moscow annexed the Crimea and resorted to proxy warfare in Eastern Ukraine.

The new Russo–Western confrontation and the rise of hybrid threats

In the Western perspective, the Russian annexation of Crimea and its subsequent military intervention in Eastern Ukraine represented a new form of hybrid warfare, involving the constant and ongoing synchronised use of a wide range of covert and overt, military and non-military instruments by Russia in pursuit of its strategic objectives (Chivvis, 2017, p. 1). Russia accomplished its bloodless annexation of Crimea with covert use of special forces without markings on their uniforms (the so-called little green men), local proxies, information warfare, psychological warfare and conventional forces massed on the Ukrainian border to deter Ukrainian and Western intervention.

The same methods were subsequently applied in Southern Ukraine, but here Ukrainian military resistance forced Russia to covertly employ a significant number of conventional forces to prevent its proxies from being overrun. The war in Eastern Ukraine has involved major use of conventional force and cost Russia more than 2,000 soldiers (Garver, 2015). In the course of the war, which, by early 2018, had settled into a pattern of continuous low-intensity fighting with no movement of frontlines, Russia also resorted to economic warfare, imposing sanctions and cutting off energy supplies to the Ukrainian state, and launched cyber attacks against Ukrainian targets. In order to deter Western intervention in support of the Ukrainian government, Russia threatened to intervene elsewhere to protect Russian minorities at risk, and significantly stepped up its patrols close to NATO air space. In addition, Russia conducted snap exercises with no advance warning, demonstrating a Russian capability to mass large troop concentrations quickly on NATO's borders, simulated air strikes on NATO countries, deployed missiles in Kaliningrad and threatened to use nuclear weapons in self-defence.

The EU and NATO have taken a long list of civilian and military countermeasures in order to coerce Russia to withdraw from Ukraine and to counter its perceived ongoing, covert subversive attempts to destabilise the West and increase support for Russian viewpoints (see Boxes 10.2 and 10.3). They accuse Russia of spreading disinformation and launching cyber attacks against critical infrastructure and private firms (Marsh, 2018), and for attempting to influence elections in several Western countries. In early 2018, the US government charged 13 Russians for interfering in the 2016 presidential election (Apuzzo and LaFraniere, 2018).

Moscow rejects these accusations, arguing that the West was waging hybrid warfare against Russia and its allies long before 2014. Russian leaders view the various so-called colour revolutions occurring in Serbia (2000), Georgia (2003), Ukraine (2004–2005) and Kyrgyzstan (2005), in which civilian protests led to the peaceful overthrow of Russian-friendly governments, as the result of subversive and covert Western activities aimed at reducing Russian influence.

Box 10.2   NATO countermeasures adopted in response to Russian actions in the Ukraine

Nuclear deterrence:

- Reaffirmation that NATO will use its nuclear weapons to respond to nuclear attacks

Conventional defence and deterrence:

- Reassurance of Central-Eastern allies and deterrence of Russia
- Deployment of four multinational battalion-size battlegroups in the Baltic states and Poland on a rotational basis (enhanced Forward Presence)
- Fighter jets on air-policing patrols

- NATO AWACS surveillance flights over the territory of our eastern Allies, and maritime patrol aircraft flights along our eastern borders
- Intensified NATO maritime patrols in the Baltic Sea, the Black Sea and the Mediterranean
- More NATO forces, exercises and training under Headquarters Multinational Division Southeast (Romania)
- Increased number of exercises

Adaptation of force and command structures for rapid crisis response:

- Larger NATO Response Force on higher readiness
- 5,000 strong Very High Readiness Joint Task Force able to deploy at very short notice
- Eight small headquarters established in Central and Eastern Europe to facilitate readiness and the rapid deployment, NATO Force Integration Units
- Prepositioning of equipment and supplies

Cyber:

- Cyber-operations centre

Defence spending:

- Pledge to increase spending to 2% of GDP; objective not in sight but total spending increased with $40 billion in 2015–2017

Diplomacy:

- Suspension of all practical civilian and military cooperation with Russia
- Maintenance of political contacts at the level of ambassadors and above
- Increased support for capability development and capacity building in Ukraine

Intelligence:

- Hybrid analysis branch analysing the full spectrum of hybrid actions, drawing from military and civilian, classified and open sources
- Enhanced cooperation with the EU to counter hybrid threats in the areas of situational awareness, strategic communications, cybersecurity, and crisis prevention and response

Resilience:

- Steps to increase member state ability to resist and recover easily and quickly from hybrid attacks, combining civilian, economic, commercial and military factors

Strategic communications:

- Enhanced to counter Russian information warfare
- NATO StratCom Center of Excellence established in Latvia

Compiled from NATO Factsheets and official documents, available at: www.nato.int

This is dismissed in the West as Russian paranoia and propaganda intended to legitimise the use of force in Ukraine (Palmer, 2015, p. 8). However, evidence does suggest that Western support did play a role in these revolutions – even if it was less decisive than Russian leaders claim (Wilson, 2006). The fact that Russian leaders expressed this concern prior to 2014 also suggests that it may be a real driver of their actions. Putin argued in 2012:

> that the notion of 'soft power' is being used increasingly often. This implies a matrix of tools and methods to reach foreign policy goals without the use of arms but by exerting information and other levers of influence. Regrettably, these methods are being used all too frequently to develop and provoke extremist, separatist and nationalistic attitudes, to manipulate the public and to conduct direct interference in the domestic policy of sovereign countries . . . the activities of 'pseudo-NGOs' and other agencies that try to destabilize other countries with outside support are unacceptable.
>
> (Putin, 2012)

Putin also accused the USA of instigating the anti-Kremlin protest movement that arose between the parliamentary and presidential elections in 2011–2012. To prevent a recurrence, the Russian government passed laws making it harder for foreign-funded democracy and human rights' organisations to operate in Russia and banned 'undesirable' NGOs posing a threat to national security (Luhn, 2015). In 2015, Russia's National Security Strategy formally designated foreign-sponsored regime change as a security threat (Bouchet, 2016, p. 1). While the latter step also served to legitimise Russian actions in the Ukraine, the countermeasures adopted since 2012 do suggest that the Russian leadership feels as threatened by 'hybrid warfare' as the West does.

Box 10.3 EU countermeasures adopted in response to Russian actions in the Ukraine

Diplomacy:

- Association Agreement completed with the Ukraine
- Suspension of negotiations over Russia's joining the OECD and the International Energy Agency

Economic sanctions:

- Asset freeze and travel restrictions
- Restrictions on economic relations with Crimea and Sevastopol.
- Economic sanctions targeting specific sectors of the Russian economy

Hybrid threats:

- European Centre for Countering Hybrid Threats in Finland supported by the EU

Intelligence:

- Establishment of EU Hybrid fusion cell analysing classified and open source information on hybrid threats

Strategic communications:

- East StratCom Task Force, which forecasts and responds to disinformation cases and campaigns, and highlights the concrete benefits of EU partnership to the Eastern partners

Resilience:

- Identification of common tools to improve protection and resilience of critical infrastructure against hybrid threats covering all relevant sectors
- Regionally coordinated management of gas shortages, in case of a crisis or a hybrid attack

Compiled from EU Factsheets and official documents available at: www.consilium.europa.eu/en

In a constructivist perspective, the Russian use of force in Ukraine initiated a process of negative interactions that will make the relationship between the two sides increasingly adversarial. Both sides are increasing their defence spending and taking actions that the other perceives as aggressive and threatening. Both sides make demands that the other deems completely unacceptable. Russia wants the West to stay out of its sphere of privileged interest and stop promoting democracy, human rights and trade agreements undermining the Eurasian Economic Union. This is not on the cards. On the contrary, the EU Global Strategy signalled a commitment to 'uphold the right' of the Eastern partners 'to determine freely their approach towards the EU' (European External Action Service, 2016, p. 33). This is a recipe for continued rivalry.

At the same time, three factors suggest escalation to a direct military confrontation to be highly unlikely. The first is derived from rational deterrence theory. The nuclear weapons possessed by the parties guarantee mutually assured destruction (MAD) in the event of war, creating a strong common interest in war avoidance. Two states with secure second-strike capabilities have never fought each other directly.

The main EU and NATO concern is Russian use of covert non-military means below the threshold required to trigger a military NATO response, such as cyber attacks, propaganda, disinformation, economic warfare and attempts to influence elections. Yet, given the difficulties that Russia has experienced in using such methods to destabilise the Ukrainian state and coerce it to comply with Russian demands (Galeotti, 2015), it is hard to see Russia succeeding in destabilising the far stronger states in the EU and NATO. There is no evidence suggesting that Russian interference in Western elections has made a decisive difference to their outcomes. Consequently, it is hard to see Russian efforts succeed now that the EU and NATO member states are aware of the threat and taking steps to reduce their vulnerabilities (see Boxes 10.2 and 10.3).

Liberal interdependence theory points to a second factor reducing the risk of further escalation: the high degree of economic interdependence between the EU and Russia. The EU is Russia's most important trading partner, whereas Russia is the EU's fourth largest trading partner (European Union, 2017, p. 6). The sanctions the two sides have imposed on each other are hurting them both (Russia more so than the EU), giving them a common interest in ending the confrontation. As most EU sanctions are linked to the Russian intervention in Eastern Ukraine, an end to the fighting would provide the EU with the argument for initiating a gradual easing of those sanctions hurting Russia the most.

Positive interaction between the two first factors limiting the risk of escalation produces a third: restraint, and a strong aversion to engage in behaviour with a high risk of inadvertent escalation. Western leaders signalled restraint throughout the confrontation, indicating that they had no intention of intervening militarily or providing military equipment to the Ukrainian government. They were slow to impose sanctions, hoping that threats would suffice to coerce Russia to stop its military involvement in Eastern Ukraine. NATO also opted for the four battlegroup-strong trip-wire posture in Eastern Europe to minimise the risk of escalation. Had NATO adopted a deterrence by denial posture, deploying seven brigades in the Baltics and Poland to stop a Russian attack on the border (Shlapak and Johnson, 2016, p. 1), Russia would have had no choice but to increase its number of troops, as these brigades would have threatened its second largest city, St Petersburg. The result would have been heightened tensions, increasing the risk of a war that no one wants. NATO and the EU have also kept a door open for dialogue and negotiation throughout the confrontation.

Likewise, Russia has consistently tried to keep its military involvement in Eastern Ukraine under the radar, using soldiers without markings on their uniforms and denying direct involvement. Russia only intervened with regular forces when it became necessary in order to prevent Ukrainian forces from overrunning its proxies. Russia has also shown restraint by limiting its frequent harassment of NATO member states to their aircraft and warships. It has refrained from harassing the ground troops guarding NATO's borders because it would create a much higher risk of escalation. The loss of an aircraft or ship will trigger a crisis, but not a war. Harassing troops or security forces in the Baltics might do so, however. The easily outnumbered and outgunned Baltic forces have a strong incentive to escalate any confrontation with Russian proxies or little green men in order to force Russia to either back down or escalate their involvement above the Article Five threshold that will trigger a military response from the entire NATO alliance.

From 'increasing concern' to 'immediate and direct' threats from the south

> Five NATO members border on the 'Middle Sea'. The situation there is of increasing concern, and we are now ready to establish contacts, on a case-by-case basis, between

the Alliance and non-NATO Mediterranean countries, with a view to contributing to the strengthening of regional stability.

Claes (NATO Secretary-General) (1995, p. 7)

Before the Arab Spring turned violent, the threats emanating from the MENA region were perceived as a source of concern, not acute dangers requiring an immediate response. During the 1990s, NATO and the EU addressed them using the same liberal IR toolbox that they were using in the east. The two organisations emphasised consultation, dialogue and partnership in their efforts to bring peace and prosperity to the MENA region. NATO launched the Mediterranean Dialogue in 1994 with Egypt, Israel, Mauritania, Morocco and Tunisia. Algeria and Jordan joined in 1995 and 2000, respectively. The stated objectives were to contribute to regional security and stability, achieve better mutual understanding and dispel any misconceptions about NATO among Dialogue countries.

In 2004, NATO launched the Istanbul Cooperation Initiative, a complementary dialogue based on the same principles with Bahrain, Qatar, Kuwait and the United Arab Emirates.

The initiative was part of an attempt to make the Mediterranean Dialogue more operational, and to enlist the members in the fight against terrorism and the threat posed by weapons of mass destruction (WMD) and their means of delivery following the 11 September 2001 terrorist attacks against the USA (North Atlantic Treaty Organization, 2004).

The EU launched its Mediterranean Partnership in 1995. The objective of the partnership was to create security, stability and prosperity in MENA by strengthening democracy, rule of law, good governance and respect for human rights, trade liberalisation and increased cultural understanding through the development of civil society organisations (Barcelona Treaty, 1995). The principle means employed to this end were dialogue, cooperation and economic support and the assumption was that the Mediterranean countries would willingly transform their societies in accordance with EU demands just as the Eastern European states had done, since it was in their own best interests. The EU consequently relied primarily on the same constructivist-style socialisation approach relying on soft power instruments to initiate a positive spiral of cooperation that was expected to foster a sense of community and common interests. A renaming of the partnership to Union for the Mediterranean in 2008 did not change this approach; the liberal assumptions, instruments and objectives remained the same.

Although the EU and NATO used the same approach in the MENA region as they had done in Eastern Europe, their results were markedly different. Whereas the approach had the desired transformative effects in Europe, it made little difference in MENA. Three factors explain the different outcomes. The first was the different motivations of the partners. Whereas the majority of the countries to the east were eager to join the EU and NATO and wanted to adopt their ways and values, this was not the case with the MENA countries. Their cultural background and traditions were different. They had no identity-driven desire to be recognised as 'real Europeans', and several of the authoritarian regimes in MENA perceived democratisation and market liberalisation as threats to their power and privileges. NATO was viewed with suspicion as an instrument of the USA, and the EU promotion of democracy, human rights and free media as a subversive attempt to undermine their power.

They consequently limited EU support to regime-friendly groups and continued to clamp down on civil society groups perceived as threatening.

The second factor was that EU and NATO had fewer and far smaller carrots. Membership, the principle attraction inducing the Eastern European states to bend over backwards to meet EU and NATO demands, was not on offer. This deprived the EU and NATO of most of the soft power leverage that they had enjoyed in their dealing with their eastern partners (Nye, 1990). Whereas the countries to the east actively sought to internalise the ways and values of the West in order to be recognised as part of the EU–NATO community (Schimmelfennig, 1998), the MENA partners had a far more transactional view of their partnerships with the two organisations. They used the partnerships instrumentally to advance their immediate security and economic interests and ignored or opposed the aspects of partnerships that did not.

The ability of the EU and NATO to coerce the MENA partners to do something against their will was limited by the voluntary nature of the partnerships, and the fact that the EU and NATO could not threaten recalcitrant partners to put their membership applications on hold. When the 11 September attacks increased the dependence of the EU and NATO on MENA partner support in the 'War on Terror', their leverage declined further still. This dependence made it difficult for the two organisations to push for economic and democratic reforms and punish MENA partners restricting democratic freedoms and violating human rights. As a result, the EU and NATO were criticised for prioritising narrow economic and security interests at the expense of human rights and democracy (for this debate, see Malmvig, 2006). While this could be regarded a cynical Realpolitik, it also reflected the fact that the EU and NATO decision makers were caught in a dilemma with limited leverage.

This brings us to the third factor explaining the limited success enjoyed by the EU and NATO: the geopolitical context and the many conflicts characterising the region. The EU and NATO were not the key players in the MENA region. Unlike in Eastern Europe, where they enjoyed a near hegemonic position for almost two decades following the end of the Cold War until Russia began to reassert itself, the EU and NATO played a secondary role to the USA in MENA. The USA was the region's principle peace negotiator and conflict manager and it was not particularly keen on giving its European allies an independent role. This relegated NATO to a marginal role, and the EU's inability to wield military power made it ill-equipped to deal with the region's violent conflicts. The failed attempt by the EU-3 (France, Germany. and the UK) to negotiate a nuclear deal with Iran in 2003–2006 illustrates the limited influence of the EU. The EU-3 continued to participate in the negotiations jointly with Russia and the USA, but it took secret bilateral negotiations between the USA and Iran to achieve the breakthrough that led to the signing of the 2015 deal that made it much harder for Iran to develop nuclear weapons without detection (Cronberg, 2017, p. 45).

This impotence prompted the Israeli Prime Minister Sharon to comment that the EU was a 'payer and not a player' in the Middle East (cited in Talal, 2007). Sharon's scathing comment reflected the poor fit between the liberal ideals and soft power methods espoused by the EU and NATO, and the Hobbesian 'Realist' realities of the MENA region (Florensa, 2015). The success of EU and NATO's soft power instruments depended on a sense of community, shared interests and voluntary cooperation that simply did not exist.

Although this criticism of the EU and NATO preference for soft power methods has some bite, it goes only so far. The attempts to create democracy, peace and prosperity in the MENA region by means of hard military power and regime change did not fare any better. The American-led military overthrow of Saddam Hussein in 2003 created a very weak conflict-ridden state in Iraq and paved the way for the rise of the Islamic State of Iraq and the Levant (ISIL) in Iraq and Syria in 2014. Similarly, the NATO-assisted military overthrow of the Gaddafi regime in Libya in 2011 resulted in state collapse and the outbreak of a civil war. This collapse turned Libya into a major destination for migrants and refugees *en route* to Europe. In the 2012–2016 period, some 565,837 arrived in Europe from Libya (Darme and Benattia, 2017, p. 15). NATO's Libya operation thus helped create the refugee and migrant crisis that shook the cohesion of the EU in 2015. The failed Western efforts to stabilise and democratise the MENA region have, therefore, helped to create the immediate and direct threats that Europe now faces from the region.

EU and NATO responses to the immediate and direct MENA threats

> Our security is also deeply affected by the security situation in the Middle East and North Africa, which has deteriorated significantly across the whole region. Terrorism, particularly as perpetrated by the so-called Islamic State of Iraq and the Levant (ISIL)/ Da'esh, has risen to an unprecedented level of intensity, reaches into all of Allied territory, and now represents an immediate and direct threat to our nations and the international community. Instability in the Middle East and North Africa also contributes to the refugee and migrant crisis.
>
> (North Atlantic Treaty Organization, 2016, para. 5)

Heightening the sense of threat in 2015–2016 was a new toxic cocktail mixing the terrorist attacks launched or inspired by ISIL in Brussels, Paris and Berlin with the unprecedented influx of migrants and refugees driven primarily by the civil war in Syria. The EU's failure to control its external borders and find a way of distributing the many people arriving primarily in Greece and Italy among its member states led several EU states to reintroduce border controls and put up border fences. It also prompted fears that terrorists could to slip into the EU undetected. In the UK, 33% of the leave voters in the 2016 Brexit referendum indicated that their main reason for wanting to leave was that it 'offered the best chance for the UK to regain control over immigration and its own borders' (Lord Ashcroft, 2016). For the EU, the situation did constitute the 'existential threat' that its Global Strategy characterised it as (European External Action Service, 2016, p. 7).

The EU countered the threat in a comprehensive manner using virtually all the tools at its disposal (see Box 10.4). The first priority was to reduce the number of people coming to the EU. The principle tools employed to this end were strengthened border controls, direct targeting of criminal networks involved in migrant smuggling and, most important of all, two agreements with Turkey and the internationally recognised government controlling parts of Libya to stop people coming into the EU from their territories. Another key instrument was a new form of partnership agreements – so-called migration compacts – with MENA and African countries to reduce the number of people migrating to Europe and to increase the returns of rejected asylum seekers to their countries of origin. In addition, the EU also enhanced its dialogues with MENA partners to improve counter-terrorist cooperation by means of capacity building and security sector reform. Compared to the MENA partnership approach employed by the EU prior to 2011, the new one was far better resourced, more comprehensive, better coordinated and far more assertive. Thus, the EU began to make development assistance and other forms of support contingent upon cooperation with respect to fighting migration and terrorism.

Box 10.4 EU counter-terrorism and migration measures adopted since 2015

Asylum:

- European Asylum Support Office renamed EU Agency for Asylum and strengthened to enable it to better assist member states in crisis situations and monitor how national authorities apply relevant EU legislation
- Hotspots: operational support to Greece and Italy helping to identify, register and fingerprint incoming migrants

Border control:

- **European Travel Information and Authorisation System** to keep track of visa-free visitors entering the Schengen Zone
- Frontex renamed European Border and Coast Guard Agency and strengthened
- Passenger Name Record directive obliging airlines to hand over passengers lists when entering or leaving the EU
- Schengen Data Base checking all persons crossing external borders
- Operations Hera, Indalo, Minerva, Poseidon and Triton in support of Greece, Italy, and Spain
- Rapid reaction pool: 1,500 border guards deployable at short notice to assist members in emergencies at EU's external borders

Capacity building in partner countries:

- Security sector reform-associated measures, such as strengthening the rule of law, improving the governance of security providers, improving border management, reforming the armed forces, and training law enforcement actors

Counter-terrorist financing:

- Rules seeking to prevent the use of the financial system for the funding of criminal activities and strengthen transparency rules to prevent the large-scale concealment of funds

Cooperation with partners in MENA and Africa:

- EU–Africa trust fund: €2bn to help deport unwanted migrants and prevent people from leaving in the first place
- Enhanced bilateral Counter-terrorism Political Dialogues with Tunisia, Lebanon and Jordan: bilateral high-level meetings to strengthen cooperation on counter-terrorism and build capacity to deal better with terrorist threats, including foreign fighters
- New bilateral partnership agreements (migration compacts) with Ethiopia, Niger, Nigeria, Mali, and Senegal leveraging all EU instruments to reduce flows of illegal migration and increase return rates
- Libya agreement: €200 to Libya's internationally recognised government to stop migrant boats leaving the country's territorial waters. EU provides training and equipment to the Libyan coastguard and support for the voluntary returns of people to their countries of origin
- Turkey agreement €6bn to stop asylum seekers from crossing, by sea, to Lesbos

Law enforcement (EUROPOL):

- European Counter-Terrorism Centre (ECTC) providing operational support for investigations following terrorist attacks; tackling foreign fighters; and sharing intelligence and expertise on terrorism financing combats terrorist propaganda and related violent extremist activities on the internet
- European Migrant Smuggling Centre (EMSC) targeting and dismantling criminal networks involved in migrant smuggling

Operations:

- EUBAM Libya plans for a possible non-executive CSDP mission providing advice and capacity building in the fields of border management, law enforcement and criminal justice
- EUCAP Sahel Mali helping the national police, the national gendarmerie and the national guard to implement security reform
- EUCAP Sahel Niger supporting the Nigerien authorities in preventing irregular migration and combating associated crimes
- EUNAVFOR Sophia captures and disposes of vessels and enabling assets used or suspected of being used by migrant smugglers or traffickers; trains the Libyan Coastguard and Navy; and helps to enforce the UN arms embargo off the coast of Libya
- EUTM Mali provides military training and advice to the Malian armed forces to counter the terrorist groups operating in the country

Foreign fighters:

- Rules criminalising the undertaking of training or travelling for terrorist purposes, organising or facilitating such travel and providing or collecting funds related to terrorist groups or activities

Arms control:

- Measures enhancing traceability of firearms and preventing the reactivation or conversion of firearms

Strategic communications:

- Arab StratCom Task Force producing positive messages about the EU's involvement in the MENA region

Compiled from EU Factsheets and official documents, available at: www.consilium. europa.eu/en

The EU succeeded in stemming the inflow of people. The agreements made with Turkey and Libya led to a dramatic drop in the number of people arriving to the EU by sea in the Mediterranean (Darme and Benattia, 2017). The downside was the creation of a humanitarian crisis in Libya. Human rights organisations strongly criticised the EU for doing too little to assist the many people stranded in Libya, and of closing its eyes to serious human rights violations committed by the Libyan authorities with which the EU was cooperating (Amnesty International, 2017). From a liberal perspective, the EU sacrificed human rights and its liberal values on the altar of self-interest. From a realist perspective, the EU put its own interests first using all its instruments of power in a legitimate attempt to achieve them. From a constructivist perspective, the EU response suggested a move away from the civilian power identity that the EU had espoused until then.

This new, more assertive approach employed by the EU to elicit more cooperation from its MENA and African powers has had mixed results. These countries have little interest in preventing their citizens from migrating to the EU or in taking them back, because it reduces the flow of remittances, which make up a considerable portion of their national income. The African countries are, therefore, demanding that the EU make it easier for their citizens to migrate legally to Europe, demands that have very little support in the EU member states (Scazzieri and Springford, 2017). Yet, even if these countries did cooperate fully and in good faith with the EU, it would not solve the root causes of terrorism and migration in the foreseeable future. The huge differences in the standards of living and the demographic pressures driving migration will increase the migratory pressure on the EU in the decades ahead, no matter what the EU does.

Box 10.5   NATO counter-terror and migration measures since 2015

Capacity building in partner countries:

- Counter IED training provided to Iraq
- Counter-terrorism training courses to Egypt
- Counter-insurgency training to Jordan, Mauritania, Morocco, and Tunisia

Intelligence:

- Establishment of a new joint intelligence and security division
- Establishment of 'Hub for the South': 100-person strong focal point collecting, assessing and analysing information on threats from the MENA region and countering them in cooperation with partner nations

Operations:

- AWACS surveillance flights supporting the Global Coalition to Counter ISIL
- Maritime force in the Aegean Sea to conduct reconnaissance, monitoring and surveillance of illegal crossings, in support of Turkish and Greek authorities and the EU's Frontex agency
- Operation Sea Guardian contributing to maritime situational awareness, counter-terrorism at sea, and maritime security capacity building in the Mediterranean

Compiled from NATO Factsheets and official documents, available at: www.nato.int

Compared to the EU, NATO played a marginal role in addressing the more direct threats from the South. It has supported EU operations in the Mediterranean and the US-led coalition of the willing fighting ISIL in Iraq and Syria, and launched new small capacity building missions in MENA (see Box 10.5). Three factors explain the Alliance's limited involvement in MENA. The first is that the threats emanating from MENA come from many different sources. It has proved impossible for the most affected southern NATO members to agree on a common course of action, because they perceive the threats differently. The lack of agreement among the southern members puts them at a distinct disadvantage *vis-à-vis* the Eastern members, who all view Russia as a direct military threat necessitating a robust symmetric military response. Second, there are no obvious military responses to most of the MENA threats. The less than successful NATO operations in Afghanistan and Libya have left little appetite for new major operations in MENA. This makes it difficult for NATO to add value to what the EU is already doing. Third, the eastern members facing Russia are actively seeking to keep NATO's involvement in MENA to a minimum, fearing that it will divert scarce resources away from the Eastern front. While they are willing to pay lip service to the need to address the threats from the south, they have made minimal contributions to Alliance activities there (Jakobsen and Ringsmose, 2018).

Conclusion: learning to live with direct threats

Two decades followed the end of the Cold War without direct threats to the national security of European states. The EU Security Strategy (European Council, 2003, p. 1) stated that 'Europe has never been so prosperous, so secure nor so free. The violence of the first half of the 20th Century has given way to a period of peace and stability unprecedented in European history.' This period ended when Russia annexed the Crimea and launched a proxy war in Eastern Ukraine. Since then, Russia and the EU/NATO members have been rearming and blaming each other for triggering the new confrontation. At the same time, the turmoil in MENA triggered by the Arab spring gave rise to a host of new threats from the south. Unprecedented numbers of refugees and migrants arriving in the EU, combined with high-profile terrorist attacks, created a crisis in 2015–2016 that the EU deemed 'existential' (European External Action Service, 2016).

This chapter has shown how the EU and NATO have sought to export democracy, peace and stability by offering partnerships to their neighbours to the east and the south. The partnership offers rested on the assumption that these countries would willingly introduce democracy, human rights and market economies, because it was in their own interest to do so.

It worked well with the Eastern and Central European countries glad to escape Soviet rule. It did not work with Russia and MENA, as these countries or states had no identity-driven urge to join the Western community and little interest in economic and political reforms that threatened their power and privileges.

In the near to medium term, the prospects of defusing the new threats seem slim. The EU–NATO and Russia remain on a collision course with both sides trying to influence the former Soviet republics caught between them to join their institutions. In MENA and Africa, the divergence in interests between EU–NATO and their partners and the scale of the problems that drive the armed conflicts, the terrorism and the migration threatening Europe leave the EU and NATO no choice but to prioritise firefighting over long-term stabilisation.

In general, however, the EU and NATO have succeeded in preventing the situation from getting worse. This applies in the confrontation with Russia and with respect to stemming the inflow of refugees and migrants, and the number of terrorist attacks committed in their member states. The rise of the new threats and their relative success in handling them has helped to strengthen both organisations. Although NATO members disagree on how to handle the threats from the east and south, the military threat from the east has given NATO a new sense of direction and common purpose, and most of the European members have begun increasing their defence spending (Jakobsen and Ringsmose, 2018). The same is true, albeit to a lesser extent, for the EU, given Brexit and the internal disagreements triggered by the migration crisis. The rise of non-military threats in the form of disinformation, cyber attacks, attempts to influence elections and the need to tackle migration, refugees and terrorism has made the EU a central and indispensable European security actor. The EU is the only actor capable of countering all these non-military threats in a comprehensive and coordinated manner; none of the member states can do this on their own. This is reflected in all the actions taken by the EU to counter these threats (see Box 10.4), and in the growing EU–NATO cooperation with respect to countering the hybrid and non-military threats facing contemporary European security. The new threat environment not only creates a pressing need for greater EU–NATO cooperation; it also facilitates it by giving them key roles in their zones of comfort. NATO can take the lead in nuclear and conventional deterrence and defence, whereas the EU can lead in the non-military domains.

The fundamental disagreements characterising the Russo–Western relations and the structural factors generating terrorism and migration in the MENA region and sub-Saharan Africa preclude any quick solution to the new threats facing Europe. The Europeans will have to learn to live with them. The no-threat environment characterising the first two decades following the end of the Cold War has gone. The good news is that the new era is less dangerous than the Cold War, where the risk of full-scale (nuclear) war was much higher than today.

Further reading

European External Action Service (2016), *Shared Vision, Common Action: A Stronger Europe. A Global Strategy for the European Union's Foreign and Security Policy*. Luxembourg: Publications Office of the European Union.

Jakobsen, Peter Viggo, and Ringsmose, Jens (2018), 'Victim of Its Own Success: How NATO's Difficulties Are Caused by the Absence of a Unifying Existential Threat', *Journal of Transatlantic Studies*, 16 (1), 38–58.

Weblinks

European Agenda on Migration Factsheets: https://ec.europa.eu/home-affairs/what-we-do/policies/european-agenda-migration/background-information_en

European Union Factsheets: www.consilium.europa.eu/en

NATO: www.nato.int

References

Amnesty International (2017), 'Libya's Dark Web of Collusion Abuses against Europe-Bound Refugees and Migrants', Amnesty International Report MDE 19/7561/2017. Available at: www.amnesty.org/download/Documents/MDE1975612017ENGLISH.PDF (accessed: 25 October 2018).

Apuzzo, Matt, and LaFraniere, Sharon (2018), '13 Russians Indicted as Mueller Reveals Effort to Aid Trump Campaign', *New York Times*, 16 February. Available at: www.nytimes.com/2018/02/16/us/politics/russians-indicted-mueller-election-interference.html (accessed: 25 October 2018).

Barcelona Treaty (1995), 'Barcelona Declaration Adopted at the Euro-Mediterranean Conference', 27–28 November, Barcelona. Available at: https://ec.europa.eu/research/iscp/pdf/policy/barcelona_declaration.pdf (accessed: 25 October 2018).

Blomfield, Adrian, and Kirkup, James (2008), 'Stay Away, Vladimir Putin Tells Nato', *Telegraph*, 5 April.

Bouchet, Nicolas (2016), 'Russia's "Militarization" of Colour Revolutions', *Policy Perspectives*, 4 (2), 1–4.

Chivvis, Christopher S. (2017), *Understanding Russian 'Hybrid Warfare' and What Can Be Done About It*. Santa Monica, CA: Rand.

Claes, Willy (1995), 'NATO and the Evolving Euro-Atlantic Security Architecture', *NATO Review*, 42 (1), 3–7.

Cronberg, Tarja (2017), *Nuclear Multilateralism and Iran: Inside EU Negotiations*. London: Routledge.

Darme, Marie-Cecile, and Benattia, Tahar (2017), 'Mixed Migration Trends in Libya: Changing Dynamics and Protection Challenges', Altai Consulting Report for UNHCR. Available at: www.unhcr.org/uk/publications/operations/595a02b44/mixed-migration-trends-libya-changing-dynamics-protection-challenges.html (accessed: 25 October 2018).

European Council (1993), 'Presidency Conclusions: Copenhagen European Council', SN 180/1/93 REV 1, 21–22 June, European Council, Brussels. Available at: www.europarl.europa.eu/enlargement_new/europeancouncil/pdf/cop_en.pdf (accessed: 25 October 2018).

European Council (2003), *A Secure Europe in a Better World: European Security Strategy*. Brussels: European Council.

European External Action Service (2016), *Shared Vision, Common Action: A Stronger Europe. A Global Strategy for the European Union's Foreign and Security Policy*. Luxembourg: Publications Office of the European Union.

European Union (1994), 'Partnership and Cooperation Agreement', *Official Journal of the European Communities*, L 327, 28/11/1997 P. 0003 – 0069. Available at: http://trade.ec.europa.eu/doclib/docs/2003/november/tradoc_114138.pdf (accessed: 25 October 2018).

European Union (2017), 'Russia's and the EU's Sanctions: Economic and Trade Effects, Compliance and the Way Forward', Policy Department Report, Directorate-General for External Policies, Brussels. Available at: www.europarl.europa.eu/RegData/etudes/STUD/2017/603847/EXPO_STU(2017)603847_EN.pdf (accessed: 25 October 2018).

Florensa, Senén (2015), 'The Euromed Dream in the New Hobbesian International Wilderness', in *IEMed Mediterranean Yearbook 2015*. Barcelona: Institut Europeu de la Mediterrània, 87–97.

Friedman, Thomas L. (1998), 'Now a Word From X', *New York Times*, 2 May.

Galeotti, Mark (2015), '"Hybrid War" and "Little Green Men": How It Works, and How It Doesn't', in Agnieszka Pikulicka-Wilczewska and Richard Sakwa (eds), *Ukraine and Russia: People, Politics, Propaganda and Perspectives*. Bristol: E-International Relations, pp. 149–156.

Garver, Rob (2015), 'How Many Russian Soldiers Have Died in Ukraine? A Glimpse at the Bloody Toll', *Fiscal Times*, 28 August.

Jakobsen, Peter Viggo, and Ringsmose, Jens (2018), 'Victim of Its Own Success: How NATO's Difficulties Are Caused by the Absence of a Unifying Existential Threat', *Journal of Transatlantic Studies*, 16 (1), 38–58.

Lord Ashcroft (2016), 'How the United Kingdom Voted on Thursday . . . and Why', *Lord Ashcroft Polls*, 24 June. Available at https://lordashcroftpolls.com/2016/06/how-the-united-kingdom-voted-and-why/ (accessed: 25 October 2018).

Luhn, Alec (2015), 'National Endowment for Democracy Is First "Undesirable" NGO Banned in Russia', *Guardian*, 28 July.

Malmvig, Helle (2006), 'Caught Between Cooperation and Democratization: The Barcelona Process and the EU's Double-Discursive Approach', *Journal of International Relations and Development*, 9 (4), 343–370.

Marocchi, Tania (2017), 'EU–Russia Relations: Towards an Increasingly Geopolitical Paradigm', *Heinrich Böll Stiftung European Union*, 3 July. Available at: https://eu.boell.org/en/2017/07/03/eu-russia-relations-towards-increasingly-geopolitical-paradigm (accessed: 25 October 2018).

Marsh, Sarah (2018), 'US Joins UK in Blaming Russia for NotPetya Cyber-Attack', *Guardian*, 15 February.

Marshall, Andrew (1994), 'Russia Warns Nato of a "Cold Peace"', *Independent*, 6 December.

Mearsheimer, John J. (1990), 'Why We Will Soon Miss the Cold War', *Atlantic Monthly*, 266 (2), 35–50.

North Atlantic Treaty Organization (1997), 'Founding Act on Mutual Relations, Cooperation and Security between NATO and the Russian Federation', 27 May, Paris. Available at: www.nato.int/cps/su/natohq/official_texts_25468.htm (accessed: 25 October 2018).

North Atlantic Treaty Organization (2004), 'A More Ambitious and Expanded Framework for the Mediterranean Dialogue', 28 June. Available at: www.nato.int/cps/us/natohq/official_texts_59357.htm (accessed: 25 October 2018).

North Atlantic Treaty Organization (2016), 'Warsaw Summit Communiqué Issued by the Heads of State and Government Participating in the Meeting of the North Atlantic Council in Warsaw 8–9 July', Press Release 2016/100, 9 July. Available at: www.nato.int/cps/su/natohq/official_texts_133169.htm (accessed: 25 October 2018).

Nye, Joseph S. Jr. (1990), 'The Changing Nature of World Power', *Political Science Quarterly*, 105 (2), 177–192.

Organization for Security and Co-operation in Europe (1990), 'Charter of Paris for a New Europe', Second CSCE Summit of Heads of State or Government, Paris, 21 November. Available at: www.osce.org/mc/39516 (accessed: 25 October 2018).

Palmer, Diego A. Ruiz (2015), 'Back to the Future? Russia's Hybrid Warfare, Revolutions in Military Affairs, and Cold War Comparisons', *Research Paper 120*. Rome: NATO Defense College.

Pop, Valentina (2009), 'EU Expanding Its "Sphere of Influence," Russia Says', *EU Observer*, 21 March. Available at: https://euobserver.com/foreign/27827 (accessed: 25 October 2018).

Putin, Vladimir (2012), 'Russia and the Changing World', *RIA Novosti*, 27 February.

Scazzieri, Luigi, and Springford, John (2017), 'How the EU and Third Countries can Manage Migration', Centre for European Reform Policy Brief. Available at: www.cer.eu/sites/default/files/pbrief_amato_migration_1nov17.pdf (accessed: 25 October 2018).

Schimmelfennig, Frank (1998), 'Nato Enlargement: A Constructivist Explanation', *Security Studies*, 8 (2–3), 198–234.

Shlapak, David A., and Johnson Michael (2016), *Reinforcing Deterrence on NATO's Eastern Flank*. Santa Monica, CA: Rand.

Talal, El-Hassan Bin (2007), 'From Payer to Player in the Middle East', *Daily Star*, 1 November.

U.S. State Department (1997), 'Minimum Requirements for NATO Membership', Fact sheet prepared by the Bureau of European and Canadian Affairs, June 30. Available at: https://1997–2001.state.gov/regions/eur/fs_members.html (accessed: 25 October 2018).

Wilson, Andrew (2006), 'Ukraine's Orange Revolution, NGOs and the Role of the West', *Cambridge Review of International Affairs*, 19 (1), 21–32.

Innovating European defence   11

Simon J. Smith

Introduction

If war is inherently a social act, the same must be said of military innovation. Even narrowing down the key terms and definitions reveals this. The subject of this chapter is the innovation of European defence, but the literature on military change has been referred to as 'revolution' (as in the Revolution in Military Affairs), 'transformation' (as in military, martial or force transformation), 'innovation', 'adaptation' and 'change in military praxis' (see Grissom, 2006).

Traditionally, the literature on military innovation was understood to be more the discipline of history and military studies than a social science *per se*. According to Grissom (2006, p. 906), this early literature was formed of 'grand historical narratives, operational histories, or bureaucratic–political case studies'. That is, until the publication of *The Sources of Military Doctrine*, by Barry Posen, in 1984. Posen stands out for bringing a social scientific approach to the study of military innovation, but is representative of only one school of thought on how militaries innovate. Since then, there has been a flourishing literature that is informed by both the disciplines of history and the social sciences.

Stephen Rosen has defined major innovation in defence organisations as 'a change that forces one of the primary combat arms of a service to change its concepts of operation and its relation to other combat arms, and to abandon or downgrade traditional missions' (1988, p. 134). This definition is appropriate because it allows us to understand innovation in terms of material, ideational and operational indicators of change. Since the end of the Cold War, military organisations in Europe have faced significant reductions in both budgets and manpower while many have also been conducting martial operations, either independently or through collective security organisations such as the EU or NATO. In short, European militaries have been asked to do more with less, which, in turn, necessitates some form of innovation. The aim of this chapter is to understand the various ways defence forces in Europe have innovated to accommodate this confluence of factors. The chapter addresses military innovation by first looking at historical, geopolitical and strategic contextual trends.

The chapter will then outline some of the key conceptual ways that scholars have sought to theorise drivers of innovation in military organisations more generally. Finally, we will apply these concepts to specific cases in order to illuminate the varied and particular approaches to innovation that European militaries have incorporated to meet their material, ideational and operational challenges.

Military innovation and the traditional approach: key lessons from history

This section illustrates some of the central themes and motivating questions that have been central to the more 'grand historical narratives' approach to understanding military innovation. It demonstrates the ways in which key historical events – in particular large-scale wars – have shaped the thinking of military strategists and organisations when it comes to how they prepare, respond and generally attempt to innovate before and after these events. It also demonstrates how scholars and theorists have come to understand the central questions and challenges that face military organisations in terms of innovation in response to socio-political, resource, and organisational concerns. Box 11.1 offers a comprehensive (but not necessarily exhaustive or mutually exclusive) indication of the challenges and questions facing modern military forces and their prospects for innovation that are considered in this chapter.

Box 11.1   Types of questions driving military innovation

Socio-political questions:

- To have democratic–political oversight of armed forces?
- What is the military for and what is the extent and range of tasks it is expected to perform?
- To pursue nuclear forces or remain conventional only?
- All-volunteer forces vs. conscription?
- The role of women in the armed forces?
- What degree (if any) do alliances play in a military strategy?
- How much to spend as a percentage of GDP on armed forces?
- To what degree will armed forces participate in frontline high-intensity tactics and operations?
- What ratio between territorial defence and expeditionary forces?
- To what degree should the military be integrated with another state's or an international organisation's military decision making, command and operational structures?

Economic and resource questions:

- Full-spectrum force versus specialisation?
- How much to spend on new capability development and R&D vs. only maintaining current force posture?

- What is your defence industrial strategy?
- To buy military capabilities off-the-shelf, develop and procure from domestic defence industry or pursue multinational military development and procurement programmes – or some mixture of these options?
- How to prioritise *quantity* vs. *quality* of military capability?

Organisational questions:

- Size of regular forces vs. dependency on reserves?
- What ratio between land, air and sea force structure (now also cyber and space)?
- The ratio of prioritisation between preparedness, doctrine and capabilities for conventional warfighting (e.g., fighting near-peer adversaries) and/or irregular warfighting (e.g., counter-insurgency)?
- To prioritise manoeuvre or attrition when preparing for future war?
- How will technology and military capabilities shape the character of war?
- To what extent will your forces be interoperable with allies?
- What percentage of your force will be earmarked for bi-lateral or multilateral military operations or peacekeeping missions?
- How to prioritise *risk* vs. *force protection*?

A central concern of military strategists and organisations has always been attempting to understand the character (not the nature) of the next war. According to Clausewitz, the famous Prussian military strategist, war's *nature* does not change but its *character* often does (1997, p. 22). As Christopher Mewett (2014) has explained, the nature of war relates to its 'unchanging essence' or, 'those things that differentiate war (as a type of phenomenon) from other things'. Thus, the nature of war is 'violent, interactive, and fundamentally political'. However, the 'character of war describes the changing way that war as a phenomenon manifests in the real world' (Mewett, 2014). Logically, our focus must be skewed towards the character of warfare, as our concern is the processes and drivers of military innovation; how and why militaries change, adapt and transform in order to be fit for (some) purpose – traditionally that of wining wars. This chapter considers how militaries – specifically European militaries – innovate in terms of both theory and practice.

In terms of traditional approaches to innovation, thinkers tended to address this question according to strict interpretations of defence and military studies. In other words, the focus was primarily on the study of military tactics, operations and strategy, the outcome of large-scale wars and any lessons learnt that could be gained. For example, they may consider if the next war (i.e., a war that may have to be fought) is likely to be dominated by defence or offence, often referred to as *manoeuvre* or *attrition*. A separate but related issue is the impact of technology and military capabilities for shaping the character of the next war. The First World War is often, as we will see below, understood as a classic example of when military strategists got things wrong – and devastatingly so – but as this section demonstrates, military strategists quite often get it wrong. A few key historical examples help to illustrate this.

In the current age, conflict is often described with terms such as *irregular* or *hybrid* warfare and fought in *grey zones*. But the traditional understanding of *regular* warfare is something that takes place between the identifiable militaries of states (usually great powers) and with finite conclusions. Of course, these are generalities and historians are always keen to point this out. Yet, before major wars, there is always a lot of uncertainty about what the next war will look like and how the combination of capabilities, technology and doctrine will affect the tangible character of the conflict that transpires.

The accepted thinking before the First World War was that a combination of speed – due to industrialisation – and advances in technology, leading to an increased lethality of weapons, would mean this next war would be deadly, mobile, offensive and short. Deadly as it may have been, the war was, in fact, a slow, bogged-down war of attrition. Military planners fundamentally misunderstood the impact of those weapons they believed to be offensive (machine-guns and artillery) but which turned out to be much more suited towards defensive tactics and operations. Therefore, a central concern that emerged from the Great War – and one that focused the minds of strategist and innovators alike during the inter-war period – was how to burst the tyranny of defence. Wartime is a critical driver of innovation by necessity, but strategists also try to use times of peace to learn key lessons from the past to innovate their forces, capabilities and doctrine.

This leads to another key theme emanating from the traditional approaches to military innovation: innovators and planners usually draw different lessons from the study of previous wars. In the inter-war period, strategists from all the great powers did exactly this. The conclusion that the French Army drew from the First World War was to further strengthen strategies of defence, ultimately resulting in the Maginot Line. The German answer was to prioritise combined arms with speed and mobility by innovating and refining their use of capabilities and doctrine towards *blitzkrieg*. During the same period, but not simultaneously, factions arose in both the USA (within the Army Air Corps) and the UK (the RAF) that looked to airpower for strategic answers on how to win wars. In short, military thinkers and strategists often prepare for the last (or wrong) war. Moreover, war and the perceived threat of war causes competition for ideas with regard to the most prudent ways for militaries to innovate.

Interestingly, capabilities were generally advancing in line with technological progress for all the great military powers. The difference was how the various military organisations chose to employ those capabilities. Michael Horowitz (2010, p. 7) has termed this 'adoption capacity theory', or the match between the financial and organisational requirements for adopting a new type of military innovation and the capabilities that a particular country might have. All the great powers were developing advanced (for the time) prototypes of submarines, aircraft and armoured fighting vehicles, but the missions they assigned those capabilities and the doctrine they applied were distinctive and tailored to their own lessons learnt.

Before we turn to the next section, two more themes that developed out of the more traditional approaches are insightful with regard to innovation more broadly. The first is that advocates of innovation often oversell (at least initially) the strategic impact of their proposed innovation. During the Second World War, both the examples of *blitzkrieg* and strategic airpower help to reinforce this concept. Although *blitzkrieg* was a highly successful military tactic, this lethal combination of combined arms and manoeuvre was not enough to translate into a strategic victory on either the Western or Eastern fronts. Moreover, Germany's adversaries were eventually able to learn and adopt these tactics as well, demonstrating again that innovation tends to happen most rapidly during war. In the case of strategic airpower, early attempts to innovate and apply these tactics were not met with the success rates that the first US Army Air Corps' advocates such as Edgar Gorrell, Thomas Milling, William 'Billy' Mitchell, and William Sherman had envisioned or asserted before the start of the war. All of this points to one final theme: certain factions of innovation may fight over the best tactics, operations and strategies, but it is war that ultimately decides.

Military innovation and the social sciences: theorising innovation

The study of military innovation began to take on a more social scientific approach in the 1980s with the publication of *The Sources of Military Doctrine* (1984). Yet, the literature has advanced and broadened considerably since then. Terriff et al. (2010, p. 7) have distinguished 'three main factors that shape the trajectory of military innovation: threat, civil–military relations and military culture'. This section aims to distinguish the various strands in this literature and to identify the key theoretical assumptions attached to each (see Table 11.1). But before this can be achieved, it is important to put forth a general definition of military innovation. Stephen Rosen has defined major innovation in defence organisations as 'a change that forces one of the primary combat arms of a service to change its concepts of operation and its relation to other combat arms, and to abandon or downgrade traditional missions' (1988, p. 134).

Building on Rosen, Grissom (2006, p. 907) offers a definition whereby three elements constitute a tacit definition of military innovation:

(1) an innovation changes the manner in which military formations function in the field. Measures that are administrative or bureaucratic in nature, such as acquisition reform, are not considered legitimate innovation unless a clear link can be drawn to operational praxis.
(2) an innovation is significant in scope and impact. Minor reforms or those that have had ambiguous effects on a military organisation are excluded, implying a consequentialist understanding of military innovation.
(3) innovation is tacitly equated with greater military effectiveness. Only reforms that produce greater military effectiveness are studied as innovations, and few would consider studying counterproductive policies as innovations.

This definition approximates to 'a change in operational praxis that produces a significant increase in military effectiveness as measured by battlefield results' (Grissom, 2006). Some literature makes distinctions between 'sustaining innovation' and 'disruptive innovation' (Farrell et al., 2013, p. 8). As described in their significant volume *Transforming Military Power since the Cold War*, 'sustaining innovation' seeks to 'improve on traditionally valued ways of war'. The latter is an innovation that seeks to improve 'undervalued ways of war, or to develop wholly new ways of war'. They also note that 'disruptive innovation' is a more sizable challenge than 'sustaining innovation', due to the necessary changes in 'vested organizational interests' and 'dominant organizational ideas about war' (Farrell et al., 2013, p. 8). Taken together, this description allows us to understand innovation as material, ideational and operational indicators of change. But we must also ask, how and from where do these changes originate? Is innovation driven by exogenous or endogenous dynamics, or some mixture of both? To do this, let us now turn to the major schools of military innovation.

The first is that most identified with the work of Barry Posen, the *civil–military model of military innovation*. Posen's (1984) work also investigated the key inter-war doctrinal developments by the German, British and French armed forces, as alluded to in the section above. However, his analysis focused on a critical explanatory variable – the dynamics of civil–military relations. He argued that this civil–military dynamic is achieved through a response to perceived external threats that, in turn, determine if and how militaries innovate. According to Posen, innovation succeeds when statesmen 'intervene in military service doctrinal development' and ideally with the support of 'maverick officers'. Furthermore, if militaries fail to innovate, they will 'gradually stagnate and ultimately fail the societies they exist to serve' (Grissom, 2006, p. 909; Posen, 1984, pp. 222–236). Clearly, in this model, innovation is derived from exogenous factors and follows a top-down logic. This model recognises military innovation as critically dependent on the influence and manoeuvring of political/civilian leadership to orchestrate change. This does include interaction between the civil–military leadership, but the former retains dominance via its access to, and control of, resources and other forms of civil authority.

Resources as an external driver of change are also at the centre of the *interservice model of military innovation* (for examples, see Bacevich, 1986; Cote, 1998; Sapolsky, 1972, 2000). Within this understanding, it is not the dynamic between the civilian and military branches *per se* – which does still exist – but the resulting competition between the distinct service branches of the military for resources (normally in a resource-scarce environment) that is the primary driver of innovation. To rephrase Rosen's definition, above: a primary combat arm of a service will change its concept of operations and its relation to other combat arms, and abandon or downgrade traditional missions, while competing for resources in pursuit of other concepts, missions and capabilities in order to stay relevant. In short, the processes here are still externally driven, highly political, but overwhelmingly *bureaucratic*, due to a mixture of high reticence towards change and the interservice component of resource competition.

The *intraservice model of military innovation* changes the focus from interservice to intra-service competition and, specifically, 'competition between branches of the same military service' (Grissom, 2006, p. 913). Stephen Rosen (1991) has been a primary thinker in this understanding of innovation. He postulates that services are not static unitary actors. In fact, they produce internal actors who 'advocate' innovation in pursuit of 'a new theory of victory, an explanation of what the next war will look like and how officers must fight if it is to be won' (Rosen, 1991, p. 20). As Grissom explains, 'innovation in modern military organizations tends to involve competition between established branches of a military service and new branches that embrace new military capabilities' (Grissom, 2006, p. 913). Again, we can see a connection to the approaches in the previous section: aircraft carrier innovation over the battleship (Royal Navy) or strategic bombing innovation over airpower seen only as tactical ground support (US Army Air Corps). Critical to innovation under this approach is the estab-lishment of 'a new arm or branch of service and opening the senior officer echelons to officers from the new arm' (Grissom, 2006, p. 914).

Terry Terriff, Frans Osinga and, most notably, Theo Farrell have been critical to the devel-opment of a fourth strand in the literature – the *cultural model of military innovation*. In the work *The Sources of Military Change: Culture, Politics, Technology*, Farrell recognises culture to be 'intersubjective beliefs about the social and natural world that define actors, their situations, and the possibilities of action' (Farrell and Terriff, 2001, p. 7). This, he argues, is a significant driver of military innovation. In their book, *A Transformation Gap? American Innovation and European Military Change*, the authors offer the concept of military culture as a vital 'shaping factor' (Terriff et al., 2010, p. 8). Military culture encapsulates those 'identities, norms and val-ues' whereby military organisations internalise their 'role and function' in response to their understanding of their external security environment (Terriff et al., 2010, p. 8).

What is significant is that military culture can actually transpire into a 'brake on innova-tion' due to its reflection of inherent biases derived from those very identities, norms and values. As Joseph Schumpeter has argued (in Sapolsky, 2000, p. 35), resistance to change in organisations is expected given that there are winners and losers in any change. Innovation, he argues, 'is a process of creative destruction. The new kills off the old' (Schumpeter, in Sapolsky, 2000, p. 35). But, unlike Posen, who argues military innovation comes from the outside, this brake can only be overcome by a credible military 'leader with authority' to advocate for the necessary cultural change. If this is a direct challenge to a military organisa-tion's 'core identity', it is still likely to be problematic (Terriff et al., 2010, p. 8). As Farrell and Terriff (2001, p. 9) understand it, 'Innovation that goes against organizational identity usually requires some external shock to military culture, such as defeat in war, in order to jolt the military into a fundamental rethink of its purpose and core business'.

Table 11.1 gives an overview of the key theoretical schools of military innovation studies, as well as some key empirical examples and leading scholars within the various conceptual strands of the literature.

Innovating European defence

Given the strands of literature outlined in the previous section, how can we then apply this to the case of Europe specifically? What is needed is an analytical framework that would allow us to cut across these literatures of transformation to provide some meaningful understand-ing around the specificity of innovation regarding European militaries. In short, what are the implied drivers of innovation?

Table 11.1 Theories of military innovation

Model of military innovation	Key theoretical assumptions	Empirical examples	Key authors
The civil–military model of military innovation	Civil–military dynamics in response to perceived external threats determine if and how militaries innovate (Grissom, 2006, p. 908).	Key interwar doctrinal developments by the German, British and French armed forces.	Barry Posen Kimberly M. Zisk Edmund Beard Deborah Avant
The interservice model of military innovation	Resource scarcity is a key catalyst for innovation. Military organisations seek to maintain their budget authority and end-strength, which requires them to maintain control over their traditional missions. This model posits that services will compete to develop capabilities to address these contested mission areas, believing that additional resources will accrue to the winner. The result is innovation (Grissom, 2006, p. 910).	Development of the Polaris submarine-launched ballistic missile system. The development of the A-10 Warthog and the 'Close Air Support Debate'.	Harvey M. Sapolsky Douglas N. Campbell Michael Armacost Owen Cote Andrew Bacevich.
The intraservice model of military innovation	Military services should not be treated as unitary actors. Instead, innovation in modern military organisations tends to involve competition between established branches of a military service and new branches that embrace new military capabilities. The innovation process begins when senior officers develop 'a new theory of victory, an explanation of what the next war will look like and how officers must fight if it is to be won'. An 'ideological struggle' ensues within the service. Advocates of the new theory work within the service to find allies and resources (Grissom, 2006, p. 913)	New special operations capabilities created by US Department of Defense during the 1980s by managing intraservice politics. The development of the Tomahawk cruise missile. The development of the M2 Bradley infantry fighting vehicle.	Stephen P. Rosen Jon F. Giese Susan L. Marquis Vincent Davis
The cultural model of military innovation	Culture (defined as 'intersubjective beliefs about the social and natural word that define actors, their situations, and the possibilities of action') is a major causal factor in military innovation. Culture sets the context for military innovation, fundamentally shaping organisations' reactions to technological and strategic opportunities (Grissom, 2006, p. 916).	The development of French and British doctrine between the World Wars. The relationship between professional military education and the professional culture of a military organisation.	Theo G. Farrell Terry Terriff Robert E. Mullins Emily O. Goldman

The first is that militaries are being used beyond their traditional Cold War remits of national and regional defence towards counter-insurgency (COIN), peacekeeping, counter-piracy, counter-terrorism, cyber security and more. In line with Posen's argument, this change is a response to the changing strategic context in which militaries find themselves. The second driver is budgets, or, rather, how much and in what way are governments paying for their militaries. As Sapolsky notes (1972, 2000), militaries are just one of many policy areas for which governments are responsible. Furthermore, this change in government priorities also reacts to social and political value changes which turn into electoral constraints (Edmunds, 2006). Finally, the third driver is the socio-technological adaptations that we see in applied operational contexts challenging traditional platforms, forcing militaries to rethink force, mass and space. As Farrell et al. (2013) suggest, there is a constant tension between the ever-changing adversarial relationship with the enemy and the resources that a military actually maintains.

There are other drivers at play. One of the most significant has been the changing nature of the Trans-Atlantic Alliance. This has three over-arching explanations. First, NATO has both enlarged and expanded geographically from its 12 founding members to a current membership of 29 states stretching much further east than during the Cold War. Second, NATO – or NATO member states acting in coalitions of the willing – have conducted military operations from Bosnia and then Kosovo, to Afghanistan and Iraq (though the latter was not a NATO operation itself), to off the coasts of Somalia and Libya. For some, like Stuart Croft et al. (2000), these operations have given NATO a new lease, and, as we will see, they have also been a key driver of innovation for many European states. Finally, we have the USA's changing relationship with Europe, from 'pivots' to 'resets', and there is uncertainty about what the medium- to long-term strategy is for the US government and where the transatlantic partnership fits into that. This uncertainty has only increased under the Trump Administration since 2017. Nevertheless, the USA remains a key transmission-belt for European military innovation, perhaps even more so than European governments themselves.

The explanatory logic contained in the four models outlined above has been evident in European innovation since the Cold War. This literature is distinctly layered, whereby military innovation and transformation is driven by state interest that is filtered through various external threat perceptions, attitudes towards alliance politics, domestic political–social agendas, and/or combat operational necessities. In the immediate post Cold War era, European governments welcomed the so-called 'peace dividend' and their militaries have been shaped less by existential threats posed by great powers as the context of European security changed to making and keeping the peace and to fighting the 'War on Terror'. At the same time, the USA was experimenting with different approaches to warfare that would attempt to build in momentum and change. European militaries have also experienced the other layered drivers, as NATO enlarged and 'transformed', as defence budgets shrank and services competed, and as European militaries found themselves in protracted but illusive combat in Afghanistan and Iraq.

However, the transformation literature fails to take into account the interlinking between layers. Rather than seeing these drivers as distinct, we should instead see them as interrelated and reflexive, whereby adaptions and innovation at the operational level may reverberate in budgets, services, alliances and even perceptions of global threats to national security. What is needed is a way that we can look at this system of military change that is able to take these linkages into account. The research project, 'The Drivers of Military Strategic Reform in the Face of Economic Crisis and Changing Warfare', led by David J. Galbreath (see also Galbreath, 2016), has suggested one framework for accomplishing this. As a result, this chapter suggests that change can be understood across the literature in three ways: *transform, transfer* and *translate*.

This approach assumes that militaries are always forward leaning, even when path-dependent and perhaps doomed to prepare for the next war in the style of the last one (see Gray, 2005). In fact, not only does competition and uncertainty drive change, but organisations naturally transform, as suggested by Niklas Luhmann (2006). All of this is to say that we should expect to see change as a necessary element of *transformation*.

Second, *transference* entails a relocation from outside a military into said military. Typically, the transformation literature has suggested that the USA and its so-called revolution in military affairs (RMA) has been a frame that has had an impact on European militaries, whether that is network-centric warfare, effects-based operations, paramilitary troops (Farrell and Rynning, 2010; Galbreath, 2014, 2015) or something more practical such as basic military kit. More often, though, transfer happens through socialisation. In their studies of military transformation, Theo Farrell (Terriff et al., 2010) and Ina Wiesner (2013) suggest that transformation often happens as a result of communication between officers from different militaries, in particular at officer training in the USA. Reporting those responsible for platforms such as networked enabledness, there is evidence that some innovations or adaptations are, in fact, learnt, especially when they are within the context of a notion or system of war. At the same time, there is often such a dependence on deploying with US forces, that there needs to be a way in which European armed forces can 'plug in' to US forces without making either less battle-ready (see Rasmussen, 2013). This dilemma fits into the capabilities gap that has arisen between US and European forces since the end of the Cold War (see Coonen, 2006). However, we should allow for the possibility that European-to-European transfer may be even more relevant than that between the USA and a European military. Although we can expect that the majority of original innovation would be located in a military that is more resourced and diverse, like the US military, this does not mean to suggest that European forces cannot be the source of innovation as well.

Finally, we can think of military change through the concept of *translation*. Already, we understand that while European states may share some basic, and perhaps even advanced, notions of war with US forces, we also can see that European states have different military traditions and strategic cultures that shape the way they think about deployment and operations. In fact, it is difficult to find a direct transfer from one military to another. Nearly 70 years of NATO suggests that the translation between the USA's and European militaries should be gradually less over time, but this does not take into account either how resourced and large the US military is and neither does it take into account the changes in European social values towards standing armies since the end of the Cold War. The RMA was translated to Europe, through joint deployments, NATO Allied Command Transformation (ACT) and its impact on the USA's and European defence industries. Network-centric warfare, perhaps a major characterisation of RMA, has been translated, however, in various different ways in Europe as a result of cultural and resources conditions. Cultural and resource conditions are difficult to separate, in as far as states will seek to resource what they find strategically and culturally important. Of the three explanations of change, *translation* is arguably the most useful in explaining military innovation in Europe.

In summary, *transform*, *transfer* and *translate* can be understood to work across the multiple levels of change established in the innovation literature review section, above. With transfer and translate concentrating on the role of social communication and learning, we should not forget that there are endogenous reasons why transformation may occur, such as to reduce or increase the number of frigates, tanks, combat soldiers, establish joint command and operations, etc. Overall, we think that endogenous and exogenous factors are fundamental to understanding changes in European militaries. To add another dimension to our analysis, let us now unpack changes in European militaries through Galbreath's three additional categories of *followship*, *frontline* and *falling* (Galbreath, 2016).

Case studies in European defence innovation

Galbreath's three groupings offer an indication of the direction of change within and across European militaries. *Followship* is change that results from a close following of other militaries, which is an accepted and understood role between follower and the leader, very often the USA. Second, *frontline* refers to those militaries that have experienced change as a result of combat operations. Finally, there are those militaries and capabilities that are *falling* behind due to shrinking budgets and reduced strategic value. Combining *transform*, *transfer* and *translate* with *followship*, *frontline* and *falling* offers a multi-level set of explanations to assess European defence innovation comprehensively.

European militaries have been changing in a variety of different ways since the end of the Cold War. For the most part, the number and role of the combat soldier has lessened even though both Afghanistan and Iraq have had a major land warfare component. The reduction in combat and support soldiers across land, sea and air services is also reflected in military capabilities, as governments were determined to fund fewer platforms, such as tank battalions, frigates, and heavy lift aircraft. While the wars of the 'War on Terror' have boosted certain elements of European militaries, the general direction of military spending on personnel and platforms has continued to decline with few exceptions (cf. Poland). Combining this decline with modern warfare as a largely asymmetric, multidimensional affair, militaries have also been seeking to work jointly across services. In his major contribution, *The Transformation of Europe's Armed Forces*, Anthony King argues that there is a 'fundamental dynamic' at play with European militaries whereby they are undergoing a 'simultaneous process of concentration and transnationalisation' (King, 2011, p. 11). According to King (2011, p. 17), European armed forces are:

undergoing a compatible but differentiated process of 'localisation'. They are concentrating at decisive locales from which they are extending out increasingly deep institutional relations to produce a new military order of multiple, interdependent nodes and interconnected transnational networks.

Jointness has also become a major part of contemporary military command and operations. In the UK, the 2010 Strategic Defence and Security Review (SDSR) determined that joint budget arrangements for operations and kit would need to be interservice procured and managed. A joint command structure makes this easier to accomplish in theory. The experience of working in Afghan Provincial Reconstruction Teams (PRTs) has also led European militaries to think about doing more in theatre with less. As a result, Sapolsky's (1972, 2000) notion of a bureaucratic politics explanation of innovation becomes challenged as jointness appears to obscure the politics behind the change.

Finally, as a result of an evolving and complex threat environment, one whereby the conceptual clarity between *defence* and *security* has been blurred, defence budgets continue to shrink but security budgets continue to rise. Militaries have a role to play in traditional and new forms of security while, at the same time, militaries have the incentive to compete for budgets in new and well-funded policy areas. While this has the potential to militarise those new policy areas, this situation also provides an opportunity to transform European militaries. The result is a combined approach to security challenges. Contemporary military operations are likely to be the results of joint commands with increasingly combined roles for civilian departments and agencies. This change, along with reduced budgets, pose different challenges for our three groups of states within the *followship*, *frontline* and *falling* categories.

Followship

The most advanced, and predominantly largest militaries fall into this category; in particular, the UK, France, Germany and Poland. None of these militaries is seeking to exponentially increase their defence capabilities and are only meeting (although not in the case of Germany) the NATO guideline to spend a minimum of 2% of their gross domestic product (GDP) on defence (North Atlantic Council, 2014). At the same time, they are in the forefront of military transformation in Europe. Yet, how they are changing is different, partly because the USA is the 'model army', but also because they have little experience of actually working with each other on the ground, even if they did contribute to the same NATO ISAF mission in Afghanistan, for example. Few common lessons are being learnt and internalised due to different national priorities and different national constraints. At the same time, there are serious financial constraints challenging innovation for these militaries as well.

Though finances are a theme throughout European defence, these states are more serious about maintaining modern militaries with the prospect of using them in the future. France and the UK have the most advanced and operationally capable militaries in Europe. They have both responded to the advances in military concepts and technologies in similar ways.

Both states have sought to incorporate networked-enabled concepts and technology into their existing operational plans and future procurement. The British military has innovated in response to a changing external threat environment post theCold War but this has seen them return to their traditional posture as an expeditionary-orientated force. The USA has been the leading transmission-belt for this innovation through its export of the RMA and by setting the operational agenda over the past 25 years. But this transferring of US innovation has also been translated and shaped by two 'domestic factors': constraints on military resources and a distinct British military culture (Farrell and Bird, 2010, p. 56).

The French military has also innovated and transformed in response to 'strategic and technological changes' with the USA as the primary external source of innovation (Farrell et al., 2013, p. 277). They, too, have sought to translate this innovation to suit their own interests, threat perceptions and operational needs. German innovation has not been driven by geostrategic factors in the main, and the biggest challenge has been the political and domestic security culture surrounding the use and the purpose of military force. Although transformation has clearly been evident, the German military has innovated its capabilities, doctrine and even its operational thresholds. Poland's transformation since the end of the Cold War has been in the realm of capabilities, concepts and doctrine, but it also had to introduce 'civilian and democratic controls' (Osica, 2010, p. 167).

For all four states, there has been concern about the state and future of their land forces. The number of those serving has declined and is planned to further decline, while the remaining soldiers in both armies are to be more operationally effective across a wide spectrum of possible deployments. By and large, these countries are the strongest European followers of the USA's broader way of war, though with much less capability and capacity than their US counterparts. The armed forces in these states, to varying degrees, are active followers and play a significant and perhaps defining role in European defence.

Frontline

Some militaries find that their ability to innovate is limited to when they are on the frontline. In this group are European states such as Italy, Spain, the Netherlands, Norway, and Denmark. These states have arguably experienced the greatest decline following the end of Cold War in terms of the number of personnel and platforms. They were militaries designed largely and predominantly for NATO's territorial defence against a possible Soviet invasion and not for the expeditionary conflicts of the sort we have seen in the past 20 years. Their evolution from conscription-based militaries to all volunteer forces (AVFs) has also played a major role in this reduction in capacity. Further, these countries took advantage of participating in the Afghan and Iraq wars to invest in modernising their forces. The result has been the eliminating (or suspending) of national service and a reduction in the number of land forces and capabilities. Tank divisions were especially hit hard as outdated technology was not replaced. Thus, the key drivers of change in these states have been their simultaneous transformation to AVF with limited expeditionary capability via interventionist wars in the Middle East and North Africa.

Italy, being the largest, has the most to gain from what is happening in the 'following' states, though Italy (like Spain and also Greece) has had its transformation project curtailed by the global financial crisis. Spain, having begun its transformation during the centre-right government of José María Aznar, sought to transform its expeditionary and peacekeeping troops through ISAF and EU Common Security and Defence Policy (CSDP) missions. The Netherlands has also played an important role in Central Afghanistan and has maintained a combat-ready ground force that was able to work with the USA and the UK especially in developing COIN capabilities during Task Force Uruzgan. As such, NATO has played a central role in shaping Dutch military innovation. The Dutch have also gone further in their naval cooperation with Belgium via the so-called Benesam arrangement, whereby the two nations have integrated command, training and basing for frigates and mine hunters in order to maintain an active naval capacity.

Finally, Norway and Denmark have both come out of Afghanistan with a clear direction for their militaries and, in particular, their armies. Norway has sought to bolster its northern borders and economic interests with new battalions, a doctrine it is familiar with from its time being one of two NATO member countries with a border with the Soviet Union. Due to its sizable commitment in Afghanistan, Denmark has also developed a more directed doctrine of transformation to work directly with the USA. They have determined that their strategic interests lie with being able to integrate with US forces to the detriment of being able to operate alone or with other European states. For all of these states, a *frontline* was an important moderniser for their militaries, especially their armies. However, beyond a frontline or a resurgent Russia, there is a limited scope or even ability to look for innovation and transformation in the way understood in the bigger European military states.

Falling

Although national military organisations do not always want to acknowledge that some 'core tasks' of their military business can no longer be achieved, for others this Rubicon has already been crossed (Galbreath and Smith, 2016, pp. 193–194). In this category are European countries that are just simply disinvesting in their militaries as a matter of political choice. Namely, countries such as Belgium, Austria, and Sweden have militaries that are increasingly designed for deployment in multinational peacekeeping operations rather than for territorial defence, although they do remain under the USA's nuclear umbrella.

For European states such as Belgium, the main driver of force transformation and reform is a lack of resources. Rather than being uniquely related to defence policy, these militaries essentially become an extension of foreign policy. Although they retain very limited military capacity, they still attempt to demonstrate their utility to allies and partners by contributing an air squadron or some personnel to a NATO, EU or coalition crisis management or peacekeeping operation (see Chapters 4 and 6 for NATO and EU operations). Naturally, especially in the case of Sweden and Austria, there are historical and political reasons why the military may be relegated the further we move away from the Cold War.

Conclusion

This chapter has described historical approaches as well as state-of-the-art theories for explaining military innovation generally, and with regard to European defence specifically. It has sought to give the reader an understanding of the type of questions and challenges that scholars of military innovation have grappled with over the past century (see Box 11.1). The first section teased out some of the larger themes that strategists and scholars have derived from studying how militaries operate, both as organisations conducting and preparing for combat operations. These themes have ranged from attempting to understand the character of the next war to a realisation that military organisations often learn different (often wrong) lessons from the same wars. How the external threat environment is perceived, combined with the inevitable competition between various distinctive 'advocates' of innovation is what drives change in defence organisations.

From the work of Barry Posen to Theo Farrell, we have seen how the study of defence innovation has assumed a destinct social-science methodology since the early 1980s. Four models of innovation were defined (see Table 11.1). The logics in these approaches portray innovation as deriving from *civil–military* dynamics, to variations of *interservice* rivalry and *intraservice* competition over scarce resources. Finally, we have seen that military *culture* is also a key driver of, or restraint on, defence innovation. An analytical framework to cut across these literatures of transformation was then provided before turning that framework on the specificity of European defence innovation. It suggested that change can be understood via the concepts of *transform, transfer* and *translate* and that European states tend to fall into the categories of *followship, frontline*, and *falling*. There are clearly challenges facing all European armed forces – not least declining budgets and personnel. Yet, there is a demonstrable shift occurring in both the global and regional political–security atmosphere. It is difficult to predict what the future operating environment or the shifting security architecture in Europe may bring. But change is the only constant in life and, therefore, some form of innovation is inevitable.

Further reading

Coker, Christopher (2015), *Future War*. Cambridge: Polity Press.

Farrell, Theo, Rynning, Sten, and Terriff, Terry (2013), *Transforming Military Power Since the Cold War: Britain, France, and the United States, 1991–2012*. Cambridge: Cambridge University Press.

Freedman, Lawrence (2017), *The Future of War: A History*. New York: Public Affairs.

Galbreath, David J. (2014), 'Western European Armed Forces and the Modernisation Agenda: Following or Falling Behind?', *Defence Studies*, 14 (4), 394–413.

Grissom, Adam (2006), 'The Future of Military Innovation Studies', *Journal of Strategic Studies*, 29 (5), 905–934.

King, Anthony (2011), *The Transformation of Europe's Armed Forces: From the Rhine to Afghanistan*. Cambridge: Cambridge University Press.

Weblinks

European Defence Agency: www.eda.europa.eu/
NATO Allied Command Transformation: www.act.nato.int/
RAND research on military transformation: www.rand.org/topics/military-transformation.html
Royal United Services Institute: https://rusi.org/
The French Institute for International and Strategic Affairs: www.iris-france.org/en/
UK MOD Development, Concepts and Doctrine Centre (DCDC): www.gov.uk/government/groups/
    development-concepts-and-doctrine-centre
US Defense Advanced Research Projects Agency (DARPA): www.darpa.mil/
War on the Rocks blog: https://warontherocks.com/

References

Bacevich, Andrew J. (1986), *The Pentomic Era: The U.S. Army Between Korea and Vietnam*. Washington, DC: National Defense University Press.

Clausewitz, Carl von (1997), *On War*, abridged edition. Ware: Wordsworth Editions.

Coonen, Stephen J. (2006), 'The Widening Military Capabilities Gap between the United States and Europe: Does It Matter?', *Parameters*, 36 (3), 67–84.

Cote, Owen R. (1998). *The Politics of Innovative Military Doctrine: The U.S. Navy and Fleet Ballistic Missiles*. Cambridge, MA: MIT.

Croft, Stuart, Howorth, Jolyon, Terriff, Terry, and Webber, Mark (2000), 'NATO's Triple Challenge', *International Affairs*, 76 (3), 495–518.

Edmunds, Tim (2006), 'What Are Armed Forces for? The Changing Nature of Military Roles in Europe', *International Affairs*, 82 (6), 1059–1075.

Farrell, Theo, and Bird, Tim (2010), 'Innovating Within Cost and Cultural Constraints: The British', in Terry Terriff, Frans Osinga, and Theo Farrell (eds), *A Transformation Gap? American Innovations and European Military Change*. Stanford, CA: Stanford University Press, pp. 35–58.

Farrell, Theo, and Rynning, Sten (2010), 'NATO's Transformation Gaps: Transatlantic Differences and the War in Afghanistan', *Journal of Strategic Studies*, 33 (5), 673–699.

Farrell, Theo, and Terriff, Terry (eds) (2001), *The Sources of Military Change: Culture, Politics, Technology*. Boulder, CO: Lynne Rienner.

Farrell, Theo, Rynning, Sten, and Terriff, Terry (2013), *Transforming Military Power since the Cold War: Britain, France, and the United States, 1991–2012*. Cambridge: Cambridge University Press.

Galbreath, David J. (2014), 'Western European Armed Forces and the Modernisation Agenda: Following or Falling Behind?', *Defence Studies*, 14 (4), 394–413.

Galbreath, David J. (2015), 'RMA, European Militaries and the Limits of Modernization', in Andrew Futter and Jeffrey Collins (eds), *Reassessing the Revolution in Military Affairs: Transformation, Evolution and Lessons Learnt*. Basingstoke: Palgrave Macmillan, pp. 156–174.

Galbreath, David J. (2016), 'Understanding Changes in European Militaries: A System Approach', *Annual Convention of the International Studies Association*, Atlanta, Georgia, 15–18 March.

Galbreath, David J., and Smith, Simon J. (2016), 'Military Capabilities and Force Transformation', in Laura Chappell, Jocelyn Mawdsley, and Petar Petrov (eds), *The EU, Strategy and Security Policy: Regional and Strategic Challenges*. London: Routledge, pp. 186–201.

Gray, Colin S. (2005), 'How Has War Changed Since the End of the Cold War?', *Parameters*, 35 (1), 14–26.

Grissom, Adam (2006), 'The Future of Military Innovation Studies', *Journal of Strategic Studies*, 29 (5), 905–934.

Horowitz, Michael C. (2010), *The Diffusion of Military Power: Causes and Consequences for International Politics*. Princeton, NJ: Princeton University Press.

King, Anthony (2011), *The Transformation of Europe's Armed Forces: From the Rhine to Afghanistan*. Cambridge: Cambridge University Press.

Luhmann, Niklas (2006), 'System as Difference', *Organization*, 13 (1), 37–57.

Mewett, Christopher (2014), 'Understanding War's Enduring Nature Alongside Its Changing Character'. Available at: https://warontherocks.com/2014/01/understanding-wars-enduring-nature-alongside-its-changing-character/ (accessed: 5 November 2018).

North Atlantic Council (2014), 'NATO Wales Summit Declaration', Press Release (2014) 120, 5 September. Available at: www.nato.int/cps/en/natohq/official_texts_112964.htm (accessed: 15 October 2018).

Osica, Olaf (2010), 'Transformation through Expeditionary Warfare: Military Change in Poland', in Terry Terriff Frans Osinga, and Theo Farrell (eds), *A Transformation Gap? American Innovations and European Military Change*. Stanford, CA: Stanford University Press, pp. 167–186.

Posen, Barry (1984), *The Sources of Military Doctrine: France, Britain, and Germany between the World Wars*. Ithaca, NY: Cornell University Press.

Rasmussen, Mikkel V. (2013), 'The Military Metier: Second Order Adaptation and the Danish Experience in Task Force Helmand', in Theo Farrell, Frans P. B. Osinga, and James A. Russell (eds), *Military Adaptation in Afghanistan*. Stanford, CA: Stanford University Press, pp. 136–158.

Rosen, Stephen P. (1988), 'New Ways of War: Understanding Military Innovation', *International Security*, 13 (1), 134–168.

Rosen, Stephen P. (1991) *Winning the Next War: Innovation and the Modern Military*. Ithaca, NY: Cornell University Press.

Sapolsky, Harvey M. (1972) *The Polaris System Development: Bureaucratic and Programmatic Success in Government*. Cambridge, MA: Harvard University Press.

Sapolsky, Harvey M. (2000), 'On the Theory of Military Innovation', *Breakthroughs*, 9 (1) 35–39.

Terriff, Terry, Osinga, Frans, and Farrell, Theo (eds) (2010), *A Transformation Gap? American Innovations and European Military Change*. Stanford, CA: Stanford University Press.

Wiesner, Ina (2013), *Importing the American Way of War? Network-Centric Warfare in the UK and Germany*. Baden-Baden: Nomos.

European security

Where do we go from here?

Laura Chappell, Jocelyn Mawdsley
and David J. Galbreath

12

Introduction

In the preceding 11 chapters we have introduced and outlined the key challenges and actors in respect to European security. As we have identified, the term 'security' has broadened theoretically and empirically in its scope since the end of the Cold War. This chapter acts as a basis for reflection regarding the actors, institutions and security threats that Europe faces presently. In doing so, we can consider where the modern day foundations of European security have come from and their evolution. From the 'simplicity' of security threats and actors during the Cold War, we now face multiple challenges with institutions designed for a different security environment, and European state leadership that has not always been able to rise to the task. The institutions studied in this book – the North Atlantic Treaty Organization (NATO), the European Union (EU) and the Organization for Security and Co-Operation in Europe (OSCE) – have tried to adapt; how far they have been able to provide security is a matter of debate. Finally, what we define as a security threat is, in itself, part of a narrative, founded on the idea of threat perception. This leads to a particular focus on what security means and which hard and soft security tools are required to try to deal with these security challenges. As has been demonstrated, Europe suffers a capability–expectations gap (Hill, 1993) and a 'consensus–expectations' gap (Toje, 2008). Hence, there is not only a dearth in capabilities, but also the political willingness to utilise those capabilities to which Europe does have recourse.

This chapter is structured as follows. To start, we highlight key contemporary trends regarding security and insecurity in Europe, using Section Three of the textbook as the basis to provide some critical insights regarding security threats and security approaches. Secondly, we will offer some concluding thoughts on the evolution and cohesiveness of the European security architecture in meeting today's security challenges. By summarising some of the key themes which came out of the three institutional chapters found in Section Two of the textbook, we will highlight the continuing issues with all three institutions and how this shapes

Europe's ability to provide for its security. Finally, we highlight the role of security leaders in providing a response to serious threats and ask whether new innovations such as Macron's European Intervention Force are a way to address challenges such as Brexit and the lack of political willingness to utilise military instruments. We finish with some reflections regarding the direction that European security is heading in, and what this means for both institutions and European leaders.

Security and insecurity in contemporary Europe

The 1990s saw an initial flurry of security initiatives, agreements and a de-securitisation of political rhetoric in Europe. It was more popular to talk about the peace dividend than to urge increased military spending. There was certainly conflict in both the Balkans and Caucasus, but for the majority of European states and citizens the decade was marked by a lack of threat. Peace deals were struck in the Balkans and even the Troubles in Northern Ireland came to a settlement. With the emergence of the EU as a security actor in the late 1990s and early 2000s, and the consequent winding up of the Western European Union (WEU), the security landscape was simplified. Gradually, the current post-Cold War European security architecture emerged, with the three institutions studied in this book enlarging their membership and taking on new security-related tasks. As Forsberg and Haukkala (2015) point out, there was no grand plan or a single peace-making event; rather, the evolution of Europe's security order was gradual and closely tied to the liberal order that emerged globally after the end of the Cold War (Deudney and Ikenberry, 1999). While there have sometimes been difficulties in managing cooperation between institutions, particularly between the EU and NATO as already mentioned, and the flaws in European defence were always well-known (Menon, 2011), so long as there were few active threats such problems were easy to ignore.

As Chapter 11 has highlighted, the ability of European militaries to innovate and adapt to changing threat perceptions and needs is patchy at best. While some have managed to track US military innovations, or learnt lessons from combat experience in the last two decades, others have largely given up. This means that there are real doubts that European military capabilities, let alone the institutional architecture within which they function, are fit to deal with what objectively can only be described as a worsening security situation. While, as we describe later in the chapter, new initiatives are being launched to tackle this problem, they are having to chase a quickly evolving security environment.

So, what are the concerns? In 2018, a European Council on Foreign Relations (ECFR) survey of citizens in all 28 EU member states found that the top five perceived threats are, 'in descending order: cyber attacks; state collapse or civil war in the EU's neighbourhood; external meddling in domestic politics; uncontrolled migration into the country; and the deterioration of the international institutional order' (Dennison et al., 2018, p. 2). Survey respondents expected the order to remain the same for the next decade, with the addition of terrorist attacks. In comparison, a similar survey in 2008 found that the top perceived threats then were: economic instability; terrorist attacks; instability in the neighbourhood; disruption to the energy supply; and cyber attacks. The ECFR survey found that there was more continent-wide agreement on threat perceptions than is sometimes thought, although fear of uncontrolled migration is strongest in the south and east, concern about Russia is most prominent in the east and the threat of terrorist attacks is strongest in those countries that have recently experienced them (Dennison et al., 2018). The question is how such threats might be countered and whether Europe's security institutions are well equipped to do so.

As Chapter 10 on changing conventional security threats showed, the concern about state collapse or civil war in the neighbourhood is merited. A low-level war is continuing in Ukraine's eastern provinces of Donetsk and Luhansk. To the south, open conflict continues in Syria's civil war, while Libya is no longer a functioning state. Moreover, while so-called Islamic State, or Daesh, may no longer hold large areas of land, enclaves of Islamist groups exist across the Middle East and Sahel regions. These conflicts have challenged Europe's security institutions, and, just as with the conflicts in the former Yugoslavia or the 2008 Georgian war, the response has been largely piecemeal, reliant on particular countries taking action, and, long term, seemingly ineffective. As Chapter 8 on human security argued, the enthusiasm for liberal interventionism in Europe has largely waned.

It is thought the conflict in Ukraine and the Russian annexation of Crimea has posed the most serious question for the European security order. As Forsberg and Haukkala (2015, p. 1) argue, 'all the key parties – Russia, the EU and the USA/NATO – are all intimately involved and at loggerheads while some of the key norms of the order, namely territorial integrity and peaceful resolution of conflicts, have been broken'. As the chapter on NATO argued, this is particularly challenging as the USA's commitment to NATO under President Trump is questioned. Suddenly, the weaknesses of the EU's Common Security and Defence Policy (CSDP) have become too important to ignore.

Arguably, Russia has never felt comfortable with the order that emerged at the end of the Cold War (Baranovsky, 2000). Charap and Troitskiy (2013) argue that as both NATO and the EU expanded to include former Warsaw Pact members and even the Baltic states, which had been part of the Soviet Union, Russia felt increasingly threatened. NATO considering offering membership to Georgia, and the EU offering an Eastern Partnership agreement to Ukraine, Moldova, Georgia, Armenia, Azerbaijan, and Belarus to strengthen ties, was simply too much for Russia. Mearsheimer (2014) is among those scholars who claim that the conflict in Ukraine can be blamed on NATO and the EU attempting to interfere in Russia's sphere of influence. Others, such as Kuzio (2017), argue that the EU was naïve not to realise that Russia viewed it, as well as NATO, as a hostile actor, with its plans to strengthen partnerships with its Eastern neighbours. There is, though, increasingly little doubt that Russia has moved from dissatisfaction with the institutionalised European security order to actively trying to destabilise it through what is called hybrid warfare (Mälksoo, 2018). European citizens are increasingly aware of cyber attacks, electoral interference and the support of anti-system parties that some argue can be traced back to Russian interference (Ziegler, 2018). It is, in short, not difficult to understand why, in this climate, the ECFR survey found that Europeans feared cyber attacks, external meddling and the deterioration of the international institutional order in 2018; especially given the increasing unpredictability of their main ally, the USA, under President Trump (Dennison et al., 2018).

The presence of both civil wars and collapsing states in the southern Mediterranean has brought large numbers of refugees fleeing the conflicts to Europe, peaking in summer 2015 when more than 1,000,000 people crossed into Europe by land and sea. Their arrival has been controversial and attitudes and responses across Europe vary widely. Some politicians, like Angela Merkel of Germany, have championed humanitarian values; others, like Viktor Orban of Hungary, regarded them as an existential threat to their states. This has meant that a coherent EU response has been noticeable by its absence (Scipioni, 2018). The member states simply do not agree. In a similar time frame, some European cities have suffered major terrorist attacks. Again, as Chapter 7 on internal security has argued, disagreements have emerged between European states on the best ways to respond to this threat. The balance between values of liberty and privacy, on the one hand, and security, on the other, is proving very hard to agree. The sense that an adequate response is not being given by, in this case, the EU, has been fuelled by the rhetoric of populist parties across Europe. While this has brought electoral success to some, and contributed to the British people voting to leave the EU in 2016, it has not, thus far, caused major damage to the EU.

The agendas of Europe's populist parties also challenge the liberal international order that underpins the institutionalised European security order. Increasingly, European citizens appear polarised between those who instinctively support that order, and those who reject it. In the bitter aftermath of the UK's Brexit referendum, these tensions are particularly noticeable (Browning, 2018). The tensions between those who view themselves as progressive, and those who feel change has come too quickly and challenges their understandings of how the world works, have also entered the field of gender politics and sexual violence, the importance of which were highlighted in Chapter 9 on gender and European security. The #MeToo campaign, which encouraged women to report sexual abuse and harassment, and which had consequences for a number of prominent men, has also sparked a backlash among those who felt threatened by it.

Kinnvall et al. (2018) have argued that to understand contemporary European security, we need to consider how Europeans are interpreting the crises around them as existential threats to the world as they know it. This brief overview of how threats are perceived and how security and politics interact suggests they have a point. Europeans had enjoyed a stable security order for nearly two decades, but now that order is being challenged, both internally and externally, at a time when Europe is facing genuine security threats. The well-known flaws of the CSDP, the unwillingness of many European states to fund defence and the over-reliance on the USA as a security provider are real problems now. All three of Europe's security institutions are struggling to be effective in this new environment. Even the norms that supported the European security order are under threat. As Forsberg and Haukkala (2015) argued, the annexation of Crimea by Russia challenged the norms of territorial integrity and peaceful resolution of conflicts that tacitly underpinned the institutionalised European security order. As Mitzen (2018) has argued, this series of existential threats, together with the inability of Europe's institutions to solve them, has created an anxious community rather than a security community. For a security order that has relied on its institutions to provide collective security for decades, this anxiety is a serious matter. But is it justified?

The European security architecture: fit for purpose?

As Chapters 4, 5 and 6 highlight, the EU, NATO, and the OSCE have had to adapt to the post Cold War security environment. NATO's transformation has developed in two directions. The first is in 'going out of area', by deploying expeditionary armed forces. This occurred initially in the Balkans in the 1990s. Significantly, however, NATO assumed leadership of the International Security Assistance Force (ISAF) in Afghanistan in 2003 (North Atlantic Treaty Organization, 2015). It also launched Operation Ocean Shield, an anti-piracy operation in the Gulf of Aden, in 2009, and Operation Unified Protector in Libya in 2011. This led to a debate regarding NATO's balancing of roles between this and its traditional Article Five collective defence task (Bunde and Noetzel, 2010; Yost, 2010). This is particularly pertinent considering Russia's current propensity to actively protect its sphere of influence, if necessary through the use of force, as the Ukraine conflict aptly demonstrated. Indeed, it appears that these two roles have been re-balanced in favour of the latter, which connects to the focus of some of NATO's Central and Eastern Europe member states. The second area relates to NATO's addition of a civilian dimension. Again, its Afghanistan experience was particularly instructive here. In particular, the creation of Provisional Reconstruction Teams, which began to be deployed in Afghanistan in 2003, integrated military and civilian personnel in order to carry out, *inter alia*, reconstruction tasks and humanitarian assistance (Maley, 2007). Indeed, the combination of military and civilian crisis management tools was stressed in NATO's 2010 Strategic Concept (North Atlantic Treaty Organization, 2010, pp. 19–22). It has also involved NATO embracing UNSCR 1325 on women, peace and security, surprisingly ahead of the EU (see Chapter 9). None the less, this has been done in a highly instrumentalised way to make NATO operations more 'effective' (Wright, 2016, p. 351). The question is whether both the civilian dimension and gender mainstreaming will be sidelined due to the renewed focus on collective defence, particularly as there is no consideration of gender in the latter. Indeed, NATO has returned to its Cold War focus.

The EU's security and defence journey has been one of creating institutions and initiatives without always finding the subsequent necessary political willingness to create capabilities or deploy operations. From the high hopes of the late 1990s, the mid-2000s onwards have proved to be somewhat of a disappointment. The problem is that EU member states diverge on the use of force in particular, meaning that potential military operations that have come up for discussion have not always been deployed. This has led to an undermining of the perception of the EU as a security provider, particularly post Libya (Menon, 2011). EU member states' failure to close defence capability gaps is also noteworthy, although the Russian invasion of Ukraine, the election of Donald Trump as US President and the UK's decision to leave the EU (Brexit), has focused minds in Brussels. Hence, since June 2016 when the latter was announced, along with the publication of the EU Global Strategy, a raft of new and resurrected initiatives designed to increase defence capabilities has been announced (see Chapter 6). Therefore, the EU is moving once again in a military rather than civilian direction. Thus, both NATO and the EU are shifting away from the civilian dimension towards military considerations due to the security threats on Europe's border.

With the unpredictability of Donald Trump, questions are being raised as to whether the transatlantic relationship, which Howorth (2010, p. 462) refers to as 'that 20th-Century life-jacket for Europeans in distress', can be relied upon. This leaves Europe with one option: to provide for its own security.

Once again this poses questions for EU–NATO burden sharing, and, in particular, unnecessary duplication between the two organisations. However, with NATO's renewed focus on Article Five and deterrence it appears unlikely that duplication will occur. Moreover, despite the EU's increased rhetoric around becoming more capable, this has yet to materialise in terms of increased political willingness to deploy substantive military operations. Indeed, of the 16 current EU missions and operations, ten are civilian, six are military and, of the latter, three are military training missions (European External Action Service, 2017, p. 2). Whether Europeans are becoming serious about defence will depend on the success of the current raft of capability initiatives to deliver results and subsequently to be used where necessary in conjunction with civilian elements. It is the EU's comprehensive approach to security that is its 'value added' component, considering it is the only one of Europe's institutions to possess both military and civilian capabilities.

The OSCE is the only European institution to incorporate both Russia and the USA. However, beyond this, the institution's distinctiveness is being challenged. As highlighted in Chapter 5, NATO has taken over arms control discussions, while the CSDP has been making incursions into areas traditionally associated with the OSCE, not least in the frozen conflicts of Eastern Europe and the Caucasus (Galbreath and Gebhard, 2010). Hence, we could argue that the OSCE is undergoing a 'fight for relevance' in the current security environment. None the less, considering the broad membership of the OSCE, and its specialisations in such areas as the protection of minorities and free media, as well as its 'quiet diplomacy' (see Chapter 5), the OSCE still has a role to play. However, the question remains as to how far Russian incursions into Ukraine and the annexation of Crimea have had an impact on the functioning of the OSCE.

Overall, post Cold War, the European institutional security architecture has undergone a degree of overlap and, thus, potential competition, regarding their security and defence roles as well as geographically where they operate. Despite this, there are still clear distinctions between them and recent events have iterated these. NATO has returned to its Article Five, territorial defence focus. Primarily, this is due to Russia's increased interest in militarily protecting what it considers to be its sphere of influence. However, it also reflects the completion of ISAF in Afghanistan, which was its primary out-of-area operation. In contrast, the EU has the comprehensive approach to security that combines both military and civilian tools. None the less, despite recent rhetoric it is still primarily a civilian actor operationally. Its geographical operational sphere is focused on Eastern Europe as well as the Middle East and Africa, which also sets it apart from NATO. Finally, the OSCE has a broad membership that enables it to engage with these members on areas that the other two institutions do not, as highlighted above. Whether this institutional division of labour provides for Europe's security is far from certain, considering the external crises engulfing the European continent.

Finding the way out of the (in)security quagmire: security leaders wanted

One of the major problems in finding a way out of Europe's inactivity relates to the lack of innovation, leadership or adequate response to the serious threats currently undermining European security. What is clear from the above section is that political willingness is the fundamental element that enables or prevents action. However, this has been lacking, particularly in respect to closing European states' well-known capability gaps, which focus on strategic enablers or deploying rapid reaction operations. While the Ukraine crisis may have partially galvanised NATO into action, the EU is still at the declaratory initiative stage. Here, we need to focus on European leaders, that is, those heads of key NATO, EU and OSCE member states.

As previously highlighted, the election of Donald Trump has proved to be problematic, not least due to a lack of predictability in the USA's actions. Trump has raised the issue of American–European burden sharing; particularly in the context of defence spending (White House, 2018). As Table 12.1 demonstrates, only five countries, including the USA, currently reach the 2% GDP NATO defence-spending target. However, asking Europeans to do more is neither new nor denotes a desire to become involved in European security issues.

Table 12.1 Defence expenditure as a share of GDP and annual real change

	2011	2012	2013	2014	2015	2016	2017e	2018e
Share of real GDP (%)								
NATO Europe	**1.55**	**1.52**	**1.49**	**1.44**	**1.42**	**1.44**	**1.46**	**1.50**
Albania	1.53	1.49	1.41	1.35	1.16	1.10	1.11	1.19
Belgium	1.04	1.04	1.01	0.98	0.92	0.92	0.91	0.93
Bulgaria*	1.32	1.34	1.46	1.32	1.26	1.26	1.27	1.56
Croatia	1.60	1.53	1.46	1.40	1.35	1.21	1.27	1.30
Czech Republic	1.07	1.05	1.03	0.95	1.03	0.96	1.04	1.11
Denmark	1.31	1.35	1.23	1.15	1.12	1.17	1.16	1.21
Estonia	1.68	1.90	1.91	1.96	2.05	2.13	2.08	2.14
France	1.86	1.87	1.86	1.82	1.78	1.79	1.78	1.81
Germany	1.28	1.31	1.22	1.18	1.18	1.20	1.24	1.24
Greece	2.38	2.29	2.22	2.21	2.31	2.41	2.38	2.27
Hungary	1.05	1.03	0.95	0.86	0.92	1.02	1.05	1.08
Italy	1.30	1.24	1.20	1.08	1.01	1.12	1.15	1.15
Latvia**	1.01	0.88	0.93	0.94	1.04	1.46	1.69	2.00
Lithuania**	0.79	0.76	0.76	0.88	1.14	1.49	1.73	1.96
Luxembourg	0.39	0.38	0.38	0.38	0.43	0.40	0.52	0.55
Montenegro	1.75	1.66	1.47	1.50	1.40	1.42	1.38	1.58

Netherlands	1.26	1.23	1.16	1.15	1.12	1.15	1.16	1.35
Norway	1.51	1.47	1.48	1.51	1.46	1.54	1.55	1.61
Poland**	1.72	1.74	1.72	1.85	2.22	2.00	1.89	1.98
Portugal	1.49	1.41	1.44	1.31	1.33	1.27	1.24	1.36
Romania**	1.29	1.22	1.28	1.35	1.45	1.41	1.72	1.93
Slovak Republic	1.09	1.09	0.98	0.99	1.13	1.12	1.10	1.20
Slovenia	1.30	1.17	1.05	0.97	0.93	1.00	0.98	1.01
Spain	0.94	1.04	0.93	0.92	0.93	0.81	0.90	0.93
Turkey	1.64	1.59	1.52	1.45	1.39	1.46	1.52	1.68
United Kingdom	2.40	2.17	2.27	2.17	2.06	2.15	2.11	2.10
North America	**4.43**	**4.09**	**3.77**	**3.50**	**3.33**	**3.33**	**3.35**	**3.28**
Canada	1.23	1.10	0.99	1.01	1.20	1.15	1.36	1.23
United States	4.78	4.42	4.08	3.77	3.56	3.56	3.57	3.50
NATO Total	**2.97**	**2.81**	**2.64**	**2.48**	**2.39**	**2.40**	**2.42**	**2.40**

(North Atlantic Treaty Organization, 2018, p. 8)

Notes: Based on 2010 prices. Figures for 2017 and 2018 are estimates. The NATO Europe and NATO Total aggregates from 2017 include Montenegro, which became an ally on 5 June 2017.

* Defence expenditure does not include pensions.

** With regard to 2018, these countries have either national laws or political agreements which call for at least 2% of GDP to be spent on defence annually, consequently these estimates are expected to change accordingly.

Indeed, as the Trump–Kim Jong-Un summit highlights, the Asian pivot remains a key component of American foreign policy.

The UK is currently focused on Brexit, which will bring about significant changes in British engagement in Europe, and also potentially in respect to the UK's position on the world stage. Indeed, as only one of two major military actors in Europe (the other being France), this has the potential to weaken CSDP in terms of diplomatic clout. It also poses the issue of how to continue to develop European defence policy. If Europeans are to go it alone, there is no institutional basis left to act as a foundation, following the termination of the WEU in 2011. In an attempt to address this problem, the French President, Emmanuel Macron, created the European Intervention Initiative (EI2) in 2018 (see Box 12.1). However, creating yet another defence body also indicates the piecemeal nature of security and defence in Europe.

Box 12.1   The European Intervention Initiative (EI2)

Macron's initiative brings together nine countries, including France, Germany, the UK, Spain, Denmark, the Netherlands, Portugal, Estonia and Belgium (European Intervention Initiative, 2018). The idea is to enhance Europe's 'collective strategic response' and to 'develop a shared strategic culture, which will enhance our ability, as European states, to carry out military missions and operations' (European Intervention Initiative, 2018, p. 2). Importantly, it sits outside of any of Europe's security organisations, although it can be used in the framework of NATO, the EU, UN or *ad hoc* coalitions. Hence, it aims to bring together those countries that are able and willing to deploy force when the need arises, without being hamstrung by institutional structures and decision-making processes which hamper such rapid action being taken. It also ensures that the UK remains engaged in European defence as well as encompassing Denmark, which has an opt-out on EU defence policy.

While Macron has taken the lead here, the German Chancellor, Angela Merkel – usually known for showing leadership in EU politics – has been slower to come to terms with the consequences of the new European security dilemma. While rhetorically she was quick to recognise the need for European strategic autonomy, Germany's military has been under-funded for decades, has important operational failings in terms of equipment, and German citizens remain very reluctant to use military force. Germany has supported Macron's EI2, although less than enthusiastically, and there have been Franco–German input papers relating to the evolution of EU defence policy (Koenig and Walter-Frank, 2017, p. 3; Mölling and Major, 2018; Westerwelle et al., 2013). Indeed, Germany's focus has been on EU defence initiatives and there is a concern that these may be undermined by EI2 (Mölling and Major, 2018, p. 5). While the German Defence Minister, Ursula von der Leyen, has altered the rhetoric around defence with the idea of 'leadership from the centre', involving increased German contributions to defence, this has not always resulted in additional troops but, rather, in the deployment of civilian capabilities (Chappell et al., 2016, pp. 174–176). This demonstrates the differences Germany and France still have in respect to the willingness to deploy force.

So, where does this leave us? There are serious flaws in the European security order; the norms that have underpinned it are being flouted, the institutions are struggling and military capabilities are weaker than desired. Of Europe's three main security powers, only France is showing much leadership beyond rhetoric. Nevertheless, there is a growing acceptance that reliance on the USA as the security guarantor, as (Western) Europeans have done since the end of the Second World War, must at least be matched by independent European security provision. Which, if any, of the current initiatives will prove successful remains to be seen.

Conclusion

The Europe of 2018 feels insecure, and there are few signs that the situation is likely to improve in the near future. Europe is facing multiple internal and external security challenges, from a more aggressive Russia, an unpredictable ally in the USA, Brexit, the refugee crisis, and multiple conflicts on its doorstep. All are difficult challenges, but made worse by the lack of agreement on how best to tackle them. Solidarity, it appears, is increasingly in short supply. The array of security challenges, coupled with the lack of solutions, has made some long-standing problems with European defence very clear. For decades, Europeans have relied heavily on the USA as a security provider and failed to invest in defence. Multiple initiatives by both NATO and the EU to change this have not succeeded. For the moment, the EU's rhetoric about strategic autonomy is both hollow and necessary as European states try to conceive of a collective defence that is less reliant on the Americans. Brexit complicates this by removing one of the EU's two military powers at an inopportune time. European military capabilities are weaker than they should be, but, more seriously, there is a lack of consensus on how to tackle the security threats facing Europe. Initiatives abound, but similarly to the mid-1990s, it is currently unclear which, if any, will be successful.

More seriously, Europe's security problems come at a time when the liberal world order that emerged after the Cold War is being challenged. Populist politicians and parties are actively trying to undermine the values that underpin it, preferring a more authoritarian style of governance, nationalist values, and conflict rather than cooperation or solidarity. The current European security order worked well in the post Cold War environment, as its institutions shared the commitment to norms such as the rule of law, democracy and international cooperation – it is less clear that it will thrive if these challengers prevail in the longer term.

Had this textbook been written in the 1990s, it would have been a very different book. Optimism was high; Europe had been largely peacefully reunited and a nuclear holocaust was no longer a threat. The big questions were about the institutional shape of European security, but these were posed in a belief that the liberal global order had prevailed and that disputes would be more a question for international law than military force. Even a decade ago, though, with hindsight, warning signs were there, few predicted the range of threats now afflicting Europe. There were hopes that the EU's engagement with its neighbours would produce a border of well-governed stable states. Instead, the opposite has come to pass. Similarly, the future is unclear. We have little doubt that were we to write this book in 2038, it, too, would look very different. Increasingly, twenty-first century European security is becoming just as unpredictable as it has been in centuries past.

Further reading

Charap, Samuel, and Troitskiy, Mikhail (2013), 'Russia, the West and the Integration Dilemma', *Survival*, 55 (6), 49–62.

Forsberg, Tuomas, and Haukkala, Hiski (2015), 'The End of an Era for Institutionalism in European Security?', *Journal of Contemporary European Studies*, 23 (1), 1–5.

Mitzen, Jennifer (2018), 'Anxious Community: EU as (In)Security Community', *European Security*, 27 (3), 393–413.

References

Baranovsky, Vladimir (2000), 'Russia: A Part of Europe or Apart from Europe?', *International Affairs*, 76 (3), 443–458.

Browning, Christopher (2018), 'Brexit, Existential Anxiety and Ontological (In)Security', *European Security*, 27 (3), 336–355.

Bunde, Tobias, and Noetzel, Timo (2010), 'Unavoidable Tensions: The Liberal Path to Global NATO', *Contemporary Security Policy*, 31 (2), 295–318.

Chappell, Laura, Mawdsley, Jocelyn, and Whitman, Richard (2016), 'The National Priorities of Germany, France and the UK', in Laura Chappell, Jocelyn Mawdsley, and Petar Petrov (eds), *The EU, Strategy and Security Policy*. Abingdon: Routledge, pp. 169–185.

Charap, Samuel, and Troitskiy, Mikhail (2013), 'Russia, the West and the Integration Dilemma', *Survival*, 55 (6), 49–62.

Dennison, Suzi, Franke, Ulrike, and Zerka, Pawel (2018), 'The Nightmare of the Dark: The Security Fears that keep Europeans Awake at Night', European Council on Foreign Relations Security Scorecard, July 2018. Available at: www.ecfr.eu/page/-/SECURITY_SCORECARD_123.pdf (accessed: 1 November 2018).

Deudney, Daniel, and Ikenberry, John (1999), 'The Nature and Sources of International Liberal Order', *Review of International Studies*, 25 (2), 179–196.

European External Action Service (2017), 'EU Missions and Operations as part of the EU's Common Security and Defence Policy (CSDP)', European External Action Service Factsheet. Available at: https://eeas.europa.eu/sites/eeas/files/csdp_missions_and_operations_factsheet.pdf (accessed: 1 November 2018).

European Intervention Initiative (2018), 'Letter of Intent', Diplomatic agreement, 25 June. Available at: www.defense.gouv.fr/content/download/535740/9215739/file/LOI_IEI%2025%20JUN%20 2018.pdf (accessed: 1 November 2018).

Forsberg, Tuomas, and Haukkala, Hiski (2015), 'The End of an Era for Institutionalism in European Security?', *Journal of Contemporary European Studies*, 23 (1), 1–5.

Galbreath, David J., and Gebhard, Carmen (eds) (2010), *Cooperation or Conflict? Problematizing Organizational Overlap in Europe*. London: Ashgate.

Hill, Christopher (1993), 'The Capability–Expectations Gap, or Conceptualising Europe's International Role', *Journal of Common Market Studies*, 31 (3), 305–328.

Howorth, Jolyon (2010), 'The EU as a Global Actor: Grand Strategy for a Global Grand Bargain?', *Journal of Common Market Studies*, 48 (3), 455–474.

Kinnvall, Catarina, Manners, Ian, and Mitzen, Jennifer (2018), 'Introduction to 2018 Special Issue of European Security: "Ontological (In)Security in the European Union"', *European Security*, 27 (3), 249–265.

Koenig, Nicole, and Walter-Franke, Marie (2017), 'France and Germany: Spearheading a European Security and Defence Union?', *Policy Paper 202*, Berlin: Jacques Delors Institut. Available at: http:// institutdelors.eu/wp-content/uploads/2018/01/franceandgermanyspearheadingaeuropean securityanddefenceunion-koenigwalter-jdib-july2017.pdf (accessed: 1 November 2018).

Kuzio, Taras (2017), 'Ukraine between a Constrained EU and Assertive Russia', *Journal of Common Market Studies*, 55 (1), 103–120.

Maley, William (2007), 'Provincial Reconstruction Teams in Afghanistan: How They Arrived and Where They Are Going', *NATO Review*, 3. Available at www.nato.int/docu/review/2007/issue3/ english/art2.html (accessed: 1 November 2018).

Mälksoo, Maria (2018), 'Countering Hybrid Warfare as Ontological Security Management: The Emerging Practices of the EU and NATO', *European Security*, 27 (3), 374–392.

Mearsheimer, John (2014), 'Why the Ukraine Crisis Is the West's Fault: The Liberal Delusions that Provoked Putin', *Foreign Affairs*, 93 (5), 77–89.

Menon, Anand (2011), 'European Defence Policy from Lisbon to Libya', *Survival*, 53 (3), 75–90.

Mitzen, Jennifer (2018), 'Anxious Community: EU as (In)Security Community', *European Security*, 27 (3), 393–413.

Mölling, Christian, and Major, Claudia (2018), 'Why Joining France's European Intervention Initiative Is the Right Decision for Germany', *Egmont: Royal Institute for International Relations*. Available at: www.egmontinstitute.be/why-joining-frances-european-intervention-initiative-is-the-right-decision-for-germany/ (accessed: 1 November 2018).

North Atlantic Treaty Organization (2010), *Active Engagement, Modern Defence: Strategic Concept for the Defence and Security of the Members of the North Atlantic Treaty Organization*. Brussels: NATO Public Diplomacy Division. Available at: nato.int/nato_static_fl2014/assets/pdf/pdf_publications/20120214_strategic-concept-2010-eng.pdf (accessed: 1 November 2018).

North Atlantic Treaty Organization (2015), 'ISAF's Mission in Afghanistan (2001–2014)', NATO website, 1 September. Available at: www.nato.int/cps/en/natohq/topics_69366.htm (accessed: 1 November 2018).

North Atlantic Treaty Organization (2018), 'Defence Expenditure of NATO Countries (2011–2018)', Press Release PR/CP(2018)091, 10 July. Available at: www.nato.int/nato_static_fl2014/assets/pdf/pdf_2018_07/20180709_180710-pr2018–91-en.pdf (accessed: 1 November 2018).

Scipioni, Marco (2018), 'Failing Forward in EU Migration Policy? EU Integration after the 2015 Asylum and Migration Crisis', *Journal of European Public Policy*, 25 (9), 1357–1375.

Toje, Asle (2008), 'The Consensus–Expectations Gap: Explaining Europe's Ineffective Foreign Policy', *Security Dialogue*, 39 (1), 121–141.

Westerwelle, G., de Maizière, T., Fabius, L., and Le Drian, J.-Y. (2013), 'European Council on Security and Defence Proposals', 23 July. Available at: http://augengeradeaus.net/wp-content/uploads/2013/07/25–07-13-Annex-FR-DE-ALL.pdf (accessed: 1 November 2018).

White House (2018), 'Remarks by President Trump at Press Conference after NATO Summit', Brussels, Belgium, 12 July. Available at: www.whitehouse.gov/briefings-statements/remarks-president-trump-press-conference-nato-summit-brussels-belgium/ (accessed: 1 November 2018).

Wright, Katharine (2016), 'NATO's Adoption of UNSCR 1325 on Women, Peace and Security: Making the Agenda a Reality', *International Political Science Review*, 37 (3), 350–361.

Yost, David S. (2010), 'NATO's Evolving Purposes and the Next Strategic Concept', *International Affairs*, 86 (2), 489–522.

Ziegler, Charles (2018), 'International Dimensions of Electoral Processes: Russia, the USA, and the 2016 Elections', *International Politics*, 55 (5), 557–574.

Index